*Islam and the Arab Awakening*

# Islam and the Arab Awakening

TARIQ RAMADAN

OXFORD
UNIVERSITY PRESS

# OXFORD
UNIVERSITY PRESS

Oxford University Press is a department of the University of Oxford.
It furthers the University's objective of excellence in research, scholarship,
and education by publishing worldwide.

Oxford    New York
Auckland    Cape Town    Dar es Salaam    Hong Kong    Karachi
Kuala Lumpur    Madrid    Melbourne    Mexico City    Nairobi
New Delhi    Shanghai    Taipei    Toronto

With offices in
Argentina    Austria    Brazil    Chile    Czech Republic    France    Greece
Guatemala    Hungary    Italy    Japan    Poland    Portugal    Singapore
South Korea    Switzerland    Thailand    Turkey    Ukraine    Vietnam

Oxford is a registered trademark of Oxford University Press
in the UK and certain other countries.

Published in the United States of America by
Oxford University Press
198 Madison Avenue, New York, NY 10016

Library of Congress Cataloging-in-Publication Data
Ramadan, Tariq.
[Islam et le réveil arabe. English]
Islam and the arab awakening / Tariq Ramadan.
p. cm.
ISBN 978-0-19-993373-0 (hardcover : alk. paper)
1. Democratization—Arab countries.
2. Social movements—Arab countries.    3. Revolutions—Arab countries.
4. Islam—21st century.    I. Title.
DS63.1.R3513 2012
909'.097492708312—dc23
2012005620

ISBN 978-0-19-993373-0

1  3  5  7  9  8  6  4  2
Printed in the United States of America
on acid-free paper

*To Saliha and Zaid Shakir*
*To Fawzia and Yusuf Islam*
*To Ingeborg and Fred A. Reed*

# Contents

*Islam and the Arab Awakening*

# Introduction

ANALYSIS IN THE heat of the action is never easy, especially as events unfold and their causes—and the future itself—remain clouded with uncertainty.

This book makes no claim to reveal secrets, to unveil what may be strategic goals, and even less to predict the future. To do so would be madness, a combination of presumption and vanity. It would also be futile. Today, as terms like "Arab Spring," "revolutions," and "upheavals" are thrown about to describe what has happened across the Middle East and North Africa, I seek only to reexamine the facts, study the realities, and suggest some lessons, not only for the Arab world and the Muslim majority countries, but also for observers of these startling and unexpected developments.

What really happened in Tunisia and in Egypt? What is happening in the broader region that makes up MENA (Middle East and North Africa)? Why now? These are the first questions that spring to mind. To answer them we must submit the recent past and the personalities involved to fresh scrutiny and evaluate the available political, geopolitical, and economic data. Only a holistic reading that encompasses these three dimensions can provide the keys needed for us to begin to understand what lies ahead. As huge shock waves shake the Arab countries, such an approach is essential if we are to make sense of the issues, if we are join hands with those societies in their march toward freedom, democracy, and economic autonomy.

As vital as it appears to give the Arab uprisings a name, we should be cautious about rushing to define them. Not knowing exactly what the components of these nonviolent, transnational mass movements are, we know even less about their eventual outcome. Like people around the world, I rejoiced at the fall of the dictators and their regimes. But after a close analysis of the facts and the objective data available, I prefer to take a position of cautious, lucid optimism. Recent history has by no means yielded all its secrets; the analysis I offer in this volume will most certainly have to be revised, refined, and perhaps challenged.

The uprisings that swept the Arab world did not come from nowhere. As early as 2003, as will soon become clear, there had been talk of democratization in the MENA zone. It had, in fact, become then-president George W. Bush's key argument for intervention in Iraq. One year later, young MENA cyber-dissidents were signing up for training courses in nonviolent protest. Institutions funded by the American administration and/or major private firms organized lectures and seminars and set up networks that would provide training for young leaders who were given instruction in the use of the Internet and social networks. How deeply were Western governments involved? What did they know? What are we to make of the fact that the governments of Tunisia and Egypt arrested cyber-dissidents or subjected them to questioning on their return from training sessions abroad? These are facts that just won't go away; they must be studied and put in context if we wish to gain a better understanding of the dynamics and issues involved.

Are we to conclude, as some believe, that the protest movements that emerged in 2010 were designed and manipulated from abroad; that ultimately, the "West," the United States and Europe, control everything? I think not. There is a huge gap between determining what was known, monitored, and sometimes planned and concluding that history can be reduced to attempts to influence the course of events. Certainly it does seem clear that the United States and Europe had decided to change their policies in the two regions. Unconditional support for dictators could no longer be a viable or effective option, especially in the presence of emerging political and economic players such as China, India, Russia, and South Africa. Reform had become imperative. What could not be controlled, however, were the breadth of the phenomenon and the extent of the sacrifices the region's peoples were prepared to make to assert their thirst for freedom.

The protest movements that erupted first in Tunisia, then in Egypt—the high-spirited tumult of Liberation Square (Midan at-Tahrir)—released forces and energy that no one could have anticipated. In countries as diverse as Yemen, Syria, Morocco, Bahrain, and Libya, women and men showed that although they could sometimes be manipulated, the mass movements they created could not be totally controlled. A barrier has been breached in the Arab world: a fact that must be acknowledged with lucidity, and without illusion. This means steering clear of both the idealism and the wide-eyed optimism of those who are blind to the behind-the-scenes maneuvers of the politicians and the conspiratorial paranoia of those who have lost their faith in the ability of human beings to assert themselves as the subjects of their own history. Such is my position throughout this study. The people of the Middle

East have proven that dictators can be overthrown without weapons, by sheer force of numbers, by a nonviolent, positive outlook. Taken together, these events tell us that something irreversible has occurred.

The moment is a historic one, as are the opportunities that will emerge as the era of dictatorships draws to an end. The outcome is unclear; the uprisings are not yet revolutions. From Tunisia to Yemen, by way of Egypt, Libya, Syria, and Bahrain, nothing can be taken for granted: democratic processes are only beginning to emerge; security is shaky while armies remain fully armed and on alert. No one can foretell the future: the tensions that followed the events in both Tunisia and Egypt show that more time will be needed before the past can be forgotten and open, pluralistic, democratic societies can emerge. But the key players involved in each society will have no choice but to face up to the real challenges and to avoid the trap of polarization, of sterile debate between "secularists" and "Islamists." More than a few fundamental questions remain to be clarified: the nature of the state, the role of religion, the basic principle of equal rights for all citizens, equality of women and men, to name a few. But the debate cannot be reduced to a confrontation between two approaches, both of which are in crisis, as I will attempt to demonstrate in this book.

The task of construction that lies before intellectuals and politicians is to identify the key issues, to define and prioritize the ways and means for carrying out social and political reform, and to foster the rise of a true civil society, far removed from warped, paralyzing, and petty quarrels. As covetous glances, both geopolitical and economic, focus on the MENA zone, such is the radical and comprehensive process of renewal for which I call.

The time has come to stop blaming the West for the colonialism and imperialism of the past or for today's attempts at manipulation and control. Arab and Muslim majority societies must jettison their historic posture as victims and reconcile themselves with the course of history that millions of women and men accelerated so massively by coming out into the streets. Their responsibility is a historic one: they must entertain no illusions about what is at stake, be wary of attempts at manipulation, and be determined to carry out essential reforms with the full participation of all citizens, women and men, from all social classes and religious and cultural backgrounds.

The uprisings have created a multiplicity of new perspectives. Choices must now be made. The timeworn "Islam versus the West" dichotomy is now giving way to multipolar relations, in which the Global South, the Islamic Orient, and Asia are assuming new and innovative roles. Though fascinating in itself, the new dynamic does not automatically guarantee more justice and more democracy. The rise to prominence of China, Russia, and India obviously does not ensure respect for human rights and pluralism. Some people are quick—too quick—to rejoice at the collapse of American power. The same people may be unaware that what might replace it (given China's new predominance and the emergence of India and Russia) could well lead to a regression in social and human rights, and to new forms of dependency. These are issues of crucial importance that call for in-depth debate over which sociopolitical models are to be developed and what new economic relations should be established. They lie at the heart of this book's overarching concern: as the Arab awakening unfolds, what role will religious references play? How should Islamic principles and ultimate goals be (re)thought? Can divergent aspirations for reform be unified, or must Muslim majority societies be restricted to the opposition between secular and Islamist ideologies? What is, today, the role of political Islam? Can Turkey be seen as a model? How are we to promote an autonomous civil state?

I will be addressing these issues, with particular emphasis on the prerogatives of civil society. In the closing section, I will analyze the ethical challenges that lie ahead and examine possible alternatives. Social and political questions, as well as those touching on the economy, on culture, and on relations with the West, will continue to be determinant and will require close examination in the light of cultural and religious references. I will suggest avenues of approach, all the while rejecting the twin temptations of oversimplification and polarization. For the Arab uprisings to flourish and to lead to toward radical change that embodies real—and realistic—hopes, we will need all the intellectual effort, all the close, constructive criticism and emancipation from Western domination we can muster.

The final section of the book consists of a series of appendices bringing together articles I wrote published in European (including Turkish) and American newspapers, in the Arab press, and also on my website, as events unfolded.[1] In them the reader will encounter a wide range of viewpoints at differing points in time, coupled with analyses that have not necessarily been developed in the first four chapters. The appendices thus form a useful and informative supplement, in the form of ongoing commentary, to the text.

The upheavals we are witnessing in the Middle East and North Africa confirm much of what I have long maintained, investigated, and repeated for several years. Readers familiar with my work on Muslim majority societies, on the presence of Muslims in the West, and on Islamic theological and legal references will be able to pinpoint the intuitions and propositions whose relevance has been confirmed by recent events. The same holds true for questions of democracy, culture, art, shared values, and ultimate goals (in both the Islamic Orient and the West), but also for the critical importance of the experiences of Western Muslims. My recent thinking on applied ethics and on the crucial importance of overcoming binary thinking has not only been confirmed but has also gathered strength and energy as we act to seize the historic occasion that lies before us.

Seen in this light, the double emancipation—of the mind and of society—must be our primary goal. The Arab awakening must not succumb to self-alienation or be subverted by a new form of colonialism that would shatter the hopes of millions of women and men. There can be no turning back; now we must hope that the peoples of the region will find their way forward, in full freedom.

# *I*

# *Made-To-Order Uprisings?*

NO ONE FORESAW them; many wondered how to describe them. When public protests broke out in the Tunisian town of Sidi Bouzid on December 17, 2010, interpretations of what had happened proliferated. The wares of a young street vendor, Mohammed Bouazizi, had been confiscated; in protest he had set himself on fire. Factors as diverse as poverty and economic hardship, unemployment, police repression, and authoritarian rule were advanced to explain his death.

The weeks that followed would bring dramatic change to the Middle East, North Africa, and the world. On January 14, 2011, the Tunisian dictator Zine El Abidine Ben Ali fled to Saudi Arabia. On February 27, after a month of confusion, a new government took office. Two months had changed the face of Tunisia. To shouts of "Get out!" directed at the despot, his family, and his regime, the people had bested the dictatorship.

Meanwhile, the world looked on in astonishment as events gathered momentum and intensity. Egyptians followed the Tunisians' lead, beginning January 25, 2011; with massive mobilizations in the now-famous Liberation Square (Midan at-Tahrir) they in turn toppled President Hosni Mubarak on February 11, 2011. Things were moving fast now, very fast. In Algeria, attempts to mobilize fell short, while Morocco witnessed a series of substantial protests called for February 20, 2011 (giving rise to the February 20th Movement). Reform had suddenly placed itself on the political agenda.

Across the Middle East the domino effect gained speed. To contain the protests the king of Jordan dismissed his prime minister (February 1, 2011) with promises of social reform. The Libyan people took to the streets and despite fierce repression, a National Transitional Council was set up on February 15, 2011, touching off a full-scale civil war with heavy support from the West and the North Atlantic Treaty Organization (NATO). Mass protests began in Bahrain on February 14, 2011, and demonstrations even took place in Saudi Arabia that March, where they were brutally repressed. The wave of protests engulfed Yemen beginning on January 27, a few weeks after two men had set themselves on fire following the Tunisian example. In Syria, sporadic demonstrations began on January 26, which turned into more organized uprisings on March 15, 2011, despite harsh repression and isolation due to virtually nonexistent media coverage and the indecision of the international community.

## *Naming*

From December 2010 through March 2011 and on into the summer of 2011 and beyond, the mobilizations that had spread like wildfire across the Middle East and North Africa continued. The mass movements all shared common characteristics—protest against social and economic conditions, rejection of dictatorship, the fight against corruption—but each one has its own very specific features, which in turn require individual analysis.

The first challenge, then, is to name and to describe what has taken place, both at its inception and in the course of its rapid expansion: were we talking about revolutions, rebellions, popular protests, or perhaps *intifadas*—uprisings—as was initially suggested in Tunisia, invoking the Arabic term now linked to the Palestinian resistance? Was it an "Arab spring," like the European revolutions of the recent past? Were they "Jasmine Revolutions," "Dignity Revolutions," or something else?

Definitions and interpretations differ widely, as if determined by the optimism of the observer. Some see recent events as the birth of a new era, as a radical turning point between past and future, and boldly speak of revolution. Others, more cautious, assert that "popular uprisings" are changing political arrangements in North Africa and the Middle East, though it is too early to say whether they will lead to a true renewal. Others see them as revolts or popular upheavals, unable thus far to bring about reforms that may or may not alter the political and economic power structure in the Arab world. Others, finally, are not convinced at all: the mass movements are controlled from abroad—had US President George W. Bush not proclaimed a democratization movement in the region?—and could only be a transition toward a new type of Western control and domination. Before us lies a broad spectrum of interpretations, ranging from a "springtime of the peoples" to a new expression of the "thinly disguised cynicism of the powerful." How are we to understand all this? What name are we to give it?

On closer analysis, the term "revolution" seems unwarranted. Can we really define the upheavals that have shaken the Middle East and North Africa as revolutions, either in terms of a transformed political order or a shift in the economic balance of power? Have the popular movements run their course; have they achieved their objectives? Clearly they have not, and it is far too soon to say that they will. Still, the extreme position that sees the omniscient and pervasive hand of the Western powers behind the mass demonstrations appears to be equally unwarranted.[1] From Tunisia to Syria through Egypt, Bahrain, and Yemen, the Western allies have clearly played a part and have attempted to control or direct the course of events, but it is impossible that they actually planned the revolts from start to finish.

As against "unfinished revolutions" and conspiracy theories, I prefer to use the term "uprisings" to describe the common character of the mass movements that have shaken the Arab countries. In them, women and men of all religions and social backgrounds took to the streets, without violence and without attacking the West, to demand an end to dictatorship, economic corruption, and denial of respect to citizens. Based on the categories drawn up by Jean-Paul Sartre[2] and still relevant today, uprising as a category can be situated halfway between revolution and revolt; once it is carried to its fullest extent and overthrows the existing system (both as political rule and economic structure) it can become revolution. On the other hand, if it is incomplete, if it is manipulated, or if it fails, it will have expressed the people's aspirations but not concretized their hopes. To speak of "uprisings" is to convey cautious optimism and to affirm that the revolts we have witnessed are already established facts, while so far the idea of revolution remains but a hope in all the Arab countries—without exception.

## *Predictable, Unpredictable*

In December 2010 and January 2011, a broad consensus emerged around the world that described the earliest upheavals as totally unpredictable and unexpected, largely because the Tunisian and Egyptian regimes had appeared so solid and unshakable. Moreover, as the European and American powers had supported these regimes for years, any fundamental political transformation seemed highly unlikely. Standing apart from the rest of the world, Arab societies for the past thirty years had been mired deeply in the status quo. Entrenched dictators headed harsh, unbending regimes that could at least be credited with preserving regional security and stability while mercilessly repressing "dangerous opponents," "Islamists," and/or "radicals." Given this state of affairs, no one could have foreseen the movements that erupted, no one could even have hoped for them: set phrases that journalists and analysts used again and again, as if to persuade the public that the immense crowds in the streets were unlike anything that had come before. For, as American president Barack Obama said, history unfolds through the political will of "people calling for change."[3] Or does it?

Any in-depth analysis of events in the region must move beyond the mass demonstrations for political reform to embrace two critical dimensions: the economic factors and the US call in 2003for democratizing the Middle East. In both Tunisia and Egypt, the two countries where the protest movement first emerged, the primary cause of discontent and mobilization was economic. Simple analysis of the social and economic realities of both countries shows that all the components of a social explosion were present. While leaders were wallowing in luxury and corruption, the prices of basic foodstuffs had soared to intolerable levels in Tunisia, in Egypt, and even in Jordan while unemployment impacted ever-widening sections of the population. Those who had jobs were forced to survive on near-starvation wages and often to hold two or three jobs to make ends meet. The situation had become intolerable; everything pointed to imminent social explosion. Though no one could have predicted that the death of Mohamed Bouazizi in Tunisia would trigger such a response to the cruel treatment inflicted on the population, the economic data did make it possible to place the meaning and the demands of the uprisings in perspective.

It should be added that the idea of "democratizing" the Middle East was, by then, hardly an original concept. It was first expressed in 2003, long before Barack Obama became president of the United States. Then-president George W. Bush explained that the war in Iraq constituted a first step toward a global democratic movement in the Greater Middle East and that Islam was by no means opposed to democracy. On November 6, 2003, he added that his involvement in the Middle East was akin to Ronald Reagan's support for Eastern Europe's struggle for democracy in the 1980s.[4] American and European strategy in the region was due for an overhaul; their wishes were no secret. Successive US administrations had made it clear that for economic and political reasons, the region's dictatorships had to change as a necessary precondition for opening up Arab markets and integrating the region into the global economy. Had these two factors not been taken into account, there was a strong likelihood that the justifications for supporting the status quo and backing the dictatorships—security and stability—would have produced the exact opposite, and would have led to a total loss of control of the situation by the Western countries. Moreover, the rise of new economic players such as China, India, some South American countries, South Africa, or even Turkey confirmed the risks inherent in inaction for the West. The West's intervention in Iraq, along with constant pressure on Iran, the crisis in Lebanon, the division of the region into Shia and Sunni zones of influence, or the stalemated Israel-Palestinian peace process were only a few of the signs that foreshadowed major changes in the region. It would be naïve to imagine that the great powers—the United States, France, Germany, Russia, or even China—were nothing more than casual observers of the growing turmoil. Their relationships with national governments, their links with the region's military establishments, their carefully calibrated dealings with each country or regime point clearly to their involvement before and during the uprisings.

Resistance movements have been encouraged, logistical support has flowed to rebel groups (as in Iran, Tunisia, and Egypt), training has been given, and significant pressure has been brought to bear on several dictatorships.[5] Nonetheless, we cannot conclude that the uprisings were directed by outside forces and that public opinion was manipulated. The protest movements have not always embraced a clear ideology; demonstrations have often gotten out of hand (as in Syria, as we shall show later). From the spark that ignited mass protests to the fall of the dictators and the emergence of new political forces in the region's civil societies, a number of imponderables must be taken into account. Though they have been neither wholly unpredictable nor wholly autonomous, the Arab uprisings are by no means a case of Western-controlled manipulation, as the most pessimistic would have it.

The best example of complexity of the issues and the forces of change may well be that of the youthful bloggers presented as the driving force of the mass protest movement. Young people trained in the use of the new communications technologies made available by the Web exploited the resources of the Internet and social networks like Facebook and Twitter to powerful effect. But the youthful protesters did not begin their training in September or October 2010, just prior the first uprisings in December of that year; they began three or four years before the events. It is useful to recall that the mass movement in Serbia, in 1998, led by a group called Otpor (Resistance) was created and led by Srdja Popović, a young man who used text messaging, the Internet, and social networks to galvanize the population against Slobodan Milošević. The movement chose as its symbol the clenched fist, which had been used in the anti-Nazi resistance, and successfully overthrew Milošević two years later, in October 2000. In 2004, Popović set up an organization called CANVAS, a training center specializing in nonviolent action and strategy. There he developed the three principles of popular mobilization: unity, planning, and nonviolent discipline. The center provided training for the young activists who were later to lead the "Rose Revolution" in Georgia and the "Orange Revolution" in Ukraine. Young politicized leaders from over thirty-seven countries flocked to Serbia for training, including many from North Africa and the Middle East. Tunisians received their training there and Mohammed Adel, one of the founders of Egypt's April 6th Movement, was trained for a week in Belgrade during the summer of 2009.[6]

Two television documentaries broadcast by Qatar-based al-Jazeera in both Arabic and English[7] revealed how Egypt's April 6th Movement had been set up three years earlier, in 2007. The al-Jazeera journalists reported on the young people's training trips to Serbia and the Caucasus, but oddly failed to mention their visits to the United States. A significant number of young activists and bloggers were given training by three American government-financed nongovernmental organizations (NGOs): the Albert Einstein Institution,[8] Freedom House, and the International Republican Institute.[9] The principles and methods of these three are identical: celebrating democratic values, mobilizing people nonviolently, and bringing down regimes without confrontation with the police or the army by using symbols and slogans to shape mass psychology and exploiting the potential of social networks and more generally, the Internet.

As early as 2004, but more systematically between 2006 and 2008, young people were trained at these and other centers in the strategy and tactics of nonviolent mobilization: social networks and the use of symbols (the clenched fist appears again in Tunisia, Morocco, Egypt, and Syria). Not by any stretch of the imagination could the American, European, or even Russian governments have been unaware of these programs. In fact, they actually funded some of them. The governments of Tunisia, Egypt, Syria, and Lebanon were also aware: some activists were arrested when they returned from trips abroad (Egypt being perhaps the best-known example) or in the course of their activities.

It would be an error to deny the powerfully indigenous wellsprings of the Arab uprisings; the Syrian people's determination to defy their country's dictatorship could hardly have been planned abroad: it clearly came from within, from the determination of the Syrian people. Even so, bloggers and cyber-activists continue to debate whether to accept US funding or to attend training sessions organized by institutions either closely linked to Western powers or within their ideological purview. These concerns were expressed by Sami Ben Gharbia, a Tunisian blogger based in the Netherlands. In a detailed article published on September 17, 2010,[10] he identified the risks inherent in accepting such funding, stressed the need to maintain independence, and warned against the manipulation of movements led by young activists against governments supported by the United States and Europe.

For the sake of history and for the future of these movements, it would be both inconsistent and shortsighted not to look closely at the connections and the preparation that preceded the upheavals in the Middle East and North Africa. Sami Ben Gharbia in his article, as well as others, cites the direct involvement of powerful American corporations. In point of fact, Google, Twitter, and Yahoo were directly involved in training and disseminating information on the Web promoting pro-democracy activism. A conference called Internet Liberty 2010, organized by Google on September 20–22 in Budapest with the participation of American and European government representatives, saw the launch of the Middle East and North Africa Bloggers Network, with organizational impetus from an institute connected with the US Democratic Party.[11] And remember Wael Ghonim, who emerged as the hero of the uprising in Egypt after his moving appearance on Mona al-Shazly's prime-time program on February 7, 2011 (just after he was unexpectedly set free following ten days' imprisonment); at the age of thirty, he was already Google's marketing director for the Middle East. Very early on, the same company, Google, helped Egypt's activist bloggers elude the government's attempts to curtail Internet activity by providing them with satellite access codes. Surprisingly, Google refused to give those same codes to Syrian activist bloggers facing pitiless repression; the "cyber-dissident" Chamy pointed this out (and regretted the strange difference in treatment) in a France Inter radio debate with cyber-activists Lina Ben Mhenni from Tunisia[12] and Mohammed Salem from Egypt.[13] It is hard to ignore Google's position throughout the uprisings as being virtually identical to that of the US government or of NATO: explicit support for the Egyptian protesters, aimed at Mubarak's rapid departure; hesitations in Syria in the hope that domestic reforms would keep Bashar al-Assad's regime in power.[14]

These basic facts and figures must be known; questions must be framed with accuracy, depth, and caution. Are the most prominent activists truly apolitical young people? (Several members of Egypt's April 6th Movement, such as Ahmed Maher, had early declared their support for Mohamed el-Baradei, the former director general of the International Atomic Energy Agency [IAEA], who was to run for president and then decided to step down.) What has been the extent of financial support from the governments and private transnational corporations that control large swaths of Internet activity?

What preparatory, behind-the-scenes role did the armed forces play in each national context? How can their nonintervention in Tunisia and Egypt (during the first months) be explained? More than a few crucial questions remain unanswered, questions that must be addressed calmly and systematically, far from radical interpretations or conspiracy theories. This is the task that awaits us if we hope to build a future free of the uncertainties and upheavals now afflicting the region.

## *Islamist or Islamic?*

The Arab dictatorships had long presented themselves to the world as a necessary evil, a bulwark against the rise of Islamism in North Africa and the Middle East. The strategy and its political justification were nothing new. Western support for autocrats and against the proponents of political Islam dates back to the early years of the twentieth century. In the 1930s and 40s, the question arose in Egypt with regard to the Muslim Brotherhood, and in Syria, Lebanon, Algeria, Morocco, and Tunisia shortly after their independence. The British, American, then-Soviet, and French governments were quite aware of the Islamist makeup of the opposition movements in the Arab world, and throughout Muslim majority societies from Turkey to Indonesia and Malaysia. Since the 1940s, Western governments have studied and clearly identified the various Islamist movements in all their diversity well before the Iranian revolution of 1979, which was soon, however, to change everything.

From a successful revolution in Iran to an electoral victory in Algeria just over a decade later, everything seemed possible with the Islamists—they had emerged as political actors who could not be ignored. A choice had to be made by the Western powers, rapidly and decisively: it would be preferable to support despots (despite the contradiction with democratic values) than deal with Islamists of whatever stripe, Shiite or Sunni, legalist, reformist, or literalist. For decades there has been an objective alliance between Arab dictatorships and the Western powers that have, without exception, supported dictatorial regimes in North Africa and the Middle East in the name of maintaining stability and safeguarding the West's geopolitical and economic interests.

That having been said, American and European policy toward Islamism has never been perfectly clear-cut. Circumstantial alliances have been concluded and openly admitted when, for instance, to oppose the former Soviet Union in Afghanistan, it proved opportune for the West to support the Taliban and Osama bin Laden.[15] Or to go one step further, the alliance with the Kingdom of Saudi Arabia, where Islam is the state religion and where the ruling monarchy claims that Islam is, by its essence, opposed to democracy, offers proof positive that the West has no problem with political Islam as such, as long as Islamist leaders promise to protect its economic and political interests. With or without dictatorships, with or without Islamism, we arrive at the same conclusion: private interests must be protected. They may be dictators or Islamists, but Western governments' best friends are those who best serve their interests.

The Arab awakening has clearly not been the work of Islamist movements. Neither in Tunisia or Egypt, nor in Jordan, Libya, or Syria were they the initiators. The mass movements took to the streets without them, against the will of their leadership, and, in any event, without their agreement. In Tunisia, the Ennahda movement joined the protests several weeks after they had begun, just as the Muslim Brotherhood did in Cairo. The same prudent attitude has been on display in Jordan, Libya, Syria, and even Yemen.

Even more interesting, the first mass demonstrations shone a harsh light on the dissensions within the Islamist organizations themselves—the very organizations that had been depicted as highly organized, tightly structured, and disciplined. In both Tunisia and Egypt, younger members of the Islamist organizations joined the uprisings first, often against the advice of the hierarchy and of the leaders of the older generation. They disregarded appeals for caution, and soon dissident voices began to be heard within the organizations themselves. Not only did the young refuse to be "patient" (as they had been advised) before joining the mass movement, but they quickly adopted sharply differing attitudes toward civil society and their own "organizational culture." Even though they belonged to Islamist organizations, they were fully conversant with web-based social networks such as Twitter and Facebook, and cultivated broad social and political relationships, taking part in virtual debates well beyond the boundaries of their religious and ideological ties. Unlike their elders, they did not see this as uncharted territory, almost naturally joining the campaign of popular protest.

During the first few weeks of the uprisings, Western and, on occasion, Arab media continued to describe the situation in terms of polarization between secularists and Islamists. Was there not the risk of a replay of the 1979 scenario when, after the effervescence of the mass demonstrations against the shah (as with the Arab dictators today), dangerous anti-Western and ultimately anti-democratic Islamists had seized power? The Israeli government was first to sound the alarm, claiming that the threat of an Iran-style outcome was too great and that Mubarak should be supported.[16] But it soon became apparent that the Islamists did not control the protestors and that the people's aspirations were stronger than the ruling regimes. The massive, non-violent, and well-organized demonstrations, which were almost totally free of anti-Western slogans, drew people from all social classes and all political, religious, nonreligious, and even antireligious social groups. Young people and women had taken a visible and irrefutable lead, and the media increasingly took notice. The presence of nonreligious people and secularists in Tunisia and in Egypt, as well as the highly visible Coptic minority presence on Tahrir Square could point to only one conclusion: a new form of opposition had emerged, with women and men rallying around new demands drawn from the core values of freedom, justice, and equality, and rejection of corruption and cronyism.

Political analysis and media coverage then underwent a radical shift. Though the Islamists may have been a cause for concern at the beginning— would the mass movements be subverted or taken over?—it now appeared that the uprisings were wholly disconnected from the religious and cultural environment in which they occurred. As quickly as the reference to Islamism vanished, so did reference to Islam, as if most of the women and men motivated by a thirst for freedom, dignity, and justice had ceased to be perceived as Muslims since their values and their hopes were so like those of the West: hence the observable discrepancy in Western and Arab television coverage of events.[17] For even though the movements themselves were by no means Islamist in nature, most of the activists, women as well as men, who were calling for freedom and justice and an end to corruption and dictatorship, did so as Muslims—and not against their religion.[18]

The reminder is necessary, for two key reasons. The first stems from what can be observed in the field following the uprisings, during the transitional period that is supposed to lead to the drafting of new constitutions and presidential elections. The presence of the Islamists is now well established; they are fully participating in the future of their respective countries. The popular movements have transformed them into opposition political groups among many, while polarization between secularists and Islamists is becoming increasingly evident. Islam as a frame of reference will surely become a determining factor in domestic political debate in the societies of North Africa and the Middle East. Some speak of a Turkish or Indonesian variant, while others point to new paths to be explored. The Islamists themselves have markedly evolved on a number of issues (though this in itself may not yet be enough): I will return to this question in Chapter 3.[19] There can be little doubt that the relation between Islam as the majority religion and the aspiration to freedom

and liberal democracy, or even a liberal economy, will emerge as considerations crucial to the future of Arab societies.

These considerations—and here lies the second reason—will impact
debates that strike to the heart of Western societies, emerging as they do from
the presence of Muslim citizens. The Arab revolts have proven that while
being Muslims in their majority, Arab citizens aspire to the same values as
do "we" in the West. As populist political parties in the West (such as the
Swiss People Party, the BNP in Britain, far right parties all over Europe or
the tea party in the United States), imitated by virtually all traditional parties, continue to present Islam as a foreign religion and Muslims as threat-
ening personifications of the "other," these women and men are proving that
such projections are as wrong as they are dangerous. It was as if Muslims, and
particularly Arabs, were by their essence fated to live under dictatorship and
entertained a natural relationship with violence. But now, hundreds of thousands of women and men have rallied—not exclusively in the name of Islam
but never against it—for democracy in a nonviolent and dignified way. That
should have been sufficient to overcome the timeworn stereotypes and the
persistent prejudices that shape the way Islam is increasingly being seen in the
West, and yet such a change is not certain. What is sure is that Arab societies
in the future, in the wake of the uprisings, will have a conclusive impact on
Western societies as a whole.[20]

## When the Other Is No Longer the Other

Relations between Muslim majority societies and American, European,
and Russian nations have been characterized historically by extremely wide
swings. Above and beyond geography, the Orient has allowed the West to
define its form as a cultural, historical, philosophical, and religious entity.
The West, and particularly the West of the Enlightenment, by a process of
projection created an imaginary Orient in opposition to which it defined
itself, the thesis that Edward Said develops in *Orientalism*:[21] the construction of the other, at whose heart lies Islam (as both religion and civilization), had the double function of establishing not only a self-identity but
the alterity of the other by way of a relationship whose components were
not only intellectual but also ideological and symbolic. Seen through this
prism, Islam was necessarily a non-Western religion, whose values could
neither be recognized nor identified as belonging to the process of intellectual, industrial, social, and political emancipation of the "Occident" of
the Enlightenment.

Ernest Renan, the French thinker and philosopher, would give the concept perhaps its most explicit form. On February 23, 1862, in a lecture on the Semitic peoples at the Collège de France, he argued, "Islam is the most complete negation of Europe. Islam is fanaticism, the likes of which even the Spain of Phillip II or the Italy of Pius V never witnessed; Islam is disdain for science and the suppression of civil society; it is the terrifying simplicity of the Semitic spirit, shrinking the human mind and closing it to every subtle notion, to every fine sentiment, to rational investigation, to ultimately confront it with the eternal tautology: 'God is God.'"[22] He went on to add: "In science and philosophy we (Europeans) are exclusively Greek."[23] Twenty years later he would reaffirm the substance of his position in his celebrated 1883 lecture at La Sorbonne: "Islamism[24] has brought nothing but harm to human reason. The minds it has closed to light may already have been closed by their own internal limitations; but it has persecuted free thought, I shall not say more violently than other religious systems, but more efficiently. It has transformed the lands it has conquered into a field closed to the rational culture of the mind."[25]

These arguments were later built upon by a majority of colonialist thinkers and political figures: a binary manner of thinking in which the emancipated Occident must civilize the Islamized Orient, seen as closed or patently backward. Economic, political, and cultural imperialism reached its culmination in historical imperialism, a monopoly on the meaning of human history that determined who was advanced and who had fallen irretrievably behind. For history had a meaning, and the emancipated, democratic West was its avant-garde, if not its culmination. Thus did history, its meaning and its teachings, come under the sway of the colonial enterprise. It might have been hoped that with decolonization, with the expansion of migration and the globalization of communication and cultural exchange, this reductive, binary, and profoundly unscientific and ahistorical vision would be overcome. Such was not the case. In fact, the opposite has occurred in our day, with the emergence of theories like Samuel Huntington's in *Clash of Civilizations*[26] that posit conflict between civilizations or proclaim the historical superiority of one over the others (particularly Islam), as in Francis Fukuyama's "end of history," from which he has subsequently retreated.[27]

These theories have been hotly debated and have met with fierce opposition by numerous intellectuals and political analysts. Nonetheless, and surprisingly, a substantial number of the ideas that inform them are today widely accepted and commonplace in public debates on Islam, Islamic civilization, or Muslims themselves. The attacks of 2001 in New York, of 2004 in Madrid, and 2005 in London have confirmed the general sentiment that Islam is a religion foreign to Western culture. Though they would not use Renan's extreme language, large numbers of Western citizens may well share his views on the essential otherness of Islam and of the Muslims. Whether they live in Muslim-majority societies or in the West, whether they live here or elsewhere, Muslims are definitely seen as being from somewhere else.

Reflections or conclusions of this kind are by no means restricted to the West. Many Muslim intellectual and political figures, in the "East" and "West," have adopted both the construct and the analytical framework as their own. They either locate themselves in a state of absolute alterity and claim, with Kipling, that "East is East and West is West, and never the twain shall meet,"[28] or become proponents of the idea that Islam must undertake in-depth and intrinsic reform if Muslims wish to emerge into modernity, to match the West's scientific and technological achievements. Both positions draw on the same basic assumption: the "East," posited as real and actual Islam, forms an entity distinct from the West. It constitutes the Other, an Other who should have the humility to learn rather than arrogantly wishing to contribute or even to formulate propositions. A large number of intellectuals from the Global South, Muslim and non-Muslim alike, have made this vision, one fraught with philosophical, cultural, and political consequences, their own. The Arab awakening suddenly seemed to bring about a change in perspective, a leap that could signal a shift in the binary paradigm I have just sketched out. Arab peoples, primarily Muslims, were rising up without violence in the name of the very same values "we" hold dear, the Western values of freedom, justice, and democracy. There may have been cause for concern that the revolts were or would become Islamist; it was rapidly concluded that their religious references had nothing to do with their actions. The Arab peoples are just like "us," they aspire to "our" values, and as a result they are no longer perceived as being Muslims. Their resemblance came at the price of deleting their religious beliefs and practices, their culture and even their history. They joined the advanced, civilized detachment of the Western-led onward march of history. No longer primarily perceived as Arabs and Muslims, they had attained the lofty status of subjects, legally and philosophically, of the Universal. At last they had overcome their backwardness and strode in lockstep with the West in its enlightened march of progress. As pendulum swings go, it was spectacular: only yesterday Muslims were the alterity against which the West defined itself; now they had become the *alter ego* of the Western Universal, allowing the West to celebrate itself. But the underlying logic of this reading remains unchanged: alterity and likeness imply a dichotomy based on power, which, whether in otherness (enabling the West defining oneself) or in like-ness (enabling self-celebration),[29] can only favor an ideologically constructed, imagined West.

Stripped of their memory and their history by the Western powers and observers, cut off from their religion and their culture, the Arab and Muslim peoples are now celebrated in their will to rid themselves of their despotic rulers. Nothing more; nothing less. The reading is a strictly political one and has been shaped in the near equivalent of a historical and economic vacuum, as if international relations and foreign influences had somehow been ren-dered secondary or obsolete. Any attempt to place events in a geopolitical, economic, ideological, or philosophical and religious context would thus be seen either as conspiratorial or as an irrelevant rejection (that of backward looking leftists, conservative Muslims, or dangerous Islamists) of the proper interpretation of history's majestic onward sweep.

This positive, highly optimistic account of the Arab awakening would not be surprising were it restricted to purely ideological self-celebration. What could be more natural in the West than to affirm that the West supports and stands shoulder-to-shoulder with the Arab peoples in their self-generated progress toward freedom and democracy? American president Barack Obama and European leaders, not to mention NATO, have repeatedly declared that they are on the side of the people. Whether they intervene in Libya or remain cautious bystanders in Syria and Bahrein, it would be cynical and unseemly to doubt their word.

More worrisome still is the repetition of the same words and the same arguments—and the same assumptions—by some of the protagonists, and a portion of seemingly committed observers, of these very uprisings. Bloggers, it is assumed, acted in full independence, driven by the broadly shared aspira-tions emanating from the Internet, and from the globalization of culture and democratic aspirations. The nonviolent, nonideological, broad-based upris-ings, with no defined political or religious leadership, are to be seen as the fusion of East and West in a kind of higher synthesis: the single civilization of the liberal democracies.[30] To raise questions about the facts, relationships, and interests at stake is seen by some as attempted manipulation by a handful of malevolent killjoys or intellectuals who see the hand of the West every-where, and therefore conclude that the Arabs can do nothing for themselves. I experienced this firsthand at a lecture I gave in Beirut on April 1, 2011: a tiny minority of the audience, which nevertheless made itself heard through the aggressive intervention of cyber-activist Nasser Weddady, strongly rejected a critical interpretation of events and questions about their homegrown, autonomous character (I was talking about the training of cyber-dissidents in the West and what was known before the uprisings took place).[31]

With one full swing of the pendulum, the other has ceased to be the other in Western eyes: certainly a cause for rejoicing. A crucial step may have been taken toward transcending the conflict-ridden polarity of the two civilizations, the Occident and the Orient, the West and Islam. The uprisings that have shaken the Middle East and North Africa can be interpreted as a celebration of transcending and of reconciliation, particularly insofar as voices echoing one another can be heard from both spheres of civilization. In political terms, democracy has triumphed, and with it the values of justice, freedom, dignity for women and men—against all despots. Such a version may well be appealing, but it is dangerously simplistic; more seriously, it is an imperialist version, if not a castrating one. Not only does it function reductively in determining that even the Arab and Muslim peoples can make the political ideals of democracy and its founding values (the rule of law, equality, justice, universal suffrage, the separation of powers, etc.) their own, but it ignores those imperatives that must govern any full reading of the facts: it is taken for granted that the Arab countries are expected to evolve, and in so doing, integrate more fully into the liberal economic order (once purged of the corruption of their ruling despots) and open their markets more thoroughly to modern technology, to global culture, and to contemporary consumerism.

The process of reconciliation, which functions by way of recognizing the *similarity* of the *assimilated* Arab and Muslim alter ego is fraught with serious consequences. In severing the ties that bind the Arab and Muslim peoples with their memory, and their traditional and religious references, the reductive vision we have been analyzing makes it impossible for them to draw on their collective cultural and symbolic capital, to use Pierre Bourdieu's term, to produce something new, something original, something distinct from the order imposed by the political and economic powers of our age. In their march toward emancipation and freedom, the respective genius of North African and Middle-Eastern societies thus finds itself denied, in the name of their accession to a common ideal viewed as superior. Their success must resemble that of the powerful, which in turn must not be called into question, for in this process of reconciliation, as a Western leitomiv, the Occident is the master, the Orient the disciple.

Such an approach is dangerous and ultimately unrealistic. The Arab peoples, like all those of the Global South, cannot and do not want to disregard the cultural and religious traditions that have defined and nurtured them. It is to be hoped that in the name of the shared values to which peoples aspire—freedom, justice, equality, autonomy, and pluralism—they will find, within their own references, the modalities that govern the production and application of these values. Not only will this procedure, this endogenous production of values and symbols confer upon them internal legitimacy; one hopes it will create new approaches, new models, contributing as it does to the constructive criticism of contemporary models of democracy. Some (Touraine, Gauchet, Huntington, Habermas, Crozier, or Gilbert) forthrightly address the profound crisis of Western democracy in the light of new economic and media power, the crumbling of the nation-state in our globalizing age, and the estrangement of ordinary citizens from politics itself. Yet all evidences indicates that only the West can legitimately voice such criticism.

To accept that the peoples of the Global South possess the capacity, based on their own referential framework, to produce new models of democracy (and management of pluralism), a new form of international relations within the existing global political and economic order, to rethink from top to bottom South-South and South-North relations in such a way as to challenge existing monopolies, to engage in original reflection on goals and on social, political, and economic ethics; to accept that the consolidation of such a collective cultural capital would entail an end to projecting and imposing a synthesis that glorifies the West and amputates other civilizations of their creative potential, we must, to put it bluntly, be prepared to have our comfortable certainties about the path to the future and the meaning of history disturbed, called into question, and even challenged. We have now reached the point where these critical paths converge.

Are Arab and Muslim societies capable of putting forward new models, of outlining the new trajectories that will be able to reconcile the practices of the present day with their long-held values? Can Islam become fertile ground for creativity or is it nothing more than an obstacle to progress, as the Orientalists have so often claimed. It is worth noting, as Jacqueline O'Rourke has pointed out in a recently defended PhD dissertation,[32] that the West's symbolic projections, as propounded by Edward Said for one, has restricted its exercise to Western tools and references alone. Said does not explore the potential of the (ideologically constructed) Orient and of Islam to question—from within— the principles, methods, and tools that the West has used to objectify them. In other words, he neither studies nor dwells on the internal references that might enable Muslims themselves to become the autonomous subjects of their history. Said's work provides a fascinating, lucid critique of the West by the West, but not a study of the Orient's particular genius as expressed through its languages, its traditions, and its aspirations.

These questions, however, are precisely the ones that the young and even the less young in Arab societies should be asking, whether they are Muslims, Christians, Jews, agnostics, or atheists. The world needs reform, not for the peoples' uprisings to be swallowed up by and to vanish in the current world order. The responsibility is a historic one, especially for majority Muslim societies. Do they have a historical contribution to make; do they share a political or economic, a cultural or ethical responsibility? Are they, as peoples, confident enough, conscious enough to believe in the positively revolutionary power of their references, in the most literal sense? Are they in a position to offer an alternative solution, a new world order, and a new grasp of ends? Are they capable of acting as the energy that drives transformation, instead of simply adapting to the current state of the planet?

After the uprisings, many of the tensions that lay at the core of Tunisian and Egyptian society could be observed. I shall return to this point, but suffice it to say that the aspirations that stood revealed then point now to what is at stake in the debate between secularists, conservatives, and Islamists. Power is part of the equation, of course, as are—in the deepest sense—visions of society torn between a conciliatory synthesis with the West and people's own singular contribution drawn from their own specific referents. This central and complex issue can no longer be eluded.

## 2

# *Cautious Optimism*

THE ARAB AWAKENING has generated theories, interpretations, and names as varied as they are contradictory. As I began to analyze developments in the countries involved—possible only on a case-by-case basis—it became clear that many questions still remain unanswered. Confirmed facts co-existed with often-unverifiable hypotheses. Making sense of events called for prudence. What was happening in the Middle East and North Africa? Why had it happened now? Were the movements that emerged spontaneous, or had one or several foreign hands manipulated not only the events themselves, but opinions as well.

## *Understanding: Manipulation or Liberation?*

In Arab societies and in the West, theories of manipulation arose quickly and flourished on the Web. Such movements could not possibly have begun without the United States and Europe guiding or even masterminding events. What we were witnessing was not liberation at all, but merely another form of control in the guise of democratization. It was, according to the conspiracy theorists, the live enactment of the program announced by George W. Bush with great fanfare in 2003. Using different methods from those employed in Iraq, the United States was now attempting to reconfigure its regional influence. Just as war had been the preferred option in Iraq, mass movements and nonviolence would now be used to undermine regional stability and bring about a Western-dependent transition under military and economic control.

Others formulated, and continue to formulate, precisely the opposite view: the faltering Arab regimes were staunch allies of the United States and of Europe, who would have no interest in overthrowing them. Uncertainty about the future was too great; no administration could wield total control over what were leaderless mass movements, let alone determine their political consequences. What we were seeing were spontaneous revolts that were even inimical to Western interests, and that heralded a new era for Arab societies: their march toward liberation.

Between these two sharply defined positions lies room for a more cautious interpretation of events, one that hews above all to the facts and subjects them to intense scrutiny. I have already pointed to a substantial body of data produced well before the uprisings.[1] The United States above all, as well as several European countries, was either aware of or directly involved in the training of bloggers and activists in the Middle East and North Africa as early as 2003–2004. Government-financed institutions and NGOs in both the United States and Europe welcomed cyber-dissidents from Tunisia, Egypt, and virtually all the other Arab countries. These institutions and NGOs cooperated directly with major American corporations, including Google and Yahoo, as well as Twitter and Facebook. The evidence, which has been verified and confirmed, reveals that the Western countries were not only aware of the activities and mobilizing efforts of the cyber-dissidents but had identified the leaders and studied their profiles and objectives.

The movement can thus not be described as spontaneous. It did not spring suddenly from nothing, taking everyone by surprise. The success of cyber-dissidence in Serbia (in which Americans and Europeans were already involved) between 1998 and 2000 clearly gave Western governments ideas. As early as 2003, the Middle East and Africa had appeared in their sights. Training sessions were organized and networks set up, becoming more structured and more widespread by 2007. In the light of these facts, we should be asking questions about the ultimate goal of training aimed at young people in countries whose governments, despite being autocratic, were allies. It was as if the United States and Europe were supporting despots while at the same time training their opponents. How to explain the apparent contradiction?

Before returning to this important question, a distinction must be drawn between the process of training leaders on the one hand, and the attempt to control events and seize historical opportunities on the other. Well before the uprisings themselves, the work of opposition bloggers had been extraordinary: they had all but colonized the Web, informing, criticizing, and spreading the message of nonviolent resistance, of opposition to dictators, and of the imperative of liberation. Their style of communication had a powerful impact on young people who had been informed and brought into action through social networking. Their psychological impact proved decisive: both the substance and the form of the call to action gave young people a positive self-image, one light years removed from the timeworn clichés about their origins and their religion. They were Arabs, they were Muslims, and they were rallying constructively and nonviolently against dictatorship. Every training session on nonviolent mobilization stressed the importance of psychology, of a positive message.[2] For the Internet-driven movement to have a hope of success, the emotional momentum, once created, had to be maintained and increased. The economic situation in Tunisia and in Egypt was dire; repression was unrelenting. Bloggers and cyber-dissidents had been at work for years. All that was missing was the spark that would light the blaze.

No one could have foreseen the suicide of Mohamed Bouazizi; no one could have imagined the impact of what he did: death by self-immolation. It was a symbolically violent act, for three reasons: Bouazizi was young; he was an innocent victim of poverty; he had no political affiliation (far from being an opposition activist, he was a humiliated street vendor). His suicide was as questionable as it was shocking in a majority Muslim society. His death provided that spark.

Bouazizi's emblematic status—that of poor, innocent, nonpolitical victim—echoed, dissimilar though it was, the self-image and commitment of the young bloggers. The full force of the emotions it released could be brought to bear on the young man; the movement caught fire. Nonviolence training lays emphasis on the necessity of positive symbols around which people can rally, symbols that can be broadly interpreted, beyond partisan interests, immune to takeover. No particular political force could lay claim to Mohamed Bouazizi's suicide.

Rapidly and massively, Tunisians answered the call. In a matter of days the movement swept the country. On December 17, 2010, Bouazizi set himself alight.[3] Less than one month later, on January 14, 2011, Ben Ali, the president of Tunisia, left the country. The political situation had shifted radically as the mass movement grew exponentially. To near-general astonishment, Prime Minister Mohamed Ghannouchi that day announced that Ben Ali had departed, and that he was taking charge. How was such a sudden departure to be explained? France, Ben Ali's foremost European ally, seemed to have been caught by surprise.

In the days and weeks that followed, startling new information was to come to light, particularly the American government's active role in operations. The United States had been present in Tunisia for a decade and had established contacts with all political groups. They knew, as well, that Ben Ali was ill and seriously weakened. As Vincent Geisser pointed out, while the US government collaborated closely with the regime in military and security matters, it had been inviting opposition figures to Washington for talks since

2006.[4] The French daily *Le Figaro*, followed by France's Canal 2, revealed that there had been close contact between the US Embassy and General Rashid Ammar, commander-in-chief of the Tunisian army.[5] General Ammar, Foreign Minister Kamel Morjane,[6] and then-general David Petraeus, commander-in-chief of the international forces in Afghanistan and soon to head the US Central Intelligence Agency (CIA), met to determine the best strategy to prepare for the post-Ben Ali era. They quickly decided to keep the army neutral (a "win-win" situation whatever the outcome):[7] it would not be called upon to open fire on demonstrators. As tension increased, the police responded with violence; on January 11, Hillary Clinton issued a communiqué denouncing the excessive use of force. That same day, France's Foreign Minister Michèle Alliot-Marie offered the Ben Ali regime French military support to crush the uprising.[8] According to a Tunisian diplomat, on January 14 the US Embassy gave the green light for Ben Ali's departure.[9]

President Ben Ali had walked into a trap. He was advised to leave, taking his family with him to safety, and make a triumphant return when the situation was brought under control. Numerous articles have detailed the dictator's last hours in Tunisia: he left the country by air and was prevented by American intervention from landing in France or Cyprus, finally being rerouted to Jeddah, where he now resides in forced exile.[10] Hillary Clinton is said to have spoken personally to Saudi Prince Nayef Bin Sultan to request that the Kingdom accept the fallen dictator.[11] That same afternoon—January 14—Barack Obama, president of the United States, applauded the "courage and dignity of the Tunisian people" and spoke of preparing the future for democracy calmly and serenely, as if to conclude that the Ben Ali era had come to an end as he declared: "I urge all parties to maintain calm and avoid violence, and call upon the Tunisian government to respect human rights, and to hold free and fair elections in the near future that reflect the true will and aspirations of the Tunisian people."[12] Overlooking the years of close collaboration with the autocratic regime, Hillary Clinton confirmed American support for the mass uprising, while Democratic senator and chairman of the Senate Foreign Relations Committee John Kerry ventured the prediction that Ben Ali's flight would "resonate far beyond Tunisia's borders."[13]

The Tunisian uprising would prove for Egyptians an emotional spark of the same magnitude that Mohamed Bouazizi's death had been for Tunisia: Tunisia was for Egypt what Bouazizi had been for Tunisia. On January 25, eleven days after the fall of Ben Ali, demonstrations called by young members of the April 6th Movement began in Cairo.[14] Declared a national holiday in 2009, the date—Police Day—commemorated the deaths of fifty policemen, and many more wounded, on January 25, 1952, when they had refused to hand over their arms to the British at police headquarters in the town of Ismaïlia. The holiday was meant to rehabilitate the reputation of the police, widely detested in Egypt, to express President Mubarak's gratitude, and to underline the commitment of the police to protecting the Mubarak regime. The day itself was rich in references and symbols of the kind that could be counted on to galvanize young people. Images of police brutality against nonviolent demonstrators in Tunisia spoke eloquently to Egyptians, who were keenly aware of how the police treated people with total impunity. The holiday had been held up to mockery in 2009, and organizations like Human Rights Watch had published reports that listed the number of arrests, missing persons, summary executions, and torture by way of denouncing the cynicism of the power structure.[15] Blogger and human rights activist Ramy Raouf was one of many who had already expressed such criticisms, in 2009 and 2010.

In designating January 25 as a "Day of Revolt," Egypt's young cyber-activists had taken the initiative. They would exploit the symbolic impact of the date to the maximum. The citizens of Tunisia had blazed the trail. It now became imperative, with the same determination and without violence, to release the emotional frustrations of the Egyptian people and arouse hopes of freedom that would go far beyond passive acceptance of the status quo. Egyptians had been suffering from the same endemic ills as Tunisians: unemployment, soaring bread and basic food prices, increasing poverty, lack of freedom, under a state of emergency that had been in force since the death of former president Anwar Sadat in October 1981 and renewed each year since. These were the elements that the young activists would draw on: they lashed out at rising bread prices, the lack of freedom, corruption, police brutality, the state of emergency, and, of course, the dictatorial nature of the regime itself. The strategy had been drawn up with careful attention to detail, using all the methods taught in nonviolent mobilization training: positive messages and slogans (as in Serbia, the clenched fist appeared on posters) aimed directly at the regime (and never at the West or other collateral forces), open symbols designed to bridge Egypt's deep internal divisions, and mass rallies called for Cairo's aptly named Liberation Square (Midan at-Tahrir). The young activists were later to provide al-Jazeera journalists with a detailed explanation of their strategy, its implementation, and the training given to many if not most of the country's youthful cyber-activists for periods of one to five years.[16]

On January 18, 2011, Asmaa Mahfouz, a young activist, posted a YouTube video in which she spoke of the victory of the Tunisians over Ben Ali and called upon Egyptians to follow suit.[17] She would not set herself alight, she said. Instead she promised to go to Tahrir Square on January 25 and demand her rights. Her intention was to mobilize Egyptian citizens, beyond political affiliation, to take a stand against police brutality, summary executions, and humiliating treatment. Those who argued that women should not take to the streets she challenged to behave like men and come out into the street to support and protect her. She laid blame for Egypt's catastrophic state of affairs on the passivity of people who did not dare to speak out and to demonstrate, quoting the Qur'an: "God does not change society's conditions until they change that which is in themselves." Appealing to the people's self-respect, she urged: "If you have honor, dignity and courage, join me in Liberation Square." The video had an extraordinary impact: tens of thousands of citizens joined her in the streets, among them large numbers of women who would soon play a key role in the protest movement. The country's political parties and groups announced their participation a few days before January 25, while the Muslim Brotherhood, prompted by its younger members, confirmed its support on January 23.

Crowds poured into the streets of Cairo, Alexandria, and other Egyptian cities, encountering violent repression, particularly in the port city of Suez. A curfew was declared and the 350,000- to 500,000-strong Central Security Forces police (Quwat el-Amn el-Markazi), under the Interior Ministry and loyal to Mubarak, cracked down on protesters. On January 26 the government suspended Internet access to prevent demonstrators from communicating via social networks, a measure later foiled with the direct assistance of Google. January 28 witnessed the first in a series of "Fridays of rage" that were to punctuate the movement, when hundreds of thousands rallied against the regime. On that same day Mohamed El-Baradei, hoping to lead the movement, returned to Egypt after twenty years abroad to a cool reception from a public unfamiliar with him. Mubarak quickly announced a change of government: too little, too late, deemed the protesters.

By then the movement had spread nationwide with astonishing rapidity. The army began to enter the cities—Cairo in particular—but unlike the Security Forces it neither intervened nor exercised violence. Like the Tunisian army, it acted only to maintain order and to prevent clashes between pro- and anti-Mubarak factions. From that moment on, the pace of events quickened. On February 1, the president announced that he would not stand for reelection in September. The following day police and Mubarak supporters, some riding camels, charged the protesters in Tahrir Square, terrorizing the peaceful demonstrators. The president continued to refuse to step down, though he offered some concessions, including transferring political authority to his recently appointed vice-president, Omar Suleiman. But the demonstrators continued to demand Mubarak's departure and the fall of his regime. On February 7, a young man named Wael Ghonim[18] appeared on television after spending ten days in jail. His appearance and his tears shed on national television, which had hitherto given the regime unconditional support, swayed large segments of the public. Huge numbers of Egyptians swelled the ranks of the demonstrators.

The American position as expressed in President Barack Obama's public statements seemed to match the climate of uncertainty that prevailed in the streets and squares of Egypt. But the American administration was in permanent contact with the high command of the Egyptian armed forces, which had been trained and funded by the United States for decades. Internal tensions in the army appear to have prevented the US State Department from taking a clear-cut position. But an odd blunder suddenly exposed these tensions: on February 10 President Obama declared that in Egypt "We are witnessing history unfold,"[19] words that sounded suspiciously like the announcement of the end of Mubarak's rule, only hours before Mubarak surprised everyone by proclaiming that he was determined to hold onto power. Had it been a case of faulty communication—or the cleverly staged exposure of apparent American ignorance of the facts, proving that the United States was not pulling the strings? Mubarak resigned the next day, February 11, on the eve of what the protestors had dubbed the "Friday of departure."

As noted, the US administration was well acquainted with the April 6th Movement and had invited some of its members to the United States as early as 2008 on the initiative of the American ambassador in Cairo, as disclosed by Wikileaks and *The Telegraph*.[20] These sources revealed that on December 30, 2008, the US ambassador, Margaret Scobey, had sent her government "sensitive" information, some of which indicated that "opposition groups had drawn up a secret plan for 'regime change' to be activated before the elections scheduled for September" 2011.[21] Several of the young activists had met with Mohamed El-Baradei in the United States in 2008 and 2009; theirs were the loudest voices when he first returned to Egypt as an opponent to Mubarak in February 2010, one year before the uprising (he then left Egypt and came back on January 26, 2011).[22]

Relations between El-Baradei and the United States had not always been cordial. The Egyptian diplomat had sharply criticized American reluctance to call for reform of the regime as a "farce."[23] But closer analysis points to relations of an entirely different kind. Those between Barack Obama and Mohamed El-Baradei are excellent; the latter has not stinted in his praise for George

W. Bush's successor. In the run-up to Mubarak's replacement, the Obama administration calculated that El-Baradei's notoriously poor relations with the Bush administration and with the United States might well prove to be an advantage.[24] As former State Department advisor Philip D. Zelikow noted: "Ironically, the fact that El-Baradei crossed swords with the Bush administration on Iraq and Iran helps him in Egypt, and God forbid we should do anything to make it seem like we like him."[25] A near-identical analysis appeared in *Foreign Affairs* magazine one year before the uprisings. Pointing out that being seen as friendly with the Americans or being supported by them was a negative factor for any political figure in search of credibility with Egyptians, Steven A. Cook, the article's author, added: "If El Baradei actually has a reasonable chance of fostering political reform in Egypt, then U.S. policymakers would best serve his cause by not acting strongly. Somewhat paradoxically, El Baradei's chilly relationship with the United States as IAEA chief only advances U.S. interests now."[26]

The US administration's apparent dithering as events unfolded might also suggest that it did not know quite what to do. The Egyptian high command was clearly split: some (the more senior officers in particular) stood for the status quo; others favored reforms. But the United States never lost touch with high-ranking Egyptian officers, some of whom had been in Washington only a few days before demonstrations broke out.[27] Anthony H. Cordesman of the Washington-based Center for Strategic and International Studies declared that there was not one but several armies in Egypt, each of them answering to different power centers in the Defense or the Interior Ministry. Forces linked to the latter preferred the status quo and were primarily responsible for the crackdown on protestors, while the high command, linked to the Defense Ministry—the US's main contact in Egypt—had decided to drop Mubarak and wanted change.

Amid sharpening internal tensions, the Obama administration brought increasing pressure to bear on Mubarak to step down. Yet on January 10, the Egyptian president announced that he would not resign, even though President Obama had, a few hours before, suggested that he would. Unnamed American officials told NBC news that same evening that several senior Egyptian officers had, that same Thursday night, threatened President Mubarak that they would "take off their uniforms and join the protesters."[28] Mubarak resigned the next day. Asked if there had been a military coup, American officials answered: "Call it clear military pressure."[29]

In both Tunisia and Egypt, close analysis reveals a context—and implications—far more complex than that of unique, homegrown mass movements springing from the desire and the mobilization of young people responding emotionally to the death of Mohamed Bouazizi or the successful uprising in Tunisia. It had taken several years—going as far back as 2004—to train and make ready a core group of cyber-activists. Not only were the US administration and certain European countries aware; they had funded the training programs and helped develop organized networks of bloggers in the Middle East and North Africa. The close relations between the US, Tunisian, and Egyptian army high commands enabled the Obama administration to anticipate and/or act very quickly as events unfolded. It is impossible to deny the troublesome facts about funding, training, and political and military interference; nor the role of private corporations such as Google, Yahoo, Facebook, or Twitter. I will be returning to this question, for it is imperative that the economic dimension of the upheavals in the Arab world not be minimized. What we are witnessing is not only a political shift toward democratization but also a clear indicator of a major shift in the region's economic structure.

But within the movement itself, bloggers and cyber-activists of both sexes have rejected American attempts to control and direct them, as well as American financial support. Some refused to meet or to be seen in the company of ex-president Bill Clinton when he visited Cairo. In Tunisia as well as Egypt there exist within civil society forces that cut across political boundaries, from Left to Right, up to and including Islamists, and that display genuine political awareness and a commitment to autonomy. They too contributed powerfully to the movement. When confronted, in both Tunisia and Egypt, with efforts at the highest levels of the state and the armed forces to manipulate or hijack the growing mass protests, they proved that the uprisings enjoyed—and still enjoy—substantial freedom of action.

Attempts to take over the protest movements are as predictable as they have been numerous (such as in Eastern Europe). But further analysis and commitment—above and beyond the wide-eyed excitement of the moment—may well open to them real prospects of democratization and liberation. So critical are the economic and geopolitical stakes that it would be shortsighted to expect Europe, the United States, Russia, India, or China to limit themselves to the role of mere onlookers. It would be equally shortsighted, given their perfectly normal penchant for interference and control, to fail to understand the unpredictable nature of mass upheavals sustained and driven by the aspiration to freedom.

Everything remains open—provided that civil society and the citizens of the countries involved commit themselves to imagining and creating a vision for the future drawn from their own history, their memory and their cultural references, their values, and their hopes. Ultimately, they must reclaim the meaning of their revolt even though they were not its sole instigators, planners, and agents. Caution and optimism must be combined with determination and commitment. The leaders of successful uprisings today and tomorrow will be defined by their clear-sighted optimism and their hard-headed dedication. Political liberation requires, above all, freeing minds, mastering emotions, and using close analysis of facts. Call it lucidity, which must be humanistic as well as political.

## Unequal Treatment

It is essential to pay close attention to how events unfolded in Tunisia and Egypt before and during the uprisings to understand what happened, and the very nature of the uprisings themselves. Significant differences can be observed; generalizations must be avoided. National circumstances must be examined on a case-by-case basis. It is equally essential to place national dynamics within the broader regional context: all the truer when we broaden our view to encompass the sources and the meaning of the popular uprisings in Jordan, Libya, Yemen, Bahrain, Syria, or Morocco, for example. Not only are domestic social and political arrangements dissimilar, but the geopolitical context has different effects in different countries, as do, a fortiori, the reactions of Western powers, the United Nations, or the international community.

The situation in the Middle East and North Africa is a complex one, involving a host of issues that go beyond the often simplistic political viewpoint that limits itself to putting forward democratization, as if no other political, economic, or strategic issues were involved. What holds true with regard to the internal dynamics of individual countries holds even truer with regard to the way the United States, Europe, or Russia positions itself. When nations have so often, and so long, been visibly supporting dictatorships in the name of frequently undisclosed economic and military interests, it would today be naïve and inconsistent, amid the general excitement, to consider the Global North's support for democratization as the sincere, unselfish expression of a newfound love for the peoples of the region entirely devoid of strategic calculations. As in any basic economic reckoning, it would seem elementary to enquire about the expectations of the parties involved and about their anticipated benefits.

Responses to the uprisings in the Arab world have been disparate, to say the least. Recall that the first mass demonstrations in a Muslim majority society took place neither in Tunisia or Egypt, but in Iran after the presidential elections of June 2009. No sooner had the election returns been made public, indicating victory for incumbent, Mahmoud Ahmadinejad, than demonstrations broke out across the country, organized by supporters of the two opposition candidates, Mir-Hossein Mousavi and Mehdi Karoubi. They lashed out at electoral fraud and a system adrift, one that had betrayed the democratic principles of equality, justice, and transparency. The protests gave themselves names that symbolized the nature of the regime: the "Green Revolution," the "Green Wave" or the "Green Sea," appropriating Mousavi's campaign color. They were also dubbed the "Twitter Revolution,"[30] as opponents of the regime used the Internet and the social networks to communicate with and to mobilize their supporters. Brutal repression followed, as the regime cracked down on anyone who had challenged the official results: demonstrators were beaten, summarily arrested, tortured, and even raped in custody, according to multiple, concordant, and confirmed testimony.[31] Public participation was widespread and drew substantial support from the West. The Tehran regime, despised by its own people, was in difficulty. Some predicted its collapse in the wake of unprecedented public participation, and the support of leading figures like former reformist president Mohammad Khatami.

The crackdown was brutal; the treatment of the opposition unacceptable. All indicators pointed to a crisis of legitimacy at the heart of the regime, a failure of institutional transparency. The ruling conservative religious hierarchy, little inclined to democratic openness, felt itself threatened on two fronts: by the religious reform movement from within, and by Western pressure from without. After the reform-minded Khatami presidency, which had seemed to open up promising—though insufficient—perspectives, the regime began to crack down on civil, institutional, and media freedoms, moving toward increasingly harsh repression of opponents.

But Iran's protest movement was quite different from the events that were to shake Tunisia and Egypt two years later. The Western view of Iran is jaundiced, an outgrowth of the efforts of Western governments and media to demonize the clerical regime. While it is imperative to criticize that regime, the restrictions on basic freedoms, and the repression of political opponents and demonstrators, the dynamics involved must be studied with proper diligence to avoid mistaken analyses and conclusions.

Iran's "Twitter Revolution" had little in common with the dynamics that were set in motion in Tunisia and Egypt. The Iranian movement arose from the ranks of upper middle-class youth in the capital, Tehran, and other large cities, who had rallied behind the opposition; however, it had very little following among the rest of the people and in rural areas. It would be a significant error not to take full account of the broad support still enjoyed by the conservatives, and by President Mahmoud Ahmadinejad in particular, among the lower classes in both urban and rural areas. In spite of fierce repression and the impact of images diffused on the Internet and by foreign television stations, support for the protests was never as massive as it would be later in Arab countries. Western political pressure and media coverage created an optical illusion when it came to grasping the facts: while Iran is in crisis, the regime continues to enjoy considerable popular support.

Furthermore, the best-known opponents of the regime, Mir-Hossein Mousavi and Mehdi Karoubi, speak from within the Iranian ideological and political system. What they denounce is a betrayal; they do not call for the Islamic Republic to be dismantled. Consequently, they fall well within the religious parameters of the state, which they do not challenge as such but which they feel are being exploited in the illegitimate exercise of power.

The complexity of the Iranian situation did not stop Western powers and their press agencies from throwing their unconditional support behind the protestors, frequently embellishing the opposition's political posture in their obsession with bringing down an Iranian regime whose political influence and alliances are seen as the source of problems in the region. The obligation to criticize the Iranian regime, its abuses and its unacceptable repression, is one thing; that such criticism be used to justify a lack of careful judgment, not to mention biased geopolitical analyses, is another. In retrospect, there is something profoundly unsettling about the American and European political and media campaigns of 2009, which supported Iranian demonstrators in the name of freedom and democracy, while at the same time silently backing the Tunisian and Egyptian regimes whose dictatorial nature had long been common knowledge.

The West, however, was quick to throw its weight behind the uprising in Tunisia, and after some dithering, in Egypt. In both countries the movements had no political coloration; protestors rallied massively, cutting across class and ideological lines, to demand that the dictators and their regimes simply "Get Out!" The real—and symbolic—strength of these movements lay in their two outstanding characteristics: the broad scope of the mobilization and its nonviolent nature. The spark of a suicide caused by the most extenuating circumstances led to a blazing bonfire. Entire populations were caught up in a fever that had taken them by surprise, and that they now lauded in self-congratulation, while people and governments in the West welcomed the "Arab spring" as the harbinger of a new era. The American government, and its European allies, pretended to be mere observers and, as events played out, to hail the people in their quest for freedom.

Matters shifted somewhat when unrest broke out in Libya on February 15, 2011, on the heels of Tunisia and Egypt (whose impact was greater), as the population staged nonviolent protests across the country. Reaction from Muammar Ghaddafi's government was immediate: the violent response of the police and the military left four dead and dozens wounded. The demonstration that followed two days later, on February 17, dubbed the "Day of Rage," saw even more violent clashes. Muammar Ghaddafi and his son, Saif al-Islam, threatened to crack down on the demonstrators, whom they described as "madmen," as "linked to al-Qaeda" some of whom had "just returned from Guantanamo."[32]

Western media were quick to propagate a particularly somber account of the repression in Libya and a sanitized version of the opposition, as Amnesty International points out in a detailed report: "Western media coverage from the outset presented a very one-sided view of events, portraying the protest movement as entirely peaceful and repeatedly suggesting that the regime's security forces were unaccountably massacring unarmed demonstrators who presented no security challenge."[33] The repressive nature of the regime was well known, of course; Ghaddafi's moody and mercurial personality left few illusions about the way he would react. He had proclaimed that he would crack down on his opponents; there was every reason to believe that he would indeed do so. A propaganda campaign was quickly set in motion, the aim of which was to present Ghaddafi—who had only recently been rehabilitated at the international level[34]—in the most negative possible light, while his opponents were absolve his opponents, who were depicted as unarmed demonstrators defying the dictator.

The reality is less edifying. When, on February 27, 2011, the National Transitional Council was set up, with the unexpected mediation of French media intellectual Bernard-Henri Lévy, details of the composition of the council, headed by former Libyan Minister of Justice Mustafa Mohamed Abdel Jalil who had defected only five days earlier, proved scanty. The United States and NATO hailed the initiative while France was the first country to recognize the Council as its interlocutor and as representative of the people of Libya, in place of Ghaddafi.[35]

The American profile in Libya had become significantly higher following the improvement of relations with Tripoli, just as it had in Tunis and in Cairo. This time, however, the Obama administration encouraged France to take the initiative. Roles were assigned according to the respective needs

of each player: President Obama could hardly justify a new military intervention or major financial involvement with the US economy deep in crisis.
But French president Nicolas Sarkozy, who had been relegated to a bit role
in Tunisia and Egypt, was given ample opportunity to refurbish his reputation as an international statesman. France would work to persuade the United
States, Europe, and other countries, up to and including the Arab League, not
only to side with the rebellion but also to provide direct military support to
the rebels, and to the civilian population threatened by massacre in Benghazi:
"Europeans, Americans and Arabs together," trumpeted Sarkozy.[36]

For the Americans, handing the initiative to France proved to be both
a bargain and a lesser evil. They could not be held responsible for opening
a new war front, nor could they be criticized for becoming bogged down.
Above all, they could continue their operations on the ground. Early on,
sources revealed that the CIA had been directly involved from the beginning
of the uprising, and even before,[37] and that it had been working continuously
and strategically with the rebels.[38]

Libyan politics are complex: Ghaddafi's power relied on a decentralized
system of clan alliances in which tribal affiliation was often more important than good or bad relations with Tripoli. But the country was also a key
regional player: liberating and then controlling it promised significant political, geopolitical, and economic benefits for all concerned, who were prepared
to accept the risks of working with a Transitional Council made up of former
Ghaddafi cabinet ministers (some of who were agents of foreign powers),
ostensibly repentant Islamists, and uncontrolled, even extremist elements.
Under France's lead, operations were launched under the aegis of NATO,
whose errors of judgment and blunders grew to alarming proportions, while
the Americans attempted to organize the rebellion, the better to profit from
the situation irrespective of the outcome.[39]

What reasons justified the Western intervention in Libya while NATO
and the concert of nations remained passive and silent in the face of the
brutal crackdown on the civilian population in Syria, particularly the confirmed fact that ten- and twelve-year-old children had been tortured? Initially
advanced, the humanitarian claim does not hold up. The strategic importance
of Ghaddafi's Libya, which had long eluded foreign control, far outweighed
the ingenuously humanistic statements of French leaders. The first protests
against Ghaddafi, whose oil wealth had restored him to the good graces of
the international community after years of sanctions, were an opportunity
not to be missed. The dictator had proven an embarrassment in four major
areas: his African policy of building economic ties and financially supporting

leaders to Libya's east, west, and south, gave them a latitude that thwarted French ambitions, and increasingly those of the United States and Israel,[40] which were becoming indisposed by the regime's budding economic relations with Ivory Coast, Chad, Sudan, South Africa, India, and China,[41] to name but a few—not to mention his open cooperation with the little-loved regime of Venezuela's president Hugo Chavez. True to his reputation as a veritable dictator, Ghaddafi could be disturbing and provocative; but for all his unpredictable and quirky behavior, he frequently displayed undeniable strategic abilities.

Recent developments cannot be overlooked: a wealthy and autonomous Libya, bordering on both Tunisia and Egypt in the process of throwing off their yoke, could have created an uncontrolled zone that would have awakened the prospect of new strategic relations between the countries of North Africa and the Middle East, thereby transforming it into a high risk area for the Western powers. Not only had it become imperative to bring Ghaddafi down; it was a matter of urgency to maintain some degree of control over the successor regime.

At the core of these competing interests lies Libya's oil wealth. Not only did Libya export more than $31 million worth of crude annually; 80 percent of the total was shipped to the European Union.[42] As an OPEC member and Africa's fourth largest oil producer, Libya enjoyed substantial autonomy vis-à-vis the West while Europe's dependence on Libyan oil production— 10 percent of French imports and as much as 25 percent for Italy—was considerable. In addition, new and promising reserves have recently been discovered. Military operations, initially presented as risk-free, could not be carried out without first consulting the oil companies such as France's Total or Italy's ENI, whose fears increased with every passing day of hostilities, as pointed out by the *Financial Times*. The stakes were high: the Ghaddafi regime's National Oil Corporation controlled the bulk of Libyan production, offering access to foreign firms through joint ventures. When they stopped production and repatriated their personnel, he threatened to turn in future to China, India, and Brazil.

The uprising in Libya, then, revealed the unspoken economic considerations that underlie the dissimilar treatments faced by the Arab countries. The wish to maintain economic and geopolitical control in Tunisia and Egypt—in the disguise of political democratization—is radically different from the intention to exert full control over Libya's political alignment while gaining direct access to the country's oil reserves. Knowing the Libyan leader's personality, it was clearly impossible to achieve these goals without direct military intervention. On September 1, 2011, the very day that France had convened an international conference in Paris to discuss the disbursement of Libya's assets and the post-Ghaddafi era (he had been defeated, but not yet found and killed), the Parisian daily *Libération* revealed a deal—dating back to March 19, 2011—between the National Transitional Council and France, granting the latter 35 percent of Libya's oil exports after Ghaddafi's anticipated downfall (Qatar, the first country to support France in its anti-Ghaddafi campaign, knew of and approved the agreement).[43] Even before Ghaddafi had been located, and while the fighting continued, French, American, Chinese, and Turkish firms had begun the hunt for contracts. France's Minister of Foreign Trade traveled to Libya with a business delegation to secure contracts (in oil, telecommunications, transport, etc.).[44] Beneath the fine words of humanitarian concern lurked cynical calculation.

To these political and economic concerns must be added the geostrategic factor. Rumors of friendly relations between Ghaddafi and Israel had grown in recent months (in the Arab world or on the Internet), even though the true nature of their relationship was very bad. As a partisan of the two-state solution, Ghaddafi never concealed his support for the Palestinian resistance; after the Arab uprisings had begun, he called on Palestinians to gather peacefully at their disputed borders. He systematically linked criticism of the United States and Europe to criticism of Israel, while he pointed to the cowardice of the Arab countries.[45] In the regional context, it was clear that Ghaddafi's policies, and his alliances with partners like Venezuela, South Africa, China, or Brazil that are far less pro-Israel than the United States and Europe, were as dangerous as his economic power and autonomy. The arrival on the scene of Bernard-Henri Lévy, who for a few days functioned as France's foreign minister, proved telling, given the man's support for Israel and his access and missions to the highest levels of the Zionist state. Rumors aside, Israel looked benevolently upon Ghaddafi's ouster, primarily because of the danger represented by his international alliances and his support for the Palestinian cause. The lure of oil combined with his outspoken anti-Israeli position in Africa (Chad, Sudan, and South Africa) must also be taken into account.

Behind the celebration of the values of freedom, dignity, and the struggle against dictatorship is concealed a battle for economic domination, control of oil production and reserves, and coldly cynical geopolitical calculation. How else is the silence over repression in Syria to be interpreted? There, nonstate media have been banned, Internet access has been cut off, and fierce repression has become the rule, as the army now fires point-blank at unarmed civilians; more than 5,000 are missing. Between the earliest demonstrations, in

February 2011, and the timid, nonconstraining resolution of the UN Security Council adopted on August 3, 2011, no significant pressure has been brought to bear against President Bashar al-Assad's repressive policies. The United States has been content to freeze the assets of the regime's leading figures— far distant from the indignation touched off by dictator Ghadaffi's actions, whose horrors were deliberately exaggerated, as pointed out earlier.[46]

Geopolitical considerations remain the decisive factor in deciding upon support or lack of support for the Arab peoples in their quest for freedom and dignity. Syria's allies Russia, China, and Venezuela (where Hugo Chavez shamelessly described Bashar al-Assad as "a humanist and a brother")[47] opposed any form of military intervention. Their position did shift during the weeks of repression: Turkey, Russia, and China finally requested the Syrian president to end the crackdown. Yet the fact remains that the regime was free to act, and to kill. From the outset, the United States spoke out in favor of internal reform (leaving the regime in power), a position that was first shared by Europe and the other major powers, including Israel.

The structure of Syrian society is a complex one. Today the minority Shiite Alawite sect rules over a country where the majority are Sunni Muslims.[48] Opposition parties and resistance currents are difficult to identify and to control. The United States, Europe, and Israel have no idea of what might be the outcome were the regime to collapse. Leftist or secularist anti-American tendencies, pro-Shiite, and pro-Iranian groups as well as Islamists form a configuration that would be difficult to manage. Despite its lack of identifiable natural resources, the regime plays a crucial role in regional strategy. Its anti-Israel stance and its support for Islamist movements like Hamas are common knowledge, but both the United States and Israel know that Israel has never had cause to fear either intervention or attack from Syria for the last thirty years, either under Hafez al-Assad's reign or during that of his son Bashar. Even after Israel destroyed its anti-aircraft missile bases in Lebanon's Beka'a Valley in June 1982, or after the bombardment of Hezbollah positions across Lebanon in July 2006 (even though Syria had promised to respond) or the air attack on alleged nuclear installations in September 2007, the regime did not respond to Israel's aggression against and humiliation of its neighbor. Indications are that the Syrian regime plays the role of a useful regional enemy for Israel: it keeps opposition under tight control (permitting no dissent) and uses violent rhetoric while never taking action. In doing so, it allows Israel to point to the permanent threat at its borders, with Syria, Lebanon, and Iran representing the axis of potential aggressors.

But the determination of the people has been and will be stronger than the wavering of politicians. Syria's immediate allies, not to mention its enemies, have gradually shifted their positions, as they came to the conclusion that the regime was in danger and unlikely to survive. Could there be a finer example of the unexpected potential of nonviolent mass uprisings? Western countries had apparently neither anticipated nor wished for what has happened. Nothing had been planned beforehand, nothing was under control: the will of the people, inspired by the examples of Tunisia and Egypt, courageous and determined, has shaken the regime and has put change on the agenda. Nothing has been definitively achieved by the mass protests that have swept the region, but it is impossible to overlook the importance of unexpected events, those that have eluded outside control, that are the product of the struggle of people for their dignity. Contrary to appearances, the uprising in Syria was not desired by its "enemies," the United States and Israel. The people's bravery and determination have forced history's hand in a country that can boast few natural resources but is geographically strategic.

In our rapid survey of the mass upheavals that have shaken the region, particular attention must be paid to Bahrain. There, protests broke out on February 14, 2011, and spread rapidly. A demonstration almost 100,000 strong (in a country whose population is 1.2 million) took place on February 23, whose participants included Sunnis and a large number of women and children. The demonstrators demanded reform of the ruling regime and an end to inequality in the application of the laws governing naturalization. Slogans called for Sunni-Shiite unity.[49] The government responded with a violent crackdown, portraying the demonstrators as Shiite radicals intent on overthrowing the regime (Shiites make up 75 percent of Bahrain's population).[50]

It became clear that intra-Muslim confessional conflict has had little to do with popular unrest. As in Tunisia and Egypt, Shiite and Sunni demonstrators joined together to demand justice, social equality, political transparency, and change in a regime built on the privileges of the ruling family.[51] But King Hamad bin Issa al-Khalifa quickly played the religious conflict card and, after having declared a state of emergency, called in his allies in the Gulf Cooperation Council (GCC) to suppress the protest movement. Saudi Arabia, the United Arab Emirates, and Qatar promptly rallied behind the regime at the same time that they sided with the rebels in Libya.[52] The stakes were double, and they were high: it was imperative to contain the Arab uprisings and prevent them from reaching even one of the oil sheikdoms.[53] Collapse of the regime in Bahrain would have sent shock waves through the entire Arabian Peninsula. In playing the religious conflict card, Bahrain, and particularly Saudi Arabia,

While it is tempting at first glance to speak of a "domino effect" in discussing the courage and energy of the popular uprisings that have spread like wildfire across the Middle East (from Tunisia to Syria, by way of Egypt, Libya, Yemen, and Bahrain), considering the differentiated approach adopted in this text a chess match seems to be the more appropriate metaphor.[57] Each country must be studied separately, but analysis must be based on the regional context and geostrategic considerations, and on the way different situations mutually impinge.

Tunisia has moved rapidly toward a democratization that, despite its difficulties, seems destined for success. In the elections to the Constituent Assembly held on October 23, 2011, 51 percent of Tunisian citizens registered to vote, and the election produced a clear victory for Ennadha, an Islamist party. Two other parties—the Congress for the Republic led by Moncef Marzouki and Ettakol (Democratic Forum of Labor and Freedom) led by Mustapha Ben Jaafar—finished in second and third place, respectively. The three parties agreed to reject the "secularist-Islamist" polarization and affirmed the primacy of cooperation and alliance. Positions were assigned under a tripartite agreement expressing the philosophy of the three groupings: on November 22, 2011, Mustapha Ben Jaafar (of Ettakol) was elected president of the Constituent Assembly. Moncef Marzouki was elected president of Tunisia on December 12; three days later he appointed Hamadi Jebali (of Ennadha) as prime minister. Of all the countries to have experienced a mass uprising, Tunisia appears to be best situated to bring about a genuine change of regime, to overcome the false debates over the nature of the state (secular or Islamic), and to avoid secular-Islamist polarization, to which I will return in the second part of this book.

The course of events in Libya has been far more troubling: the armed forces of NATO threw their full support behind an armed rebellion. Under French and American authority, they were successful in tracking down Colonel Ghaddafi on October 20, 2011. The erstwhile Libyan strongman was taken alive, then lynched in circumstances that showed little respect for basic human rights. Though Ghaddafi had been a bloodthirsty dictator, he should have been brought to trial. The images of his lynching were as inhuman as they were unbearable.[58] A few days later, on October 24, the president of the National Transitional Council (NTC) announced that Shar'ia would form the "basic law" of the land, and went on to make striking references to divorce, marriage, and the legalization of polygamy. The proclamation conveyed a twofold message: (1) an affirmation to Libyans of the total independence of the NTC and its new leadership, and (2) a warning to the West to could construct an interpretation of events that would justify their regional policy as a reaction to Iran's genuine influence and to the significant presence of Shiism. The additional credibility gained from Shiite resistance to Israel's policies (Iran's clear-cut positions; Hezbollah's resistance to Israel's July 2006 aggression against Lebanon), as well as refusal to cooperate with the United States, also had to be factored into the equation.[54]

Neither the United States nor Europe reacted to the Bahraini regime crackdown. The Arab League's claim that the conflict was a religious one and that the population's demands had nothing in common with those of the peoples of Tunisia, Egypt, or Libya came in for sharp criticism.[55] Economic considerations, regional stability, and access to oil triumphed over support for democratization. Political rhetoric and media coverage—more akin to propaganda stressing the dangers of the mass protests in Bahrain—were clearly designed to undermine the legitimacy of the pro-democracy movement in an extremely sensitive part of the world.

A documentary aired on al-Jazeera English (covering both the demonstration and the repression) created tensions between Bahrain and Qatar, even though the latter, alongside Saudi Arabia, had been quick to support the current regime. The documentary was not broadcast on al-Jazeera's Arabic-language channel.[56] Support for protesters calling for justice, the rule of law, and democracy appeared to depend on national and regional considerations. Though uncertainty remains, the situation in Tunisia and Egypt seems to be relatively under control—and far different from in Libya, where a battle for economic and geopolitical advantage is being fought, and more different still from the situation in Syria (a useful objective ally) and in Bahrain (where regime change would entail major and unpredictable consequences). Young people in Bahrain and in the petro-monarchies as a whole have not been trained in the techniques of nonviolent mass mobilization. In any event, the absence of democracy, prevalent conservatism, and religious literalism do not bother the Western powers in the slightest, any more than they have the slightest connection with the declarations of support or condemnation the Arab countries are continuously unleashing at one another. Analysis has shown that the spontaneity and the apparently positive nature of the so-called Arab spring should be qualified, or at least placed in a broader context. Though understandable, an outburst of national enthusiasm restricted to a sole country without taking regional realities into account would be a risky proposition: in a state of political intoxication, it is often difficult to distinguish between a historical opportunity for liberation and cynical manipulation.

downplay its current and future role in determining the country's reorientation and reconstruction. Curiously, the two declarations did not disturb Western governments in the slightest, as they seemed to confirm that the sole purpose of the NATO intervention had been to support the civilian population and that Western participation had been strictly limited to that mission. The words of Mustafa Abdul Jalil provided proof positive that the United States, France, and the United Kingdom had made no attempt to influence the political outcome in Libya. Indeed.

The following weeks were to reveal that political and economic dealings between the new Libyan authorities, the United States, France, and the United Kingdom had been intense and often fraught with tension. The Western Powers remain deeply involved in Libya and in close touch with all the country's political forces (which was the case, as I noted, well before the fall of Ghaddafi). The economic agreements and reconstruction contracts signed provide clear proof that NATO support was far from simply humanitarian, and that Western governments intend to play a determinant economic and political role in Libya.[59] The stakes are particularly high, and the democratization process in Libya has been far from transparent. Only over time will the shape of the new regime emerge, given the clan and tribal relationships that make up the country's social fabric. Months after Ghaddafi's fall, the militias are refusing to lay down their arms until they are given guarantees on power sharing. Nothing can be taken for granted.

Despite a recent agreement ensuring him immunity, Yemen's president Ali Abdullah Saleh continues to mobilize his followers and allies to blunt the thrust for democracy in Yemen. The armed forces, along with tribal alliances, continue to play a key role and, once more, no one can predict the outcome. Determined to pursue a nonviolent course, the people of Yemen, who have made so many sacrifices to liberate their land, are far from being assured of a democratic future. In the heart of the Middle East, the country seems to have been forgotten, as though its struggle for liberation were less meaningful than those of other countries. A democratic, united, less corrupt Yemen would have a substantial regional and geostrategic impact, but the struggle for this has been ignored. In Bahrain, the Sunni and Shiite mass movements continue as these groups seek their own freedoms, but spotty media coverage has been given to these efforts; as 2012 unfolds, little if anything has changed, with women and men continuing to shout their rejection of the status quo.

Events have taken an equally sobering turn in Egypt. The victory of the Muslim Brotherhood in the recent legislative elections and the surprising second-place showing of the Salafist an-Nur party appear at first glance to

## On the West, on Politics and the Economy

All the elements enumerated earlier, whether analyzed sequentially (preparation of the uprisings, the attitude of the West as events unfolded, etc.) or simultaneously (integration of economic and geopolitical data to shape a coherent political understanding), call for circumspection. It is essential to avoid hasty conclusions and to adopt a global approach to the complexities of the Middle East and North Africa.

Amid the celebration of the "Arab spring" and its contagious optimism, much has been made of the advent of democratization in the Arab world, as if that alone would be sufficient to explain the true nature of the historical upheaval unfolding around us. Overnight, the United States, Europe, the major press agencies, and the world's mainstream media lavished praise on the nonviolent mass movements that would at long last unlock the door to liberty, and that could actually aspire to establish democracy. But an intriguing element seems to be missing from this otherwise positive narrative: if liberal democracy has suddenly become so wonderful for the Arabs, how can the long-standing, unconditional support of the Western powers for dictatorship be justified? How can we explain that such support stops short of some countries, the petro-monarchies, for instance? By asking these two questions we can broaden our analytical perspective, and avoid the political over-optimism or naivety brought about by economic and geopolitical carelessness or blindness.

For the West, the democratization of the Arab world has never been an end in itself. What matters above all is regional stability and securing Western economic interests. For decades Tunisia, Algeria, Morocco, Jordan, and—crucially—Egypt stood guard over the geopolitical and economic interests of Europe and the United States. American and/or European military bases were established in Morocco, Algeria, Tunisia, and Egypt, not to mention Jordan, Saudi Arabia, Qatar, and others. The creation in 2008 of the United States Africa Command (Africom) base and military headquarters (located in Stuttgart and commanded since 2011 by General Carter Ham) to coordinate military operations and surveillance throughout Africa, underlines the importance of these strategic ties. The "war against terror" opened the door to an even larger scale military presence, with American bases on Arab soil carrying out wholly autonomous military and surveillance operations directed by Washington alone. As early as 2003, the US Central Command (Centcom) directed most American military operations in Iraq from its sophisticated command center in Qatar.[87] Bahrain constitutes another crucial element, as it is home port to the US Fifth Fleet, which was directly involved in the Iraq and Afghanistan wars[88] and operates in the strategic areas of the Persian Gulf, the Red Sea, the Sea of Oman, and parts of the Indian Ocean. Governments that were more often than not dictatorial and that depended on the United States in case of danger facilitated American penetration of the Arab world. Israel's presence and surveillance capacity have always been one of the cornerstones of the United States' unfailing support for Israel in the region.

Above and beyond the familiar military and geopolitical arguments lie economic interests. Certainly oil (in Iraq, Libya, Algeria, and the oil-rich kingdoms of the Arabian Peninsula), natural gas (in Qatar, Saudi Arabia, Iran, and Algeria), iron and lithium (a substance crucial to modern and future industry, found abundantly in Afghanistan) have focused attention and justified policies that did not always agree with human rights. The Western powers have contrived to protect their access to these and other mineral resources by ensuring a secure environment for contracts awarded to European and American multinational corporations.

For years, the United States and Europe invested heavily in protecting their own economic interests, stability, and security in the Arab world. If an equation that contained no unknowns (profit, stability, security) could be insured by dictatorships (like those in Tunisia or Egypt) or by kings who swore by strict, conservative Islam (as in Saudi Arabia), then such regimes were considered de facto reliable allies. The uneven response to the Arab uprisings by the US and European governments indicate that nothing has changed.

Noam Chomsky could not be clearer when he states that the United States will never permit the processes of democratization to develop fully: the stakes are too high, and the consequences potentially too dangerous. Arab popular opinion dislikes the American presence, a fact the Americans are fully aware of: hence their preference for pliable political leaders or the military (as in Egypt even now). Chomsky sees nothing new on the horizon in terms of US long-term strategy. In his view, the Obama administration, like those before it, will find a way to prevent the process from being carried through and will, at best, permit only managed democracies to be set up. Such "democratic" transformations have been frequent in recent history: Chomsky lists Somoza's Nicaragua, the Shah's Iran, the Philippines under Marcos, Duvalier's Haiti, Chun's South Korea, Congo's Mobutu, Romania's Ceausescu, and Indonesia's Suharto.[89] All these regimes were supported in the name of well-defined economic interests, and all were later dropped in the name of democratic ideals (but always masking the imposition of a new kind of relationship and of control).

The Arab world is no exception. The rhetoric changes to suit new circumstances, while the basic strategy remains intact: calls for justice and democracy are selectively celebrated depending on the vital interests at stake. Europe and the United States claim to have intervened in Libya following an Arab League request for the establishment of a "no-fly zone" over the country to prevent the Ghaddafi regime from bombing civilians and resistance fighters. In responding to the request, the West interpreted the UN resolution in a way that went well beyond the Arab League's wishes. Later, through its Secretary General Amr Moussa, the League criticized the way its request had been exploited.[90] When the same Arab League had earlier called for a no-fly zone over Gaza where the civilian population was being bombarded daily by the Israeli air force, its request was not acted upon, nor even discussed. Libyan oil, it seems, is thicker than Palestinian blood.[91]

Why has such a sequence of events unfolded in the Middle East and North Africa? However we wish to view the actual autonomy and significance of the uprisings that have taken place, the question remains relevant. Why, in supporting and funding seminars in nonviolent mobilization, did the United States prod some Arab countries toward the goal of democratization first articulated by George W. Bush in 2003, while most of those countries' regimes already fully supported American policy? For what reason, assuming that the Obama administration was truly taken by surprise, did it not lend firmer support to its friends in Tunisia and Egypt, and attempt to protect them, if the risk of seeing them slip out of its control was so great?

It should be recalled, first, that the Ben Ali (in Tunisia) and Mubarak (in Egypt) regimes were drawing to an end; the time had come to consider the question of transition. However true, simply to state the fact can hardly explain why such a simple realization should have led the United States to take a risk of such magnitude. All evidence indicates that the old formula— "security + stability + economic interest"—that had long enabled the United States and often Europe to dominate the Arab world was no longer applicable. Major American corporations were active in the region, but the criteria applied for protecting their profits (support for pro-Western dictatorships and control of the oil, natural gas, arms and consumer goods markets) were adversely impacting the policies of Western multinationals. Factors ranging from corruption, obsession with security, and the structural limitations of a 400-million-strong market had made strategic change an urgent necessity.

One decisive element is hardly ever mentioned in discussing and analyzing the Arab uprisings: the looming shadow of China, and to a lesser degree the shadows of Russia, India, Brazil, South Africa, and Turkey.[92] The Russian

and Chinese governments were hesitant in their support for the Arab protest movement. They criticized the West's intervention in Libya and opposed
any intervention in Syria. Chinese economic strategy in the region has been
bearing fruit for years now: it extends to an impressive array of industrial
activities, cutting-edge technologies, and services. The Chinese government
is unlikely to be embarrassed by human rights rhetoric contradicted by facts.
In fact, China has no "human rights rhetoric" masquerading as a conscience.
The presence of Chinese economic agents in the Middle East is noteworthy
for its noninterference in local politics and its efficiency. China's dynamism is
striking, and its security guarantees and military power are confirmed by figures: its military budget increased by 12.5 percent from 2010 to 2011, and the
US National Security Council's Strategic Assessment Group predicts that "by
2020 China will achieve military parity with the United States."[93]

The three flaws commonly associated with the West—European colonialism, American imperialism, and their unconditional support for Israel—have
never afflicted China. As early as 2000, Yasser Arafat suggested that China
appoint a permanent envoy to the region, which Jiang Zemin's government
eventually did.[94] In May 2006 the Chinese president had no hesitation in
inviting the Hamas Foreign Minister Mahmoud al-Zahar to the China-Arab
cooperation forum in Beijing, despite alarmist criticism from the United
States, which describes the group as a "terrorist" organization and continues to attempt to isolate it.[95] Its independence in the Israel-Palestine conflict
while keeping close and visible contact with all the region's main players has
strengthened China's ideological and economic credentials in Arab society,
where public opinion strongly favors Beijing over Washington. The invasion
of Iraq by the United States and Great Britain proved to be a decisive factor
in changing perceptions: China kept out of the conflict and sharply criticized
US doublespeak on human rights after the Abu Ghraib prison scandal—just
as it had done over Guantanamo.[96] Its criticism was well received in the Arab
world. In 2008 China signed an agreement to purchase oil worth an estimated
US$3 billion ("the first major oil deal Iraq has made with a foreign country
since 2003," reported the *New York Times*)[97] that reconfirmed and expanded
the terms of an earlier agreement signed in 1997, though China had not been
a party to the conflict. A US Center for Strategic and International Studies'
(CSIS) study entitled "China and the Middle East" examines in detail the
phenomenal growth of Chinese economic programs in the region, describing
them as "economic growth without significant political liberalization."[98] In a
wide-ranging summary, it discusses prevailing views of China's growing influence and its "peaceful rise" regionally and globally. Over and above China's

military capacity, it points to the rapid transformation and adaptation of Chinese commercial, energy, and technological expertise.

Between 1999 and 2006, trade between China and the Middle East soared, according to International Monetary Fund statistics, growing from $US9 billion to $US78 billion. Since then, exponential growth has continued.[99] A similar pattern can be observed in North Africa (particularly in Algeria and Morocco). The Chinese presence in the region represents a major challenge for the United States, as Beijing has not only developed ostentatious ties with declared foes (particularly Iran) of the United States but has also courted American allies, particularly Saudi Arabia (where trade has increased fivefold in the last decade), Algeria, and even Israel (which has established military and technological cooperation with China). A book aptly entitled *The Vital Triangle: China, the United States, and the Middle East* suggests that more holistic attention be paid to the Chinese regional presence, as it represents a significant regional economic, military, and strategic challenge.[100]

Far removed from the celebration of democratic values, a genuine economic and ideological war is being waged throughout the Arab world, in Africa and in Asia. While the United States has attempted to develop a more aggressive policy of economic and military penetration, new players are blunting the American strategy. Not only is China well received in the Arab world (which considers it to be more pro-Arab and pro-Palestinian than pro-Israeli); so are Russia, Brazil, South Africa, and, more visibly, Turkey. India, an emerging power, has also begun to draw attention. During the Tunisian and Egyptian uprisings, the Indian government attempted to remain neutral.[101] Its commitment to political noninterference, its economic ties with Iran,[102] its frequent support of Palestinian rights (despite a threefold rise in joint projects with Israel over the past fifteen years), and its burgeoning economic ties with regional countries (not to mention the 5 million Indian immigrant workers residing there) lend India a particular stature and draw direct and indirect criticism from the United States[103] while preserving a largely positive image in the Arab world. The rise of strong, multifaceted competition has put the markets of the Western multinationals in danger: the status quo has become untenable; without in-depth reform, the tide threatens to turn against the United States and Europe.

It has become increasingly obvious that to focus strictly on political factors (the attainment of democracy by the Arab countries) is not only reductive but also highly deceptive. Regional dynamics and the interests involved cannot be understood by restricting analysis to a strictly political and media account of events. The stakes are high, and critical: in economic terms the Middle East will remain for some years to come a key geographical area in the competition between the United States, Europe, China, India, Russia and new arrivals like Brazil, South Africa, and Turkey.

The Arab awakening must be seen and interpreted in the light of the latest economic and strategic information available. Political freedom—and democratization—cannot assure a country or even a region of autonomy: economic security and independence are the fundamental conditions for preventing the establishment of ostensibly democratic but economically subservient Arab states.

The very instrumental presence of powerful multinational corporations at every stage of the process that climaxed in the mass uprisings points to the need for extreme vigilance and redoubled caution before drawing conclusions. Broader democratic freedoms could well give rise to a restructuring of the regional economy, to reforms less concerned with democracy than with reorientation that would in turn lead to restricted freedoms and a slowing of the social and economic development in the countries of the region. The imperatives of liberal economy would be quite likely to turn against the prospects of liberal democracy. This is Arundhati Roy's conclusion: the Arab awakening must be seen primarily as a way to open the Middle East to the neo-liberal economy.[104]

Barack Obama's address at the State Department on May 19, 2011,[105] bitterly disappointed the Arab world.[106] It was a fascinating, revealing, and above all unsettling performance. After hailing the popular movements in Tunisia and Egypt, the president devoted fully half of his speech to economic matters and to the commitment of the United States to "support" the democratization process by injecting substantial amounts of money via the Bretton Woods institutions, the World Bank and the IMF. The logic could hardly be clearer: provide financial support, assume control, and ensure long-term dependence through debt. To the countries of the Global South that had attained political independence in the 1940s and had long since been forced to recognize the consequences of economic imperialism, the return of the old model was patent. Today the question arises: sixty or seventy years later, what, if anything, has changed? Could the Arab awakening have created the conditions for a tragic leap backward into a "new" old-style dependency?

A fair question. But above and beyond political analysis, the issues defined earlier—the creativity of people inspired by their own history and cultural references—cannot be overlooked. When, as I have noted, both Left and Right, whether intentionally or not, validate the notion that the Arab and Muslim majority peoples are stepping up to "our" values, "our" democratic requirement, and are at last joining the linear progress of history, they are in effect laying claim to history—an ideological imperialism that goes to extraordinary lengths to keep people from reconciling themselves with who they are, and with their own genius. To be free, they must reproduce what already exists. Never, of course, must they challenge the economic diktats that make a mockery of the prerequisites of democracy and are driven by interest and profit alone.

The Arab world, so rich and yet so divided against itself, now finds its own weaknesses staring it in the face. So long ideologically alienated, it suffers from grave economic and strategic inconsistencies, not to mention religious tensions. It is all well and good to criticize the power of the United States, Europe, China, Russia, or India, but the criticism will be wasted if the weakness, the challenges, and the failures of the Arab world are not held up to scrutiny.

## What Lies Ahead for Muslim Majority Societies?

The world watched the Arab awakening with surprise, and often with satisfaction. At last, the Arab countries would emerge from their cocoon, free themselves from dictatorship, and attain democracy, greater freedom, and justice. What the Right- and Left-wing opposition parties and the Islamists had, for a half-century, been unable to achieve, youthful bloggers, cyber-dissidents, and ordinary women and men from all walks of life had been able to accomplish peacefully and with lightning rapidity. The strength of the mass movements, particularly in Tunisia and Egypt, lay in their capacity to unite people beyond political divisions. Putting aside their affiliations with this or that trend, women and men united in a ringing "No" to dictatorship. The mass effect, the impact of hundreds of thousands of citizens taking bravely to the streets, brought about a surprisingly rapid result.

The second great strength of the movement was the clarity of its message, focused from the beginning on the dictator and his regime. Slogans like "Get out!" or "The people want the fall of the regime!" were chanted over and over again, day after day. There was no mention of anything but the yearning for freedom, the urge for justice, and the quest for dignity. Despite the dozens of dead, the repression, and the police blunders, positive messages filled with humor and hope could be heard. Training in the techniques of nonviolent mobilization may well have been a key factor. The focus on a simple message, on symbols that transcended political or religious ideologies, on massive gatherings and well-planned discipline gave the Arab peoples a breath of life that some thought them no longer capable of, so accustomed had they become to submission to dictatorial regimes with a kind of culpable passivity. They people had said "No!" They had rebelled.

Once the regimes had fallen, however, the movements whose strength had been their lack of ideological leadership were rapidly to lose their momentum. The power of the masses in defying the regime had become the prime cause of their weakness. Civil society indeed existed in Tunisia and in Egypt, but such was the weight of the dictatorship that intellectual and political debate were circumscribed for lack of freedom, or focused entirely on opposing the regime. The uprisings, and those who propelled them forward, had a clear idea of what they no longer wanted, but they struggled to give expression to their social and political aspirations, beyond the slogans that called for an end to corruption, cronyism, and the establishment of the rule of law and democracy. Debate over constitutional reform, an election calendar, and the renewal of political life quickly conveyed the impression that differences of opinion on formal and procedural matters had become the dominant considerations.[107]

Citizens found themselves caught up in the debate over the future of countries that were deeply immersed in an examination of the status of the old regime, the place to be accorded to Islamic references (should the notion of Shari'a be included in the constitution), equality between women and men, the judiciary, to name but a few. More and more political parties sprang up: in Tunisia, some 115 had been registered by October 2011 (with 1,500 lists competing in the October 23 Constituent Assembly elections);[108] more than twenty were registered in Egypt, with numerous candidates squaring off in the upcoming presidential elections.[109] Civil society is in a state of ebullition/ ebullience; debate is pointed and often tense, revealing divisions and contradictory interests. The people had united to express their rejection of autocratic regimes; but when it came time to shift from rejection to concrete proposals, squabbling soon broke out among political factions and intellectuals.

This was the pattern throughout the Arab world. The uprisings made it possible to create surprising and sometimes improbable alliances in Libya (where the rebel movement brought together elements of the former regime, members of the Muslim Brotherhood, secular leftists, and tribal chiefs), in Yemen (former communists took to the streets alongside Islamists), in Syria (where secularists rub elbows with former communists and Muslim Brotherhood), or in Morocco (where the February 20th Movement brings together such disparate elements as the Islamists of al-Adl Wal-Ihsân, and the radical left of the Unified Socialist Party and Annahj Addimocrati). Fascinating as they are, the constantly changing alliances should not mask one of the principal challenges to the transition toward the rule of law and true, transparent, and necessarily regulated political pluralism: civil society must learn to envision its own development in order to acquire the capacity to put forward a genuine model of political organization.

Those who most stand to profit from the turmoil and tensions of the transition are invariably the least democratic, the least well intentioned. First among them is the military, which remains everywhere powerful and influential; then elements of the former regime who are working to turn the uprisings to their own advantage. Nothing new here either: democratization movements in West Africa faced similar challenges in the late 1980s and early 1990s. There, such movements often consisted of little more than setting up election procedures, creating political parties, and establishing a legal structure: an approach that very soon revealed itself to be limited, if not dangerous. The populations concerned had not been taught democratic practices; civil society had not achieved the necessary degree of autonomy, had not acquired the tools to carry out critical and contradictory debate.[110] Similar challenges are still facing Arab society.

These and similar concerns cannot be excluded from the central question that has emerged in the tension engendered by the mass upheavals: how do Arab societies ultimately see themselves? The answer to this question will determine the backdrop against which any potential process of political liberation will probably unfold. Without going too far back in history, we can identify the forces that have gradually shaped the Arabs' collective political conscience. There is nothing new about the polarization between nationalists (often nurtured by Western ideas in the way they challenged existing systems, or by socialism or Marxism in opposition to colonialism and imperialism) and political Islam (whose religious connections sought to present it as distinct, in its very essence, from the West). The dichotomy dates back to the 1950s in both North Africa and the Middle East.

With the collapse of the communist model in the late 1980s, a small paradigm shift took place, bringing the advocates of secularization and the Islamists, whose outlook was primarily legalist (nonviolent and reformist), into direct opposition. Under the deadening weight of dictatorship, which all political tendencies opposed, Arab political thought seemed trapped in an equation in which there were no unknowns: the only choice was between two modes of understanding, two models, two hopes. The life of ideas in society found itself impoverished as the parameters of debate constricted. Arab politicians and intellectuals appeared—as they still do—to have assimilated the binary frame of reference and the concept of otherness brought with it by

Orientalism. Over the debate pitting secularism against Islamism loomed the complex relationship between Islam and the West.

For the past half-century, it is as if the Arab world's self-perception in terms of its ideological and political choices, led nowhere but to that tension, to the imperative to choose between two visions, two totally opposing models. It was not uncommon, in debates between Arab citizens and intellectuals, to hear views expressed that could have come straight from the universities, think tanks and social circles of Washington, London, Paris, or Berlin. In like manner the Islamists shaped and reduced their religious references to suit their relation with the West, which either insisted on total otherness, or introduced similarity (to avoid rejection or fear). In both Tunisia and Egypt (in addition to pressure from the West that betrayed its fear that Islamists would hijack the popular uprisings), the same polarization has emerged in a fashion that more resembles caricature.[111] The Arab self-image, torn between similarity and alterity with regard to the dominant civilization and/or ideology, points to the essential question: the alienation of contemporary Arab thought. A three-cornered relationship (dictatorship, secularism, Islamism), shared opposition to dictatorship, and the obsession with adopting mutually exclusive positions (secularists vs. Islamists) make it impossible for either to indulge in in-depth reflection about the crisis that afflicts them both. This defensive posture, which cuts across all ideological and political lines, may well provide the best definition of Arab thought today. It hinders the emergence of an alternative, of a forceful alternative vision originated by peoples liberated from dictatorship to become the subjects of their own history, and not objects fashioned by an ideological construct that is as confrontational, binary, and barren as it is artificial.

The sequestration of Arab thought, which increased in the aftermath of the fall of communist regimes in Eastern Europe and around the world, appears to have had a similarly reductive impact on the way the real, actual conditions of democratization are seen. Debate over political models, the relationship between state and religion, the articulation of the political sphere and that of the law, or that of the public and private spheres is fascinating. But can it be called the heart of the matter, if the socioeconomic dimension, the power and class relationships, are not examined and taken into account? The success of the proponents of the market economy in the Arab world can be attributed to their success in having invited political figures and intellectuals to debate a state model from which, as we will see, any criticism of economic ideology, any analysis of the balance of social power within society has been expunged. Secularists and Islamists—as if unconsciously agreeing to disagree—have fallen into the trap and now, in the era of globalization, have fallen into the kind of argument that could only be carried on within the framework of the nation-state, as it was understood in the early twentieth century.

There can be no true democratization unless it is accompanied by the striving for greater social equality and economic justice. Meanwhile, critical, creative economic thinking appears to have deserted the Arab political debate, as could be easily ascertained after the uprisings. Only by reconciling the political with the economic can the deadlock of a timeworn dialectic be broken, thus opening the way to a more comprehensive approach based an open, far more challenging triangle whose components are the state, the economy, and the cultural and religious references of the people. The trap of national, if not strictly nationalistic, thinking must be avoided; the trap that makes it impossible for most contemporary Arab thinkers, be they atheists, secularists, or Islamists, to formulate broader social, political, and economic perspectives, which should be conceived and elaborated in the light of the history of the Arab world and of its cultural and beliefs, and from the standpoint of South-South and South-North relations and of regional and international dynamics. One of the greatest tests facing the Arab awakening, and perhaps its prime weakness, is the tendency to look upon itself, and to couch problems in terms of national political regimes, and to envisage the solutions of liberation and democratic independence on an essentially nationalistic basis. In the era of globalization, to locate the kind of true democratization that would bring autonomy and freedom at the strictly national level is, for the countries of the Global South, a contradiction in terms, a mental illusion: a point to which I will be returning.

Yet another challenge confronting Muslim majority societies must not be downplayed: the increasingly tense relations between Sunnis and Shiites. Relations between the two branches of Islam have never been simple: their history has been punctuated by competition, quarrels, and even conflicts.[112] There have also been periods of calm and collaboration. In the Middle East, the conflict with Israel has frequently brought Sunni and Shiite Muslims together. Between 1980 and 1988, the war between Iraq and Iran (which had become the champion of Shiism following the 1979 Islamic Revolution) gave the first evidence of opposition between Iraq, claiming to defend Sunni tradition, and Shiite Iran. The divide deepened, evolving into sharply polarized positions, after the invasion of Iraq in 2003, as Vali Nasr has noted.[113] The violent bomb attacks on Iraq's Shiite population fired sectarian imaginations and led to a series of events at the regional level that directly or indirectly contributed to widening the divide. The United States and Europe have systematically stigmatized Iran at the international level, while the Iranian government has systematically denounced the compromising attitude of Saudi Arabia's Sunni regime, particularly since Mahmoud Ahmadinejad took office in 2005. Notes published by Wikileaks in the *New York Times* and the *Guardian* revealed, for example, that in April 2008 Saudi Arabia urged the United States to attack Iran and to "cut off the head of the snake."[114]

Attitudes toward Israel have been another factor in the upsurge of regional tension. Iran styles itself as the defender of the Palestinians and criticizes the cowardice and the compromises of the Arab states, as illustrated by the December 2008–January 2009 attack and massacre in Gaza.[115] When Israel attacked Hezbollah in July 2006, the Lebanese group's fierce resistance won it near-victor status, enabling it to represent Shiites as the most courageous opponents of Israeli policies in the region.[116] Whether measured in credibility, regional autonomy (from the United States), or resistance to Israeli policies, the war of influence favors the Shiites and is generating increasingly sharp tension.

While the Shiites comprise only 10 percent to 15 percent of the world's Muslims, their percentage is much higher in the Middle East, perhaps as much as half the population divided among the regional countries.[117] Those boasting Shiite majorities possess huge oil and mineral resources, in addition to their great strategic importance, as Noam Chomsky aptly points out.[118] Iran's policy of expanding its influence in Iraq and Afghanistan (not forgetting its ties with Bashar al-Assad's Syria), the critical position of Lebanon, and the Shiite majority's resistance in Bahrain (where power is in Sunni hands) are political indicators of what Vali Nasr has termed the "Shia revival." The growing influence and prominence of Shiism are bound to have consequences on the way the countries of the region react to the Arab awakening. In Bahrain, Iran views Saudi Arabia's and Qatar's support for repression of the mass movement[119] as an attempt to smother Shia resistance, while Saudi Arabia's support of the rebellion in Syria is a clear attempt to circumscribe Iran's sphere of influence.[120]

Among the factors that exacerbate tensions between Sunnis and Shiites in the region, and throughout the world, are the struggle for religious influence, possession of regional mineral resources, and, above all, the question of attitudes taken toward the West and toward Israel. These contradictions, as we will see, represent one of the principal challenges facing Muslim minority societies; they also reveal a critical weakness, which the United States, the European countries, and Israel have been able to exploit successfully in anchoring their presence in the Middle East. The fears of the petro-monarchies about advancing Shiism, their uneasiness in the face of permanent criticism of their religious hypocrisy, their dishonorable alliance with the United States, and their lack of courage on the Palestinian question combine to play into the hands of foreign powers that are able to assert control over the region by accentuating its divisions.

Religious scholars, particularly from among the Sunni ranks, have taken contradictory positions. Fear of the Shiite revival has led some Sunni authorities to sound the alarm in an effort to limit Shiite proselytism. Among them was the influential Sunni Sheikh Yusuf al-Qaradawi, who caused a surprise among his friends and supporters when he warned against the Shiite colonization of Sunni majority societies. In his view, though the Shiites are Muslims, they are members of a "sect" whose influence must be restricted. Ayatollah Muhmmad Tashkiri, vice-president of the International Union of Muslim Clerics (al-Qaradawi is its president), criticized the statement as "dangerous," one that reflects the implicit influence of the petro-monarchies, particularly Qatar, where al-Qaradawi resides.[121] Yet only a year before, the same al-Qaradawi had attempted to call upon Sunnis and Shiites to unite and to put an end to sectarian killings among Muslims in an appeal issued in conjunction with former Iranian president Hashemi Rafsanjani on al-Jazeera's Arab-language network.[122]

The contradictory attitudes on display reflect the weight of the religious, political, and geopolitical issues linked to the strained relations between Sunnis and Shiites. These issues are, in turn, one of the principal obstacles facing Muslims in the Middle East and the world over (Sunni-Shia relations are critical in Syria, Pakistan, Afghanistan, Asia, and even in the West). The wars for influence and the contradictory attitudes to the Arab uprisings must likewise be seen through the prism of intra-Muslim tension, which is capable not only of weakening national and regional movements for independence and liberation, but also of thwarting and even annihilating them. Contemporary Muslim thought must face up to this reality and deal with it in all its theological, political, and geostrategic complexity.

From deep within Middle Eastern and North African societies have emerged challenges and obstacles: powerful mass movements that lack clear leadership; limited self-awareness combined with a binary vision of political realities steeped in narrow nationalism; disregard for hard economic facts and global dynamics; Sunni-Shia tension. Whatever the schemes and the manipulations of the Great Powers, the future of the Arab awakening will depend on the capacity of each society to take its fate into its own hands, to develop new approaches, and to open new perspectives. No one can deny it: the collective conscience and intelligence of the Arab world are now in crisis. That it is capable of developing the intellectual and psychological resources to face up to and to overcome the crisis is no less certain. Now the time has come for the young people who carried forward the Arab awakening to shape and to determine—beyond their mastery of technology and technique—a vision, a project, an alternative.

## 3

# Islam, Islamism, Secularization

THE PURPOSE OF this book is to situate Islam as a religious and ideological reference in the Arab awakening now unfolding, the idea being to analyze its component uprisings in the light of recent history, of their likely causes, and, of course, of their broader political, economic, and geostrategic context. Each one of these dimensions alone would justify full-fledged analysis, something that lies beyond the scope of the present work. My main purpose in these pages is, rather, to gauge what role Islam as a reference will and can play at this critical moment in the evolution of the Arab world.

Irrespective of how the facts are interpreted, it is clear that something has changed in the Middle East, and that the process is irreversible. Country-by-country analysis reveals that debates over the place of Islam in society tend to focus on two main themes: the compatibility of Islam with democratic pluralism and religious diversity and, more specifically, the role of Islamist parties (which are everywhere present) in the societies now liberated from dictatorship. Though these concerns may have seemed absent from the slogans that gave birth to the uprisings and drove them forward, they are omnipresent in the period immediately following the fall of the dictatorial regimes, now that the door to democracy is being opened by the drafting of new constitutions, and by parliamentary and presidential elections.

It is essential to grasp the historical and ideological content of these crucial questions if the role of Islam in the mass revolts is to be given its proper place.

## Islam and Islamism

Many of the intellectuals and researchers who have studied the Muslim majority societies have spoken of "Islams" to underscore the diversity of religious observance that occurs in different social and cultural contexts.[1] However, the label is problematic religiously, and also in terms of what is subsumed by the notion of "Islamic civilization" itself. As Arab and Muslim societies have entered a phase of renewal, it is important to understand how unity and diversity function within the Islamic reference.

By way of prelude, in the body of Islamic teachings and prescriptions, there are certain source texts upon which all Muslims agree, be they Sunni or Shiite, Eastern or Western. Islam's two scriptural sources (the Qur'an and the Prophetic tradition—the Sunna) are recognized by all schools of thought and constitute the bedrock of Islamic belief. From these sources a number of principles and practices have been extracted and categorized, and they constitute the core of Islamic teachings, upon which all traditions and schools of jurisprudence agree: the six pillars of faith (*arkân al-imân*) that constitute the creed (*al-aqîda*) and the five pillars of Islam (*arkân al-islâm*) that detail the rituals (*'ibadât*: prayer, fasting, etc.). Taken together, these elements, along with obligations and prohibitions (regarding food, drink, behavior, etc.), represent the core of Islam for all the world's Muslims: it is thus entirely legitimate to speak of one Islam on the primary religious level.

How then to account for the diversity? It is manifested at a second level; in the way the two scriptural sources—the Qur'an and the Sunna—are read and interpreted. Though Muslim scholars are unanimous on the structure and the categorization of the basic principles (the four fields listed above: scriptural sources, the pillars of faith, the pillars of Islam, and the main obligations and prohibitions), they differ widely in their interpretation of the texts and in secondary principles. Apart from the two main traditions, Sunni and Shiite, more than thirty legal schools (including both Sunni and Shiite traditions) have existed over the course of Muslim history, arising from a multiplicity of legal interpretations (fundamentals aside). Diversity also flourishes in the process of interpretation itself: there are traditionalist, literalist, reformist, rationalist, Sufi, or political trends, none of which are mutually exclusive: a Muslim can be literalist and political, reformist and Sufi, for example.[2] How far removed from the binary opposition of "good Muslims/bad Muslim" or "moderate Muslim/fundamentalist Muslim."[3] Reality is far more complex. If Islam is a unified whole with regard to its basic principles, countless interpretations exist as to secondary prescriptions and to the objectives attributed to the texts themselves.

Yet another level of diversity exists. Muslims have, over time, settled in different lands and encountered new cultures. Numerous elements from these cultures have been integrated into the Islamic reference, invoking the legal ruling that governs social and cultural affairs: "The primary principle (in these fields) is permission."[4] There is, then, a variety of cultures nurtured by Islamic principles, each of which powerfully influences the way these principles are lived and implemented—while, of course, the fundamentals remain unchanged the world over. The dynamic operates in both directions. African, Middle Eastern, Asian, and today, American and European cultures constitute a second level of diversity at the heart of Islam itself. What is meant by the concept of "Islamic civilization" is precisely this: one single Islam, a diversity of interpretations, and a plurality of cultures. The same body of references and values nurtures the diversity of interpretation, or cultural and artistic expression. "Islamic civilization" can be seen as a single, fundamental religious reference expressed diversely through different historical periods, intellectual perspectives, and cultures.

Though awareness of Islamic diversity may not be widespread, it is relatively easy to acknowledge the diversity of Muslims—traditionalists or rationalists, reformists or Sufis—the better to understand that Islam, as a religion, cannot be reduced to the behavior of one or of a small group of its faithful. Everything changes however, when it comes to the study or consideration of political Islam, seen as a monolithic category that represents—a fortiori since September 2001—radical Islam and violent extremism. The oversimplification is as dangerous as it is frequent; in its reductionism, it fails to assign concepts and dynamics their just place in history, depriving them of the contexts that lend them meaning and justification.

The elements that were to shape contemporary political Islam appeared in the late nineteenth century. Jamal ad-Dîn al-Afghânî (1838–1897) and Muhammad 'Abduh (1849–1905),[5] two reformist thinkers operating respectively in Turkey and Egypt, from the 1870s onward, strove to conceptualize alternatives at the collapse of the Ottoman Empire and of (primarily British) colonialism. The Islamic reference appeared to them to be the key factor that would enable them to break free from foreign domination. The solution would be a return to the Qur'an, using the rich, open Islamic tradition of independent legal reasoning (*ijtihâd*); national languages (Turkish, Arabic, or others) would be revitalized; the people would be educated according to their own spiritual and intellectual references, combined with scientific knowledge and philosophy; the division of Muslim nations would be rejected in the struggle against cultural and political colonialism.

The reformers' vision, at once pan-Islamic and fiercely anti-colonial, was to have a powerful impact on twentieth-century Islamic thought.[6] Principal among the thinkers who followed were the Syrian Abd al-Rahman al-Kawakibi

(1855–1902), the Lebanese-Egyptian Muhammad Rashid Reda (1865–1935), the Turk Said Nursi (1878–1960), the Algerian Abd al-Hamîd Ben Badis (1889–1940), the Tunisian Muhammad Tahar Ibn Ashûr (1879–1973), the Indo-Pakistani Muhammad Iqbal (1877–1938), and later, the Moroccan Muhammad Allal El-Fassi (1910–1974). Their path was to adopt a strictly religious approach (by proposing to follow reformist paths), to educate both the general population and the elites (by doing so methodically), or, on the political level, to struggle against British, French, Italian, or other forms of colonialism. In the eyes of these thinkers, Muslims had to rediscover the living force of their religious teachings, to develop a critical outlook, and to free themselves from the alienation produced by colonialism. In this sense, Islam as a religion was called upon to play a key role in the liberation and the political, cultural, and economic future of the Muslim majority countries. It would also act as a unifying factor against the divisions imposed by the colonial powers.

With his creation of the Muslim Brotherhood, Hassan al-Banna (1906–1949) gave sharper definition to what would come to be known as "political Islam" on "Islamism." Profoundly influenced by the first generation of reformist thinkers, he threw himself into the re-islamization of his country—Egypt—first at the local level, and then in resistance to colonialism, participating in anti-British demonstrations at age thirteen, in 1919.[7] In 1928, four years after the abolition of the spiritual caliphate exercised by the Ottoman Empire, he created the Muslim Brotherhood, assigning to it quite specific objectives: a return to Islam, programs of mass education, social and economic reform, implementing Islamic legislation, and, in the long run, setting up an "Islamic state," something that could happen only after the departure of the British. His thought transcended national boundaries: the Muslim Brotherhood (which saw itself as a Sufi order as much as a solidarity-based social and educational organization, without defining itself as a political party)[8] quickly acquired affiliated branches in the Sudan, then Syria, Lebanon, and Palestine, where members of the Brotherhood had been dispatched to oppose and to resist Zionist designs.[9] The intellectual and ideological ingredients that were to define contemporary political Islam were all in place before the Muslim Brotherhood was founded, but it successfully united them around its organizational structure and program. By the late 1940s it had as many as 1.5 million members, supporters, and sympathizers.

From its inception, the philosophy of the Muslim Brotherhood was nonviolent and legalist.[10] Hassan al-Banna was determined to work within the framework of the law and rejected those suspected of committing acts of violence in the organization's name, particularly in the assassination of a judge, or of Egyptian Prime Minister Mahmoud al-Noqrashi Pasha in January 1949. About the killers he wrote: "They are not Muslims, they are not Brothers."[11] He set up a "special organization" with the twofold objective of responding to state repression, seen as masterminded by the British colonialists who pulled the strings behind King Faruk (Hassan al-Banna threatened the British that he would call upon the people to rise up if they did not leave Egypt) and taking part in the resistance alongside the Palestinians (the game played by the British, who had concluded secret agreements with Zionist terrorist groups, was more than ambiguous).

Such is the context, that of social struggle and resistance to colonialism, in which the birth of political Islam and of the Muslim Brotherhood must be placed. In both its principles and its actions, the organization would remain nonviolent until the early 1960s. Slogans that invoked the Qur'an as a constitution, jihad as resistance, or martyrdom as the supreme ambition of action must be understood in the context of the anti-colonial struggle. Similar slogans, with similar messianic tones, can be found throughout the Global South in Christian, Muslim, Marxist, or more broadly atheist resistance movements.

Political Islam was not monolithic. The initial signs of dissension appeared after the first crackdowns, and after the imprisonment and torture that younger militants saw as proof that the legalist strategy had failed. After the coup d'état staged by the Free Officers Movement in Egypt (1952), Colonel Gamal Abdel Nasser (1918–1970) began his ascension to power. Drawing support from the mass base of the Muslim Brotherhood, of which he was a member, he ousted General Mohamed Naguib on November 14, 1954, consolidated his power, and began to suppress former allies who had now become his opponents. Several Muslim Brotherhood leaders were executed; thousands were jailed. In Egypt's prisons bitter debates raged, divisions deepened: How could the disaster be explained? What religious stance should be adopted toward the new rulers? The British colonialists had been non-Muslim usurpers, but what of Nasser? Could he still be considered a Muslim after having other Muslims (not all members of the Muslim Brotherhood) executed and tortured?

The younger—and more radicalized—had come to feel that the true Muslims were those who had been imprisoned, repressed, or executed, and that Nasser was a tyrant, no more a Muslim than his supporters: a view the first generation of Muslim Brothers, rallying around new guide Hassan al-Hudaybi (the successor to al-Banna), himself imprisoned, did not share. They asserted that Nasser, along with all the oppressive elements and their allies, active or passive, direct or indirect, were and remained Muslims (*mus-limûn*) while they, who were suffering imprisonment for the social and polit-ical goals, defined themselves as Islamists (*islamiyyun*). The distinction is a critical one: the first generation of Muslim Brothers refused to claim affili-ation to Islam for themselves alone, at the risk of casting "outside of Islam" those who did not agree with them. Whatever their political positions and moral lapses, individuals must not be excommunicated (*takfir*): such a judg-ment lay with God alone, never with men.[12] Contemporary use of the concept of "Islamism" by its protagonists themselves can be said to have originated in the debates that took place in Nasser's prisons. For them, it was a matter of distinguishing themselves—the "Islamists," as defined by their social, cultural, and political agenda—from "ordinary" Muslims who remained Muslims even in spite of their relatively low political awareness and relative laxity in the practice of their faith. Clearly this was no mere semantic argument as it involved critical theological and legal criteria that decided who was a Muslim and who was not.

Within the Muslim Brotherhood itself, where several trends of thought co-existed, the decisive split was not long in coming. The organization's Guide, Hassan al-Hudaybi, laid out the Brotherhood's historical position in a book explicitly entitled: "[We are] preachers, not judges."[13] It was meant as a reply to the younger generation, which had only recently joined the move-ment (just before the Free Officers Revolution, during the repression and after the death of Hassan al-Banna) and could no longer accept imprisonment and torture. They were drawn to the thought of Sayyid Qutb, who had joined the Brotherhood in 1951[14] and whose positions were harsher and more radi-cal. According to him, there could only be two alternatives: societies founded on Islam, and those of *jahiliyya* (the pre-Islamic period of ignorance). A "true believer" could not choose the latter without risking the loss of his status as a Muslim. The Brotherhood had thus come to comprise trends ranging from fidelity to the organization's original, legalistic tradition to the radicalization that followed Nasser's repression in the early 1950s. Some, disheartened, left the organization and/or founded new Islamist groups: al-Gama'a al-Islamiyya (Islamic Groups), Tanzîm at-Takfir (Order of Anathema), Takfir wa-Hijra (Anathema and Exile), Tanzîm al-Jihâd al-Islâmî (Order of Islamic Jihad), and others. They may have agreed on objectives, but their understanding of Islam and their methods of action displayed fundamental differences.

The brief overview of the early decades of political Islam is richly instruc-tive. Islamism began as a legalist, nonviolent movement based on a strategy of reform from the bottom up (educating the masses), the ultimate aim of which was to transform the "top" (reform society and change the structure of the state). Failure and repression brought about changes. Goals and methods were rethought. Analysis points to two key conclusions: first, the organizations themselves changed from within in response to historical shifts; second, the diversity of outlooks was such that it would be wrong to posit Islamism as a monolithic whole. The same internal divisions and diversity of views are likewise present in all Muslim majority countries: in Morocco, Algeria, Tunisia, Libya, Syria, and Lebanon, as well as Turkey, Indonesia, Malaysia, and others.

Though political Islam displays common features, Islamist movements are themselves extremely diverse, and must be studied in their diversity. Broadly speaking, seven contentious questions have frequently caused tension and splits among different Islamist tendencies: (1) the definition of who is a Muslim and of that person's rights; (2) the use of violence: the majority of the world's Islamist organizations are legalist and nonviolent, while some have legitimized the use of violence to overthrow a tyrant; (3) the definition of sharī'a: Is it a closed legal or an open corpus of principles potentially compatible with foreign references such as democracy (which some Islamists accept while others do not);[15] (4) the issue of whether an Islamist political party should be created or retain the status of a religious and social organization (a question that has preoccupied, if not undermined, virtually every Islamist trend); (5) the role of women in the organization as well as in Muslim majority societies (some trends remain very conservative, others are more open); (6) relations with people of other beliefs (or no belief) within society: their presence, their role, their involvement; (7) relations with the West: Are there other options than opposition?

Debate has often been intense; disagreements sharp. Islamist groups have frequently been at odds. Among them the same fault lines that exist in Christian political organizations can be observed: trends that range from something similar to Liberation theology (to the left of the traditional political spectrum), Christian democracy (of the left or the right, depending on the country), and conservative and/or fundamentalist movements (clearly on the right). To reduce political Christianity or political Judaism to a single ideology or a single political stance would be a glaring analytical error. The same applies to Islamism, which must be defined, contextualized, and analyzed on a case-by-case basis, by organization and by country.

There is not an Islamist current that has not undergone changes, even radical ones, over time. In this respect, Islamist organizations are like all political ideologies and their supporters: they resemble one another in that their understanding of issues, political priorities, bargaining power, and, of course, opportunities tends to shift according to circumstances. Even the most radical groups, whose objective was once national liberation, have revised their strategies. In fact, one of the characteristics common to all such movements was that they might—like the Muslim Brotherhood—have branches in different countries, but their methods, priorities, and objectives were for all intents and purposes set at the national level. Seen from this perspective, al-Qaeda (whose ideologue Ayman al-Zawahiri first criticized then opposed the Muslim Brotherhood because, he claimed, it had "betrayed the cause of Islam") made a qualitative leap in its approach, beginning in the late 1990s. The assassination of Anwar Sadat on October 6, 1981, by Lieutenant Khaled al-Islambûli (leading a group of men who were all members of Tanzîm al-Jihâd al-Islâmî) brought Hosni Mubarak to power. He immediately declared a state of emergency that was to last for thirty years, until his resignation in February 2011. Throughout his rule, his policies were to prove harsher than his predecessor's. Ayman al-Zawahiri would repeatedly explain why it was necessary to favor global jihad: the point was not to unseat a despot, whether in Egypt, Tunisia, or elsewhere (at the risk of installing a successor who is far worse), but to strike those who manipulated the autocrats as if they were playthings, that is, the United States and Europe. The al-Qaeda position is a marginal one at best; it has come in for denunciation by virtually all other Islamist groups and movements. But it was successful in attracting individuals who have acted through clandestine cells in Muslim majority societies, in religious communities in the West, and even within structured Islamist organizations in many countries.

The Arab awakening has shown how far removed such movements are from young people's concerns and aspirations. In fact, the Islamism of violent extremism is the antithesis of the nonviolent movements that swept the Arab world. Those who rose up did so in the name of justice and freedom, against dictatorship and corruption, in a resolutely nonviolent manner and without taking an anti-Western position. Many young people belonging to other Islamist trends took part in the mass protests, sometimes against the wishes of the hierarchy, which either held them back or rejected the terms of participation. In the Islamist parties and organizations themselves, tension between generations and differing interpretations of the popular uprisings brought to light real divisions previously concealed by the unity necessitated by resistance to dictatorship. The reference to Islam and the role of the Islamists have touched off debate in every Arab country where uprisings have shaken old structures to the core. Some commentators, like Olivier Roy, even speak of "post-Islamist revolutions;"[16] others see them as a "third age" of Islamism, as exemplified by the rise of Turkish Prime Minister Tayyip Erdoğan's AK Party; others have suspended judgment, fearing that the Islamists have remained the same and may seize control of the revolutions to their own advantage. No one can predict the future. But it is clear that every Islamist current in the Arab world is going through a crucial period in its history. The way each movement handles the crisis will largely determine its future.

## *Secularization*

There can be little doubt that the notion of "secularization" is one of the conceptual references that have nurtured the deepest misunderstandings between West and East. The term, along with its French equivalent, *la laïcité*, describes two entirely distinct historical experiences, depending on whether it is applied to the societies of the North or of the Global South. The process that led to the separation of church (later, of religion) and state enabled Western societies to achieve religious tolerance and democratic pluralism. While it began with the Renaissance and the rise of humanism, the Age of Enlightenment—impelled by the great British, German, and French philosophers—gave more tangible form to the objectives of separation. While the Catholic Church, which at the time held a dominant position in many European societies, often enjoyed discretionary power over the affairs of state and imposed its dogmas, prescriptions, and philosophy on public life, philosophers and thinkers attacked its citadel and called into question the legitimacy of its monopoly on political power. Thinkers like Locke and Hobbes, Kant and his critical reason, Montesquieu, Rousseau, or Voltaire,[17] following in the footsteps of the Renaissance humanists, probed the underpinnings and the prerogatives of both church and states, challenging the authority of the religious hierarchy to manage the state and public affairs. Though religion had a part to play in the private lives of citizens, who must be free to choose their faith, it could not interfere in the public sphere, which must be subservient to another authority possessing a different kind of legitimacy. The process of secularization began slowly—and often in confrontational terms—in the name of respect for shared rationality, of equality of all citizens, and of universal liberties.[18]

It was an era of bitter debate and struggle; individuals were condemned, imprisoned, excommunicated. Gradually, however, the process became institutionalized in the organs of the state, the medical bodies, the universities, and others. It was a landmark achievement. Not only did the church no longer exercise direct authority over the affairs of state, but the state was obliged to guarantee equal rights for all citizens and to respect individual beliefs and religious practices. Two fundamental liberties—(individual) freedom of conscience and (collective) freedom of worship—were won by hard-fought struggle waged in the name of secularization and its institutionalization through a secular legal framework. Secularization made it possible to democratize the public sphere, enabling all (initially male) citizens to enjoy their rights and to receive equal treatment, irrespective of their religious or philosophical beliefs. Secularization, in other words, led to the merging of political democracy and religious pluralism in the public sphere.[19] Obviously the process was perceived as positive, as under the Old Regime religion had wielded almost exclusive authority over the state, citizens were denied their rights, and religious minorities (Protestant, Jewish, or Catholic depending on the country) were often victims of discrimination, or repression.

In societies that were Arab and Muslim majority, history took a different course. Secularization, far from being linked with the march toward freedom, became identified with the threefold experience of repression, colonialism, and the assault on Islam. The case of secularization in Turkey provides a telling illustration. In the 1920s Mustafa Kemal Atatürk imposed secularism, by compulsion and without popular consultation. In 1924 he created a single party (the Republican Peoples Party) and, inspired by enlightenment France, enforced secularism not by separating religion and state but by placing religion under state control.[20] The Religious Affairs Directorate, which he established that same year, supervised and controlled the prerogatives and the religious discourse of Muslim scholars. Between 1924 and 1937,[21] when secularism was officially enshrined in the constitution, it was expeditiously and unilaterally enforced while the military, as guardian of the institutions of the state, exerted increasingly greater power if not oppression. Though Atatürk invoked the ideals of the Enlightenment, his conception of secularism fell far short of realizing its aims or of opening up in Turkey the same perspectives. His secularism could not be described, as in the West, as a happy combination of democratization and religious freedom. Backed by the military, the single party enforced its line, turning the secular order adopted by the West on its head. While religion had guided the affairs of state under the Ottoman Empire, Turkish secularism sought to submit religion to the unilateral, repressive, ideologically oriented will of the state. In point of fact, Turkey's historical experience had little affinity with European or American secularization: in the US experience, secularism meant the acquisition of rights, freedom, and equality; in Turkey, it was experienced as rule by an authoritarian military regime under which freedoms were few, as the regime was essentially anti-religious and anti-Muslim.

Decades later, Tunisia's president Habib Bourguiba praised Atatürk's Turkey as an example for the Muslim world. Turkey, in his eyes, represented the first secular Muslim state, the "yeast" of his own revolution and of his march toward a Tunisian model.[22] Yet Bourguiba refused to marginalize the Islamic religion and insisted on invoking it at every turn (including the 1959 constitution, proclaimed "in the name of God") [23] while brandishing his status as "supreme combatant" (a title that in its Arabic wording, *al-mujâhid al-akbar*, directly evokes Islamic terminology, drawing on the same root found in the word *jihad*) against French rule or distancing himself from the Turkish prototype, declaring, in 1973: "We have not acted in the same way as some peoples who have turned their backs on Islam, who reject the use of the Arabic script, claiming to belong to a noble Indo-European race. They have broken with everything Semitic."[24]

But these noteworthy differences of opinion did not change the nature of the Tunisian regime toward democracy and religion. The regime was a dictatorship, one that used religious symbols to ensure a certain level of legitimacy, but whose actions militated against religious expression, while expressing a desire for strict control. As early as 1956 Bourguiba began to criticize Muslim scholars (*ulama*) for their backwardness, abolished the religious courts, and promulgated the Personal Status Code that disqualified any legal reference to Islam. Zitouna—both the mosque and its venerable traditional teaching institution—was subjected to government tutelage to the profit of the secular universities. In March 1964, Bourguiba went as far as to break the Ramadan fast on television during the daylight hours, arguing that the economic constraints of the modern age must prevail over the outdated practice of fasting.[25]

Bourguiba was quick to present his program of forced secularization and his secular model as achievements, particularly with regard to human rights and economic growth. More thorough analysis indicates, as François Burgat and Augustin Jomier have noted,[26] that these achievements tended to be more theoretical than real; above all, the regime exploited them to sell its "secularist and feminist" model to the West. France became one of the first countries to praise the Tunisian model, which granted women unparalleled rights. Tunisia's status as a dictatorship could be conveniently overlooked, as done by Henri Guaino, special advisor to President Nicolas Sarkozy, who let slip in January 2011 that the country was "a form of dictatorship; a secular one, but a dictatorship, it's true....At the same time, Tunisia has been, since Bourguiba, the country that has made the greatest efforts to educate and empower women."[27]

It may have been more difficult for the Tunisian people, subjected as they were to autocratic rule, to grasp the positive aspects of secularism as it was applied under Bourguiba.[28] The day-to-day experience of dictatorship, the lack of freedom, the repression, and the attacks on religion appeared to be the outstanding features of the Tunisian model, which was a carbon copy of the Turkish example (up to and including state control of all religious expression). Even though the "supreme combatant" had fought against political colonization, he seems to have accepted French ideological domination, borrowing that country's ideals and vocabulary but without respecting the principles of freedom, equality, and justice that should have accompanied them. What has remained in Tunisia of "secularization"—or, in French, "la laïcité"—as experienced in its historical reality, beyond the sloganeering and propaganda about human rights and women? Remaining is a frequently negative connotation in which the imposition of a model borrowed from the colonial rulers is linked to a repressive, antidemocratic, and antireligious policy that harked back to the fierce anticlericalism of certain French secularist intellectuals—and these individuals, historically, by no means represented the totality of the currents that promoted secularism.[29]

Similar examples abound in virtually all the Arab countries in the postcolonial period. Each of the "liberators," from Bourguiba to the FLN in Algeria, from Nasser to the secular socialist Baath Party regimes in Iraq and Syria, or the Pahlavi dynasty in Iran displayed the characteristics listed earlier. They boasted that they had instituted secularization and the separation of state and religion. But in reality these were dictatorial regimes whose policies were often more antireligious than those of the former colonial powers, repressing faith-related demands and enforcing a system in which religious authorities were kept under tight control, in a state of total subservience. This was no alliance of democracy and pluralism in the guise of separation of religion and the state; religion was subjected to the state, with no democracy and no pluralism.

Given the variety of historical experience, reactions are equally varied to the way the terminology of secularism is used. But except for an elite, for a tiny minority of intellectuals frequenting the corridors of power, most people in Muslim majority societies, particularly Turkey and the Arab countries, generally understand "secularization" as models of the dictatorial, anti-Islamic regimes that have been influenced by or imported from the West; any debate over the place of religion and the state must take this into account, instead of falling into a sterile and counterproductive terminological dispute.

It is worth noting that, above and beyond the participation of Islamist parties, which notoriously oppose secularization as being antireligious, reference to religion is reemerging in both social and political debate. Eighty years after the Kemalist revolution, Recep Tayyip Erdoğan's Justice and Development Party (AKP), with Islamist origins, today governs Turkey and has been twice reelected, while reducing the prerogatives of the military. In the aftermath of the uprisings in Tunisia and Egypt, as well as in Libya and Syria (but also in Lebanon, Morocco, Yemen, and Jordan), appeals to Islam as a reference have become commonplace. Olivier Roy believes that we have entered what he calls a "post-Islamist" phase, and then adds, "we are not finished with Islam."[30] Current changes must not only be taken into account, but also the ongoing presence of this reference in the contemporary Muslim conscience.

Everything possible must be done to avoid a doubly distorted debate: first, between Arab protagonists who share the same historical experience but who ideologically oppose one another via a terminology that is foreign to their religious references and, above all, to their history; second, between "West" and "East," between "North" and "South," each of which is imprisoned within sets of definition, idealization, and even demonization that prevent constructive dialogue and make agreement of substance impossible (primarily because of misunderstanding over form).

## Hollow Debates, Real Issues

In the early stages of the uprisings in Tunisia and Egypt, a number of primarily Western intellectuals, politicians, and journalists posited a present and future role for Islamism in the mass protests. The dictators, from Ben Ali to Mubarak and from Ghaddafi to al-Assad, echoed this refrain, claiming that the leaders of the rebellions were radicalized Islamists. Their claims were belied by facts; the young people who spoke for the protestors had almost no connection with Islamists, and even less with extremists or radicals. The uprisings were broad-based nonviolent movements with no specific political affiliation. Yet questions had begun to surface in the countries concerned, given that Islamist parties (Ennahda in Tunisia, the Muslim Brotherhood in Egypt, Libya, and Syria) had joined the demonstrations and appeared to be the opposition groups best organized to capture a leaderless mass movement. On January 30, 2011, Rached Ghannouchi returned in triumph to Tunis.[31] In Egypt, the Muslim Brotherhood set up the Freedom and Justice Party, headed by Muhammad Morsy,[32] and, following internal disagreements, one of the Brotherhood's highest profile members, Abdel Moneim Abul Futuh, left the movement and declared his candidacy in the upcoming presidential election.[33]

The debate and discussion that followed the uprisings opened the path to constitutional reform, the election of new parliaments, and the preparation of presidential elections; they also revealed divisions between political forces. Suddenly, polarization became the watchword: everywhere, "secularists" and "Islamists" found themselves at odds. United against dictatorship, the supporters of the two camps began to unearth the old fears and the old slogans that set "theocracy-loving Islamists" against "secularist Western puppets." By its very nature, the resulting polarization ruled out an in-depth dialogue over the positions and aspirations of the two broad groupings; the arguments used to defend their positions, in Tunisia and in Egypt, were more like caricatures, the result being that the protagonists spoke more and more at cross-purposes, undermining as they did the potential collective creative power of the newly liberated peoples. Had the intention been to invite intervention, it would have been hard to find a more effective way to encourage the Western powers or the military to take over or manipulate the popular movements. Yet it is the leaders themselves who, on their own initiative, perpetuate these sterile divisions. The forces of change in civil society and the political parties must break with what has become an unhealthy polarization, break with the alienation that has them speak of themselves (and of their political opponents) as if they were speaking from abroad, and reconnect with their own history, their own religious and cultural references, and the aspirations of their people. Having broken free from political dictatorship, they must free themselves from the intellectual straitjacket and the false divisions that prevent them from exploring new ways and new horizons together.

The world has changed. Some former categories must be revised, reexamined, perhaps even discarded. And yet, some people continue to refer to secularization and secularism, or to Islam and political Islam, in terms either directly borrowed from Western definitions and categories, or little better than ideologically generated caricatures. The institutionalization of secularism does not and cannot be meant to imply opposition to the religious reference and to its presence in the public sphere.[34] Such an interpretation is not simply a Westernized one; it draws on secular ideological currents in France, Germany, the United Kingdom, and the United States. Though occasionally echoed by a Francophile or Anglophile elite in the Arab countries, it does not address the real issues raised by secularization in a contemporary society. These issues focus on distinguishing between authorities and the powers they wield. Divine power, emanating from above, must be differentiated from human power, negotiated from below. The religious authority of a church, a doctrine, sacred texts, or scholars applies to those who believe in it. It must not be confounded with the authority vested in states or individual human beings, which must be freely and openly granted by the people.

Secularization can be defined as the process by which the two authorities have been set apart, and which has led to the separation of state and religion. Religious authority applies to the order of faith; it organizes worship (or the church) and requires that individual conscience subscribe to it: it belongs to the private sphere. Collective participation in the delegation of authority negotiated among women and men concerns social and political organization, and belongs to the public sphere. The distinction between the two spheres is well established, yet it should be drawn with caution as the line of demarcation between the two remains indistinct; many of the mechanisms of collective structuring, as well as public cultural references are directly influenced by the religions of the majority. This occurs to such an extent that more than a few Eastern Christians, like the Copt Makram Ubayd in Egypt or even Edward Said,[35] an atheist from the Christian tradition, acknowledged that they were of Muslim culture, so powerfully did this culture shape social intercourse in Arab civil society. For the same reason, Western societies speak of themselves as being of "Christian culture," even in their respective public spheres, as Pope Benedict XVI implied in his Ravensburg address of November 2006.[36] In this respect Jürgen Habermas, Charles Taylor, and Tariq Modood are correct in noting that no public sphere is entirely culturally and religiously neutral, whether in the East or in the West.[37]

Muslim countries need to set aside the pointless, counterproductive, and empty quarrel over the conflict between secularization and Islam and/or Islamism (which masks important issues by reducing to so-called essentials the relations between religion and state, glossing dangerously over the substantial variances in historical experience that separate the two civilizations); far from these warped controversies, Muslim countries must give serious and sustained consideration to the relationship of Islam to authority in its many forms. From the outset, Muslim scholars in their work of interpretation distinguished between divine authority on the one hand, as expressed in the texts bearing upon the credo (*'aqîda*), worship (*'ibâdât*), and religious duties and prohibitions (*wâjibât, muharramât*), and human authority on the other hand, which, in social affairs (*mu'âmalât*) must manage the primary sphere of the permitted through consultation (*shûrâ*) and a majority decision-making process. The distinction between the two levels of authority is absolutely not foreign to Islam; it is, in fact, an essential teaching in a religion that has neither a clergy nor a religious hierarchy. These legal stipulations can be found in the works of the founders of Islamic legal philosophy (*usûl al-fiqh*: the fundamentals of Islamic law and jurisprudence), figures like Ja'far as-Sadiq or ash-Shafi'i,[38] in both the Sunni and Shiite traditions.

On the fundamental level, the principle has never been set aside. It is imperative for contemporary parties to the debate to revisit its substance and its meaning in the light of their own references and history. The philosopher Alain de Libera, a specialist in medieval history, has even claimed that the separation of authorities (the goal of secularization) was introduced into Western and Christian thought through the influence of Islamic philosophical and legal thought thanks to the free flow of critical intelligence that flourished early among the Arabs and the Persians. Going further, he states: "The conflict between religion and philosophy was imported into the West by the Arabs. With Saint Augustine (late fourth century), philosophy was defeated, only to return to its rationalist vision thanks to the Arabs."[39] What de Libera has said of philosophy, which the Arabs never feared to translate from Greek and Latin—can and must be said of the relationship between legislation and its philosophy. The Islamic tradition makes the differentiation of authority before God and among men an integral part of the very essence of its religious, legal, and cultural dynamism.

As the French philosopher Alain de Libera notes, the underlying question is whether to accept the use of rationality, of critical debate, of human creativity in science, philosophy, in the confrontation of social and political opinions. The history of Islam and of its cultural and social references demonstrates that rationality, criticism, recognition of the status of the individual, and of social and political dissent (up to and including the legitimate challenge of particular dynasties, despots, or religious castes) are an integral part of Islamic civilization. The principled position of Ibn Rushd (Averroes), whose *Decisive Treatise*[40] criticizes state authoritarianism, is not at all remote from the stance of his predecessors, the Muslim scholars of the dominant Islamic legal tradition, who rejected any attempt by the state to impose any particular school of jurisprudence. Mâlik ibn Anas (711–795), who in the name of jurisprudential pluralism stood steadfast against the efforts of Caliph al-Mansûr (714–775) to declare his work, *al-Muwatta,* as the state's sole legal standard, or Ahmad ibn Hanbal (780–855), who resisted attempts by the state to impose a single doctrine on the createdness or uncreatedness of the Qur'an, stand out as examples.

How curious, and disturbing that in the West only Ibn Rushd's position is credited (undoubtedly because of its philosophical proximity to Locke's

*Letter concerning Toleration*)[41] to the detriment of scholars who, despite their courageous struggles and stands, have gone unrecognized as thinkers and intellectuals. Even more disturbing, in Muslim majority societies, Muslims themselves accept what amounts to a reductive and biased reading of the history of Islamic thought. This is no small matter: it locates outside the purview of religion the distancing of oneself from the state, criticizing it and opposing its despotic character (politically, doctrinally, legally, and religiously)—in keeping with a very "Western" way of what a secular "thinker" or "philosopher" should be. In so doing, it overlooks the critical rationality and political independence of Muslim scholars like Mâlik ibn Anas and Ahmad ibn Hanbal, whose courage cost them years of imprisonment (though, historically, they were far from the only ones). They are seen as too "religious" to be recognized as having early drawn a distinction between the two authorities, divine and human, doing so not only as Muslim scholars but also as legal philosophers, according to the categories of the Western social sciences.

Muslims must reconcile themselves with this aspect of their history; they must study it anew instead of either ignoring their own past and their own being, or seeing themselves through the prism of the West's reductive view of Islam, its values and its multiplicity of tradition. It is time to rediscover how the two powers—the divine and the human—are articulated, but also to relearn the ways of relating to knowledge, and to the independence of rationality and science. Hunke goes so far as to affirm, not without reason, that the Islamic universities established in Europe in the Middle Ages were the "first secular universities," given their approach to religious, philosophical, and scientific knowledge.[42]

As Arab societies awaken, as peoples achieve political liberation, to invoke Islam means to liberate minds through the acquisition of knowledge, autonomous rationality, critical thinking, and freedom of thought: the very definition of pluralism, responsible citizenship, and civil society that functions as an interface between institutions and the state. A return to these sources (without denying that the experience of the West can also enlighten and enrich internal debate in Muslim majority countries) must make it possible for contemporary societies to move forward, while remaining faithful to their heritage,[43] and while discussing the fundamentals of democratization: the role of the state, of the religious reference, the substance of general and civic education, the rights of women, and the prerogatives of civil society.

What could have been more normal than for Islamist parties and/or movements, in their opposition to colonialism in the early twentieth century, to insist on the role of the state and on its "Islamic" character by invoking the nation-state? In their eyes, it was necessary to call upon Islamic ideology in the struggle to break free from the colonial yoke and from cultural imperialism. They were as much the products of a long tradition as the inheritors of a specific historical and political context. Their struggle was a two-pronged one: nationalist on the one hand (even for the pan-Islamists), as they wanted to end foreign rule and restore their country's independence; ideological and religious on the other hand, as it challenged the rulers' claims to a monopoly of universality, and of the means and ends of success. Political Islam is a product of its time. It reduced the Islamic heritage and the categories by which it understood itself, the better to seize hold of the principles and means that it needed, at a precise moment in history, to differentiate itself from the other: the West, and its colonialism and its domineering, restrictive secularization. Above and beyond the slogans that rejected the Western model (and the often relevant criticism of its flaws and contradictions), the conditions of thought historically imposed upon the Islamists drove them to limit the scope of their own traditions and the breadth and depth of their long history to the immediate imperatives of the questions before them.

Now, in the aftermath of the Arab awakening, the time has come for real debate to begin instead of the empty controversies that pit secularists and Islamists against one another on grounds that are as artificial as they are ideologically and politically motivated. Such a debate, based on national specificities (religious, philosophical, and cultural) must not oversimplify the complex interaction of the two authorities, divine and human. They should focus on the relationship between the state and collective ethics, with particular attention being paid to popular education, individual freedom, the equality of citizens (and of women and men), and, of course, political and religious pluralism. The uprisings must be understood in their regional context, and in the light of international political and economic relations, in the Global South as well as in the North. Such are the prerequisites for enduring success, as opposed to symbolic though short-lived victories.

We would then be far from today's conflict of ideas, which conveys the impression that little has changed since the early twentieth century and the struggle for independence. Today, at the epicenter of globalization, the challenges have become far more complex and interdependent; national independence can no longer guarantee freedom and autonomy. The recent experiences of Western democracies are showing that economic globalization, new technologies, migrations, and emotional policies that feed on fear can lead to democratic regression, to the curtailment of liberties, to a restrictive rereading of constitutions. These are the issues that must be addressed today.

## *Interlocking Crises*

Muslim majority societies in Africa, the Middle East and Asia must be examined without bias. Their prospects and their aspirations are immense, their potential boundless, their missed opportunities seemingly countless. Today these societies find themselves locked in a series of complex and multidimensional crises. To study each of them in detail would be beyond the scope of this book—but it is of crucial importance to focus on the crises touched off by the polarization of political debate over the issue of secularism versus the primacy of the Islamic reference.

The result has been to reduce, impoverish, or even shift the debate away from the core issues, and to provide the two hostile camps with an excellent excuse for escaping self-criticism; as though the protagonists of contemporary Arab and Muslim intellectual and political life could avoid assessing the deficiencies and contradictions inherent in their own positions. Their alienation is twofold: first, the respective positions—in the societies of the Global South as a whole—seem naturally justified and accredited by the presence of the contradictory opinion; second, the discussions taking place derive their meaning only from the way in which they relate to the West, finding either justification in alignment or credibility in rejection and differentiation.

It seems clear that "Oriental" societies, from Africa to Asia, cannot avoid the process of representation of self and of others that has emerged from the construction of "the Other," as posited by Edward Said in *Orientalism*. In Arab and Muslim majority societies, the "other" is also constructed by the refraction of that society's positive or negative relations with the West. The debate is warped; self-criticism is often lacking.

For all that, the dynamics of political liberation and of ideological revival, not to mention the movement toward independence and autonomy, combine to demand that this critical process be carried out systematically. Now is the time to draw up an initial list of the questions and issues that seem central.

## *Advocates of Secularization*

On close examination, the arguments put forward by the advocates of secularization in Muslim majority countries (both those who have recently shed dictatorship and those who have not) often appear oversimplified, disconnected from reality, and even fraught with contradictions. Who could deny that these oft-repeated ideas (above all the need to separate the political and religious spheres, as if this were the crucial question in Arab societies) are the product of an elite that has remained historically and ideologically very close to its former colonial rulers, their thought systems and values. The very choice of this issue, as though it were a vital priority, is part and parcel of the ideological agenda of the former colonial rulers who sought to convince the colonized that their backwardness was the fault of Islam's inability to keep the political and religious spheres separate. Anxious to escape responsibility for their political and economic domination, the colonists—and the intellectual occupying powers—shifted the terms of conflict to the religious and the cultural spheres. Today's elites—very often Anglophiles and Francophiles—continue to apply the same logic, even though direct colonial rule has come to an end. It could hardly be clearer that intellectual and cultural imperialism has by no means ended, and that on occasion the Global South's elites sustain and even reinforce it.

Even more disturbing, though hardly surprising, is the gap, not to say the disconnect, between the elites and the very people they claim to represent and to protect. To the people they praise democracy, freedom, equality, and human rights; a closer look reveals that the promoters of these fine and worthy ideals are often out of touch with the people to whom they speak. Or if they aren't, like some grassroots movements on the left of the political spectrum, their influence is marginal at best. Worse yet, these circles had been—and still are—close to the inner circles of autocratic rule or to the military (such as in Egypt, Tunisia, Syria, or Iraq). They may have collaborated with dictators, accepted institutionalized cronyism, or benefited in one way or another from corruption, that cancer that corrodes and destroys democratic processes. Against religious conservatives and the West, the secularist elites claimed, among themselves, to hold religiously liberal and tolerant positions. This by no means meant that they were politically liberal: some of them worked hand in glove with the worst dictatorships while promoting the values of secularism, democracy, freedom, and justice, which had become theirs by default as, in the West and by simple deduction, they stood against any overlapping of religion and politics. To this day the same circles find it immensely difficult to establish veritable communication with the population and to put forward a coherent vision of democratization.

Relations with the West remain the Achilles heel of those who claim that only secularization can solve the problems of Arab and Muslim societies. It is as though the source of tension lies somewhere between the idealization of the West and commitment to a critical process whose tools (rationalism, analytical objectivity, etc.) are still perceived as issuing from the North. Quite superficially, members of the elite accept that strictly rationalistic, "secular" criticism must be more objective (and necessarily less biased) than an analysis that uses religion as its point of departure. Such arguments—so commonplace that they have become truisms in the West—are accepted quite uncritically in the societies of the Global South. Having laid claim to democracy and freedom without attempting to make life consistent with them, the elites have also laid a vice-grip on the tools of objective and scientific thought (in the Marxist sense) while relegating their opponents to a dangerous subjectivity, to unscientific forms of thought that are too religious to be modern. An imagined West has thus taken shape from within the ongoing debate in the Global South, while the tools of knowledge (secular thought with its "objective," "rational," "critical," and "modern" approaches) are mobilized to consolidate power, ideological domination, and cultural imperialism.

The willingness to employ putatively objective tools can be observed even in the work of certain intellectuals who have sharply criticized ideological representations of "the other" as a construction designed to buttress domination. When an author as multifaceted and compelling as Edward Said deconstructs the mechanisms of the West, he employs at the same time the critical instruments perceived by the West as uniquely valid, effective, and objective, thereby disqualifying the tools put forward by the other, by the Muslims, those subjects now projected as objects. The only Muslim thinkers Said stoops to mention—as representing the voice of "the other"—are those who have already been favorably received by the secularized West because they share the same objectives and utilize the same tools (while, like his examples Adonis or Rushdie, having little impact in the Muslim majority world). As a result, Said's argument turns against itself: though he claims to be interested in the other not in that other's actual being but in his projection, his choice is a highly selective one, coming as it does from an Arab, Palestinian, and American intellectual. It is, in effect, a projection justified by his own ideological position: a position that owes more to power than he is prepared to acknowledge and, disturbingly, he seems unprepared to assume responsibility for. In truth, his is a posture that is frequently encountered among the partisans of secularization who, while often voicing harsh criticism of the West's political and economic formulae and imagined prerogatives, remain captives of their own references and conceptual tools, often displaying a culpable, oftimes unfathomable ignorance of their own history, and of their cultural and religious traditions.

By presenting the debate over secularization as the primary challenge, the secularized elites of the Arab world not only display their disconnectedness from their memories and traditions, but also present a thoroughly distorted image of the fundamental dysfunction that afflicts Western society as a whole. Without even being aware of it, they sometimes endorse the populist rhetoric that reduces the multidimensional crises spawned by economic, technological, and cultural globalization to the relationship of the citizens in their diversity with the state or the nation. Uncritically they accept the ideological void that is the hallmark of traditional Western parties, whether of the right or the left. The end of political ideology in the West, the biased debate over identities and immigration, the absence of fundamental debate over social and educational policy, and over the nature and limitations of the neo-liberal economy have had a powerful impact on the meaning and direction of the Arab uprisings—and vice versa. Do the secularist intellectuals of the Global South have an alternative to propose for their own countries? Over and above the simulacrum of a debate pitting them against religious conservatives and Islamists, do they have a vision of society drawn up for the people, with the people, and in the name of the liberation of the people? The debate over secularization and political Islam is to the secularists of the Global South what the foreigner (and today, the Muslim) is to the populist xenophobes of the North: a pretext, and an alibi.

The true challenge of the day is to choose the right battle—to mobilize the creative energy of the peoples in the attempt to find real solutions to real problems. The march toward democracy in the Global South entails a thorough reconsideration of the three "fundamentals": economic (and agricultural) policy, educational policy, and cultural and media policy (in the general sense). The secularist elite would be well advised to acknowledge that it truly has nothing new to offer in these three vital policy categories. At the risk of sounding repetitious, there can be no true political democracy without a profound restructuring of the economic priorities of each country, which in turn can only come about by combating corruption, limiting the prerogatives of the military, and, above all, reconsidering economic ties with other countries as well as the modalities of domestic wealth distribution. Concern for free, analytical, and critical thought must take the form of educational policies founded upon the construction of schools and universities, revising the curriculum and enabling women to study, work, and become financially independent. Despite their parents' fulsome declarations, the children of the secular elites often end up pursuing their studies in the West. While progressive statements about women have never troubled entrenched traditional and patriarchal attitudes within those elites, their fine words must at last be translated into genuine social and educational policy at the local and national level. These are the issues; they must now be addressed.

Much has been made of alternative media and the "Internet culture," of social networks and virtual relationships. Given that they helped generate mass mobilizations strong enough to overthrow regimes, any humanist thinking worthy of the name, particularly if it defines itself as secular, must study and assess today's "Internet culture" and, more generally, the media. Though it has empowered the masses, this same cult tends to relieve individuals of their personal responsibilities, hidden as they are behind virtual relationships, anonymity, and an obsession with surveillance, manipulation, and conspiracy. The Internet, paradoxically, may represent the marriage of communication technology and regression in human interaction; of the power of networking with the dispossession of the person. When combined with a certain fascination for the West, it may exert a powerful influence on young people who enjoy little freedom, have no social opportunities, no educational prospects, and no jobs. The consequences can be serious; just how serious can be observed in the timeworn debate between secularists and conservatives or Islamists, which is not only inappropriate but is also a historical blunder.

## *Defenders of Tradition, Religious Conservatives, and Islamists*

Traditionalist, literalist, and conservative religious organizations, as well as Islamist movements and parties, have more often than not accepted the terms of the warped debate between "secularists" and "Islamists"—and occasionally imposed these terms themselves. Their point was to challenge the legitimacy of those who claimed to be speaking for the people. If the (literalist or Islamist) supporters of tradition are often right when they point out that the secularists belong mostly to a Western-influenced elite cut off from the population, their own critical arguments only deal at a superficial level with the real issues that have undermined Muslim majority societies in general and Arab societies in particular. They are more concerned with giving "Islamic" legitimacy to their rhetoric than with providing concrete answers to contemporary challenges. Once again, they may be sincere and well justified in fearing alienation or Westernization. The fact remains, however, that in the confrontation of ideas, religion is more frequently exploited to provide symbolic credibility and power than it is employed as an inspiration and a reference by minds that refuse to deny the complexities of reality. The endless conflicts between secularists and the advocates of "tradition and Islamic references" make it impossible for them (as for the secularists) to take critical stock of a century of struggle, achievement, and failure.

In the first place, it is difficult, just as it was with the secularists, to dis-cern any concrete or innovative contributions made by the conservatives, and a fortiori by the Islamists, on the three broad issues outlined earlier. What concrete proposals have they developed to reform the economic policies of the societies of the Global South? Terms like "Islamic economy" or "Islamic finance"[44] are bandied about, but in the realm of fact, on the national and international levels, no real alternative that can claim to originate in Islamic ethics has been put forward. Much the same can be said of educational policy, which should be concerned with the training and the intellectual and critical autonomy of people. The conservatives and the Islamists may indeed be closer to the population than the secular elite, but they are lacking in terms of need management. Their social work is important, but what are their proposals for public instruction and education? The reforms they would enact are primarily structural, focused on religious instruction, which—even in private Islamic institutions—continues to be marked by the lack of a critical approach to teaching methods and curricula.

Recurring in such institutions, these features point to an absence of global vision: they tend to concentrate on religious instruction using tra-ditional methods of rote memorization, give undue weight to purely scien-tific disciplines (medicine, engineering, computer science, etc.), and relegate the humanities to a subsidiary position. A similar dearth of innovative cul-tural policies is also striking, as is their inability to meet the challenges of the new media environment. Aside from criticism of the West and its cul-tural imperialism, the ways and means advanced by the conservatives—in the petro-monarchies, for example—and by the Islamists to conceptualize new, forward-looking cultural and media policies are striking in their poverty; projects that deliver on their claims can be counted on the fingers of one hand in North Africa and the Middle East.

In the realm of facts, the political rhetoric and vision of conservative traditionalists and Islamists have more often than not been trapped in themes relevant in the early twentieth century when the struggle for decol-onization made it normal and necessary to think in terms of the nation-state. Against the French, British, Dutch, or Italian colonial rulers, it was of vital importance to envision the structure of a free and autonomous state that would emerge from the cultural and historical references of the people fighting for independence—precisely what the slogans of Islamist and pan-Islamist movements wanted to express when they referred to the "Islamic state." Behind the label that identified the state as "Islamic" lay the desire for reconciliation with their heritage and the imperative to break free

from Western domination and to chart an original path leading to independence. Traditional classics like al-Mawardi's *al-Ahkâm al-Sultaniyya*
or Ibn Taymiyya's *al-Siyâsa al-Shar'iyya*[45] were revisited in the light of the
challenges facing modern states. The aim was to gain (or claim) "Islamic"
legitimacy for political projects, state models and structures. An example is Saudi Arabia, where the idea of democratic elections was—and still
is—seen as contrary to Islamic tradition. The issue has been a subject of
fierce debate among the various Islamist trends since the 1940s (within the
Muslim Brotherhood in Egypt, and between different currents of thought
in North Africa, the Middle East, and Asia). The early stages of the Iranian
revolution were also marked by intense exchanges of ideas over the specific
features of the "Islamic Republic,"[46] exchanges and contradictions that still
fuel the respective positions of conservatives and reformists within the system itself.

Perspectives and visions have, alas, progressed little; it is difficult to distinguish what identifies the political models of the literalists and the Islamists.
Furthermore, the Islamists continue to insist on the concept of sharī'a being
enshrined in the constitution, as they did in Egypt after the mass uprising.[47]
But it is difficult to imagine how the term would be understood and implemented: as a general orientation—a path toward justice—or as a closed system
restricted to the penal code?[48] Above and beyond the question of inclusion in
the constitution, the source of so much impassioned debate, the issue of the
sharī'a reveals little about the programmatic intentions of the conservative
and/or Islamist trends. The political choice can be as broad as the gap that
separates the Saudi model, where the sharī'a has constitutive force,[49] and the
intentions of the current Turkish government,[50] for which sharī'a is understood, as explained by Recep Tayyip Erdoğan, as a striving for less corruption,
and for greater equality and freedom.

Caution is indicated—caution and critical assessment of people's true
aspirations. No one can deny that the movements sweeping the Middle East
have evolved rapidly in several fields: those involved may be finding it difficult
to escape from the constraining references to the nation-state and their own
nationalist commitments (with a concomitant failure to consider wider issues
such as South-South cooperation), but their positions on democracy, wom-
en's participation in public life, capitalism, or relations with the West have
shifted rapidly.[51] Opinions may differ on whether the changes have been positive or negative, but the fact remains that these political currents are neither
static nor one-dimensional, even though they have yet to provide pragmatic
responses to the challenges of the day.

The Arab awakening has not yet penetrated the petro-monarchies, where kings and governments wield a literalist, conservative version of Islam— an excellent example is Bahrain where the uprising was summarily crushed. Even better examples are Saudi Arabia and Qatar, whose regimes remain hermetically sealed despite a limited political and media opening (al-Jazeera). But nothing truly innovative can be expected from their interpretations of Islam and its application to the daily lives of their subjects.[52] For all their limitless financial capacities, these regimes share a long list of deficiencies, ranging from curtailed freedoms, limited democratization, extremely slow improvement of the status of women, and perennially backward educational models.

Much the same can be said of Islamist movements in North Africa, the Middle East, and, in fact, in all Muslim majority countries. A rapid overview of recent history shows that the greatest difficulty encountered by Islamist organizations and parties has not been to remain in opposition (where resistance to the regime added to their credibility), but to exercise power (which often led to a loss of much of that credibility). Whether as the governing party (as in Iran, Sudan, Somalia, or even Palestine) or when sharing power (as in Algeria or Morocco), Islamist organizations and parties often appear to have compromised themselves or, at minimum, to have been inconsistent with the principles they espoused while opposing the regime. They may have been a grassroots presence (by providing social services, medical and educational assistance for the poor) while in opposition, but once elected (whether as a majority or as a minority participant in a governing coalition) they failed to deliver on promises.

The concrete experiences of the Islamist movements should make it easier to evaluate their real and symbolic strength: they are much more successful in opposing than in developing credible proposals for the future. Their historical resistance to colonialism, their debate with the secularists, their rejection of the West (in a repulsion-attraction relationship), the legitimacy derived from their hostility to Israel all conferred upon the Islamists the legitimacy of a moral counterweight; but these very accomplishments did not allow them to make a hard-eyed, critical assessment of their own political program. Consequently, after the fall of the tyrant whose very existence had unified their ranks in opposition, the Islamists experienced an implosion. In Tunisia, and even more glaringly in Egypt, when confronted with the choice between joining the protest movements and imagining the post-Mubarak era, the Muslim Brotherhood split into five distinct subgroups. The older generation disagreed over the prerogatives of the organization itself and of the newly founded Freedom and Justice Party. When its leader Abdul Futuh decided to run for president in defiance of the Brotherhood's leadership he was forced to quit the organization. Simultaneously, younger members felt free to set up another party or support a non-Brotherhood candidate.

Opposition to the regime, far more than the strength of their vision, was what had united the organization's diverse currents. On May 18, 2011, Muhammad Morsy,[53] president of the Muslim Brotherhood's newly created party, delivered a lecture at Oxford about the movement's future prospects. In it he summarized the arguments that the organization has been repeating for fifty years (about the constitution, democratization, the rule of law, and relations with members of other faiths). Nothing new, nothing forward-looking was said about economic, social, or political issues (poverty, education, employment, women); nothing was ventured about the regional outlook (the dominant economic order and dynamism, South-South relations, etc.). It was in the context created by the binary opposition and the implosion of the Muslim Brotherhood that the Egyptian Salafi Front made its appearance on Cairo's Tahrir Square. While the demonstrators justifiably feared that the uprising might be taken over by former regime figures or by the military, the Salafi Front (or Islamic Front, made up primarily of literalists, and then the party an-Nour) replicated the binary relationship in an attempt to monopolize the Islamic reference and thus the religious legitimacy of the movement.[54] In such circumstances, it is difficult to emerge from the role-playing phase. The same kinds of deficiencies can be observed in Tunisia, Syria, Libya, and Morocco.

The long-awaited and vital debate over future prospects, democratization, and international alliances is still far away. Like the secularists, conservatives and Islamists alike shun the test of self-criticism, preferring to confine themselves to an empty, outdated, and counterproductive paradigm. Even discussion of the Turkish example has become polarized: Can the Turks be described as Islamists, or has the post-Islamist era begun? Posing the question in those terms is as reductive as it is simplistic: Is Turkey an example of democracy or an example of an Islamist project for democracy? Thus phrased, it skirts the main issue. Of course Prime Minister Erdoğan comes from Turkey's Islamist movement, but what is most compelling is his government's commitment to overcoming the futile opposition between secularists and Islamists by putting forward a pragmatic policy of all-around reform.[55] President (and former foreign minister) Abdullah Gül, energetic and competent Foreign Minister Ahmet Davutoğlu (architect of the "zero conflict with our neighbors" foreign policy), and the government as a whole are implementing a multidimensional policy that must be analyzed and criticized for what it is.

The fight against corruption and cronyism at home, reducing the pre-rogatives of the military; increasingly orienting foreign relations toward the Global South;[56] stepping up trade with China, India, Brazil, and South America (even as the European Union dithers over its possible integration); acting as a mediator in the Middle East (with regard to Iran) and adopting firm, critical stance toward Israel (thus winning international admiration among Muslim popular opinion): these are the elements that make Turkey a model for Muslim majority societies in North Africa, the Middle East, and Asia.[57] Turkey is now the world's seventeenth-ranked economic power; its growth rate is Europe's strongest (8.1 percent in 2010 according to the World Bank).[58] In an inversion of roles, the European Union may now need Turkey more than Turkey needs it.

Turkey, it should be remembered, took clear, strong positions on the Arab uprisings, sometimes remaining more cautions, as in the case of Syria where it held back for seven months before beginning to articulate its position. The Turkish prime minister was among the first to praise the Tunisian people, to call upon the president of Egypt to step down, and to support the Libyan resistance movement. Though he took some time to distance himself from Bashar al-Assad's repressive regime, his government was quick to welcome Syrian oppositionists and to allow them to organize resistance from Turkish soil.[59] He also saw that training sessions (in politics, management, religious ethics, etc.) were set up for young Arab activists, mainly but not exclusively from Tunisia and Egypt.[60]

The ambitions and wide-ranging activism of the present Turkish government warrants a far more detailed analysis of their objectives and strategies. Does Turkey represent the path that future Arab democracies should follow? Clearly Turkey has been waging war against corruption and renewing its education policies; but what of the prospects for its capitalist economy? The question must be raised: Is the country's economic policy bound by its openly productivist objectives, or is the Turkish leadership attempting to stabilize the economy before moving ahead to introduce an ethically sustainable alternative?[61] Has contemporary Turkey been faithful to its history and traditions; is it proving successful in safeguarding its spirit, its specificity, and its cultural creativity? Has it achieved anything more than thoroughly—and apparently successfully—integrating itself into the global economic order, into the dominant global culture, and accepting the prevailing productivist logic? Does its commitment to strong economic growth and a new strategy of international relations represent a step forward, a means to an end—or an end in itself?

These are the issues that lie at the heart of any discussion of the Turkish model, whether it is viewed positively or critically. The same issues are of utmost relevance to the future of the Arab awakening and to the capacity of Arab societies to explore new paths, new ways of posing questions, new ways of charting the development of civil society, to create a new paradigm in international relations. The Turkish model, I am convinced, should be seen as a means rather than an end—precisely the question I will take up in the fourth section of this book.

# 4

## *The Islamic Reference*

THERE ARE TWO types of analysis of events that can be considered as inappropriate, mistaken, and ultimately counterproductive. The first is that the social, political, economic, and cultural influence of Islam in Arab and Muslim majority societies can only be appreciated through a particular prism: that of the various Islamist organizations, a reductive approach if ever there was one. The protestors who have been the driving force behind the Arab awakening are, in their overwhelming majority, Muslim; they have not been acting against their religion but with it, and quite often in its name. They would like their society to evolve in a way that would allow them to live in a manner consistent with their attachment to tradition and also with the challenges of the modern era. As noted earlier, it would be awkward to analyze events as nothing but a historical way station along the road leading the peoples of the Middle East and North Africa to Western style modernity, with an identical view of freedom, democracy, and knowledge, all culminating in a slightly Hegelian manner, in a superior synthesis of history as embodied in the Ideal of the West.

As Olivier Roy, the French sociologist, notes: "We are not finished with Islam." It now remains to see what will be the nature of the Islamic reference now, in the heat of the uprisings, and beyond. Will it continue to stand as the West's alterity, to play the "other" while perpetuating a historical relationship founded exclusively on the balance of power, on trauma and tension? Will it simply vanish, merging into the new "single civilization of the civilized" (in the words of former Spanish prime minister José-Maria Aznar)[1] that is the ultimate stage of globalization? What are the prospects? Given that globalization of the economy, of culture, and of communication is generating crises that no society can avoid, the key issue is twofold. Is the West, even with its culture, and with all the means at its disposal, in a position to eliminate the tensions that plague the very order it has been instrumental in creating? Can other civilizations—China, India, South America, and the Muslim majority societies—contribute to building the future by offering another vision, other priorities and other goals, and in so doing help to find solutions and to reform our world?

The second of these two questions—the one that sees Islam as a civilization and as a religion—now assumes its full importance. What, in the onrush of globalization, amid the blurring of former landmarks, and as tensions proliferate, can the Islamic reference hope to offer on the political, social, economic, and cultural levels? What can and must be its ethical contribution? To objectively recognize that people are attached to Islam does not necessarily mean that the Islamic reference will automatically enable them to break free from the restraints that hold them back. Likewise, the temptations of fatalism and conspiracy theory that we mentioned in the first part must be resisted, lest we be transformed into passive spectators to history as it unfolds.

The challenge that analysis represents is clear-cut: can the Arab individual in particular, and Muslims in general, emerge as subjects of their own history by refusing to view that history as a representation produced by the West or as an instrument of its power? To be successful, that person—and Muslims in general—must reconcile themselves, deeply and always critically, with the core and the essence of their tradition, and ask the questions that will make it possible for them, should they so decide, to define themselves as contemporary and autonomous Muslim subjects. The same reference must commit them to participating fully in history, making them active subjects endowed with free thought and masters of their fate. Becoming a subject in the full light of history is an imperative. If the expression "active subject" seems redundant, a "passive subject" of history is a contradiction in terms.

The Muslim peoples must fully assume the status of subjects and contribute actively to the debates and the challenges of our times. It is imperative that citizens, intellectuals, *ulama*, Muslim women and men in general undertake an intellectual and practical commitment to put forward a vision of a fairer, more equitable world. They must struggle to bring about more transparent democracies, governments more heedful of their people and less under the control of financial lobbies or media conglomerates that function in the most undemocratic way. How to ensure that secularism does not become the pretext or the most effective means—beginning with the distinction between religious and state authority—by which, in the long run, ethics are driven out of political, economic, and/or cultural action?

Such constructive criticism is already being carried out by thinkers in the West, but it would have an entirely different meaning and potentially different tangible consequences if it were developed and formulated by drawing upon Islamic references and with a perspective of putting forward visions and projects from within. Twenty-three years ago the Swiss sociologist Jean Ziegler wrote about the inversion of perspectives and the true contribution of the apparently defeated in history.[2] The "victory of the defeated" can be described as their ability to view the conflicts and contradictions of their time in a different way, to experience the satisfaction of self-reconciliation and the essence of singularity while suggesting an alternative that the "dominant" group had not thought of, or to which it was blind. Ziegler's formulation is compelling. But the challenge of today would also seem to be that of emerging from a relationship based on power. The double victory—of the defeated and the victor—would be to recognize that common challenges warrant bringing to an end relations based on rejection and/or domination, and to open the door to a real encounter, one respectful of diversity and equality: an encounter of singularities facing challenges of high complexity. At this precise historical moment, Muslims will only have proven the singularity of Islam when they have been able to demonstrate its universality.

## The End of Political Islam?

The end of political Islam has been predicted time and time again for more than twenty years. The trajectory followed by the regime in Iran, the crises in Algeria, Egypt, and elsewhere, pointed to the conclusion drawn by Olivier Roy (followed by Gilles Kepel): "the failure of political Islam" and its inevitable end, which had already begun.[3] Scholars and analysts are, however, sometimes unclear about how exactly to define and outline the notions of "Islamism" and "political Islam." At both ends of the semantic spectrum, it is essential to know at what point the reference to political Islam ends. Can it be termed political Islam when a tiny group of violent extremists that has no organized structure to speak of, no articulate political vision, kills innocent people in different parts of the world? At the opposite end of the spectrum, has the evolution of the Turkish "model," from Erbakan to Erdoğan, along with the thoroughgoing transformation of the Justice and Development Party (AKP) removed it from the category of political Islam? In like manner, what of the changes that the Islamist movements have undergone in the twentieth and early twenty-first centuries: do they still represent political Islam? How to describe the ideology enforced in the petro-monarchies, particularly in Saudi Arabia, which asserts that democracy and the principle of elections itself must be rejected in the name of Islam? Is this not a political ideology oriented and nurtured by a specific understanding of Islam? Is there not a temptation to attach the "Islamist" label to any political movement that invokes Islam while taking a position—sometimes in uncompromising terms—against the West?[4]

Before announcing the end of "political Islam," we must first agree on a precise definition to understand what is subsumed by the term. Scholars and analysts, both political scientists and sociologists, have thus far failed to reach a consensus. Who could doubt that all Islamist organizations or movements have undergone substantial changes during the twentieth and early twenty-first centuries? A simple comparison of the arguments used by the pioneering opponents of colonialism, al-Afghani and Abduh, and those of contemporary Islamists shows that the range of opinions and strategies has greatly expanded over the course of their historical experience, in both success and failure. Over nearly a century the official leadership of Egypt's Muslim Brotherhood (the Guidance Bureau: Maktab al-Irshâd) has undergone substantial development over questions like democracy, women, political pluralism, and the role of civil society. In addition to the changes at the leadership level, the organization has been constantly stressed by generational conflict arising out of contradictory visions and strategies. Has the newest generation of Muslim Brothers jetti-soned the paradigm of their elders? Are they no longer "Islamists?" Such a conclusion might be extreme, but it must be admitted that the legalist incar-nation of political Islam has undergone a mutation, not only in the terminol-ogy it employs, but also in the substance of its ideology and the priorities it sets in its political commitment. After a nearly a century marked by obstacles and threats, how could it have been different? The same general pattern can be observed from Morocco to Egypt, from Tunisia and Algeria to Libya, Syria, and even farther east, to Pakistan, India, Indonesia, and Malaysia.

Seen in this light, the Iran experience is instructive. Influential person-alities, from the philosopher Abdolkarim Soroush to former prime minis-ter Mir Hossein Mousavi, had supported the 1979 Islamic revolution before modifying their views and developing, from within, positions critical of the regime and calling for indispensable reforms. If some have ceased to recog-nize a political role for Islam in the light of what they consider to have been a negative experience, others, like Mousavi, Mehdi Karoubi, and most of the reformists claim to have remained faithful to the founding ideology but oppose what they see as a betrayal of its spirit by the present regime, where a portion of the religious hierarchy wields authoritarian control. They have another vision of what the Islamic Republic should be, but they would by no means wish to drop the notion of "Islamic" from their political outlook. In fact, they were to invoke it in demanding more transparency, an end to arbitrary arrests, censorship, and the cronyism of the clerical caste: for them, such practices run counter to religious principles and betray the principles of the 1979 revolution, which set out to moralize politics in the name of Islam, not to use it to monopolize power.[5] To such an extent, according to Reuters and the Israeli daily *Haaretz*, that Barack Obama could see little difference between the policies of Ahmadinejad and Mousavi: with either man, future relations promised to be fraught with tension.[6] The regime is far from shaky; it can be expected to exercise a decisive influence in the region for years to come—alongside that of its Lebanese ally, Hezbollah.

No less compelling is the Turkish example. The evolution of the positions of current prime minister Recep Tayyip Erdoğan away from those of his long-time mentor, former prime minister Necmettin Erbakan, seems clear-cut and in some respects, radical. When he took office, Erbakan, an economist by training, wished to create a counterweight to the G8 (the eight more industrialized countries in the world), in the spirit of early twentieth-century Islamism and the pan-Islamism that had inspired it. In the spring of 1996 he directed Turkey's foreign and economic policy southward and eastward, inviting Egypt, Iran, Pakistan, Bangladesh, Indonesia, Malaysia, and Nigeria to join the D8 ("Developing Eight").[7] It was anticipated that the participating countries, all with Muslim majorities, would work together to shift the center of gravity of their economic relations. Erbakan noted at the time: "Trade among European countries is between 70 percent and 80 percent, while trade among Muslim countries is only 7 percent. We must increase the percentage."[8] The intent was clear: in addition to carrying out an Islamization policy at home, a new "Islamic" power bloc was to be created through economic means within the existing world order. Though the project fell through, it pointed to what would distinguish Erdoğan from his former mentor. Where Erbakan had adopted an Islamist and deeply anti-capitalist approach (though not a communist, he spoke of "another way"), Erdoğan's priorities were different. He turned toward the West and the European Union, petitioning to integrate Turkey into a union that would be primarily economic. In accepting secularism, carrying out constitutional reform, and steering away from former Islamist slogans, he appeared to invert priorities: Turkey must now assume a strong position in the international economy and follow the globally accepted rules in order to gain recognition as an indispensable political player (hence the "zero problems with our neighbors" policy).

In its domestic policy, the AKP is a conservative party that strives to remain faithful to Islamic religious and moral traditions. It by no means shares the literalist reading of religion that prevails in Saudi Arabia (the AKP advocates reformist Islam)[9] but a similar political and economic configuration can nonetheless be detected: an emphatic ideological reference to Islam (reformist in Turkey, literalist in Saudi Arabia) accompanied by an acceptance of the neo-liberal capitalist economic order. It can be observed that whenever such a configuration appears in a Muslim majority country, there is hesitation in the West to stigmatize that country by defining it as "Islamist"—as though being less anti-capitalist made a country less Islamist. In other words, Islam is acceptable, and can be assimilated into the respectable categories of political science, on condition that it accepts the laws of the market. In the process, it is often forgotten that such Islamists can be conservative and on occasion, not terribly democratic, as in the petro-monarchies where acceptable conservative, neo-liberal despots can always be found.

Nothing new here. The same argument has dogged Islamist movements since their inception in the early years of the twentieth century, and even as far back as al-Afghani's pan-Islamism, which was considered extremely dangerous as it combined anti-colonial resistance with the call for political and economic unity in the Muslim world.[10] Many years later Hassan al-Banna, the founder of the Muslim Brotherhood, launched a large-scale agrarian reform movement in southern Egypt, developing small and medium-sized enterprises designed to escape the confines of the market economy. The experience was a resounding success, although it was undone several years later when Gamal Abdel Nasser dismantled the alternative banks and firms in the name of his idea of "socialism."[11] In this perspective, political Islam can be seen as quite close to the principles of the Christian liberation theology that was formulated in the 1970s by Franciscan priest Leonardo Boff and Archbishop Dom Helder Camara (both Brazilians) and by the Peruvian priest Gustavo Gutierrez.[12] Sayyid Qutb wrote a fundamental critique of capitalism, as did the Iranian Ali Shariati, often described as an Islamo-Marxist, who defended the same approach as one of the initiators of the Islamic revolution.[13] But Islamists, both from within the Muslim Brotherhood and in Muslim majority countries, did not always put forward such positions: far from it. Not all Islamist movement leaders shared the concept of socialist Islam expressed by Mustafa as-Siba'i, one of the leaders of the Brotherhood in Syria. Over time, and through successive incremental shifts, the dominant trend among the world's Islamists—of both older and younger generations—appears today to center on the call for political reform while either enthusiastically or reluctantly, for all their verbal criticism, accepting the pre-vailing economic order.

Beyond any doubt, ideas and discourse on issues as central as democ-racy, law, atheism, and women have evolved. Could it be said that since what once defined political Islam has changed so thoroughly, given the consensual acceptance of economics as the decisive factor, it is no longer possible to speak of "political Islam?" Such a conclusion would be overly bold and certainly too hasty. Islamism may well be caught up in a process of mutation, but many of its basic tenets still speak to the populations of the Muslim majority coun-tries. The debates that emerged in the aftermath of the uprisings in Tunisia in Egypt are evidence enough. The supporters of political Islam enjoy a widely recognized historical legitimacy stemming from their opposition to dictator-ship, the years of prison, torture, and forced exile. In any event, with or with-out Islamists, Islam remains to this day a reference in the social and political lives of the people. What will determine the future of the Islamic reference as such will be the inspiration and energy it instills in the people who are rising to face the challenges of their time: the role of the state, freedom, pluralism, technological and cultural globalization, and—obviously—the crises now shaking the global economic order. The fact that Islam itself is being called into question is a clear sign that political Islam is not dead but is facing a new conjuncture and stands poised to undergo a profound shift brought on by the dynamics of history and the new political, economic, cultural, and broad geostrategic environment.[14]

## Toward the Civil State

One of the distinguishing features of political Islam in the early twentieth century was its call for the creation of an "Islamic state." Methods and strat-egies might differ ("bottom up" for the Muslim Brotherhood, "top down" by revolution for other organizations, and as happened in Iran), but the aim remained the same. The structure of the state was conceptualized in Islamic principles (as drawn up by the classical Sunni and Shiite traditions) and articulated around the core concept of "Islamic law," meaning shari'a. It was no accident that late nineteenth- and early twentieth-century Islamist orga-nizations expressly sought to revive Islam's social and political heritage. As the Ottoman Empire was being dismantled and broken up into numerous smaller countries, and as Western colonial rulers expanded their control, it became essential to visualize the paths and the stages leading to independ-ence and, in the long run, to reunifying the *Umma*, the Muslim spiritual community, understood—or idealized—at the time as a political entity, which the Ottoman state had symbolically, though imperfectly, represented. It was only normal for the movements that identified themselves as Islamic to organize their action in pursuit of two priority objectives: the national and state structures that had been imposed upon them in the aftermath of the1885 Congress of Berlin and the potential for transnational dynamics, as reflected in the pan-Islamism of al-Afghani and later, of the international expansion of the Muslim Brotherhood at the time of Hassan al-Banna.

To the Islamists of the day, the "Islamic state" comprised a threefold response—religious, political, and cultural—to the imposition of Western models. It was understood as a call to resistance to the plans of the colonialists; they, in turn, were seen through the prism of imperialism, with aims that seemed crystal clear: consolidating the political and economic dependence of the colonized countries, enforcing secularization, fighting Islam (and its forces of resistance) and traditional cultures in general. Confronted with a multidimensional threat of this magnitude, the Islamists were convinced that only by referring to Islam could they resist Western imperialism and the three-pronged assault of colonialism—a perception shared by all Islamist movements. The state, defined as "Islamic" was, according to them, the only structure that could ensure the political independence, religious identity (as opposed to secularization, implicitly directed against Islam), and cultural specificity of the emerging Arab state entities. It was an ideological response, driven by circumstances, which must be assessed in the light of the prevailing issues of the day. The same pattern prevailed until the Iranian revolution, which would be the last revolutionary expression of political Islam within the strict framework of the nation-state in opposition to a pro-Western dictatorial regime. The Iranian experience, failing as it did to fulfill the idealistic aspirations of many Islamists, was to have a powerful impact on both Shiite and Sunni movements and organizations. Factors like globalization, the absence of a genuine pan-Islamic movement and the emergence of new forces (possessing new capacities) explain why the understanding, the vocabulary, and even the objectives of the Islamists have, from the end of the last century to the present, taken new forms.

As noted earlier, some Muslim scholars and leaders—like Sheikh Yusuf al-Qaradawi or Tunisian leader Rached Ghannouchi—have readily accepted the democratic principle. For them, it is not in contradiction with the idea of Islam as a political project.[15] Still, the Islamist leader of the Algerian Hamas party, Mahfoud Nahnah, appears to have been the first no longer to speak of an "Islamic state" but of a "civil state."[16] It was not long before several Islamist movements replaced "Islamic" with "civil" in describing themselves, all the while avoiding terms like secularization, secularism, or nondenominational as such concepts continue to carry a negative connotation in the broad Arab and Muslim conscience.[17] In his on-the-spot (and highly optimistic) analysis of Egypt's January 25th uprising (which he considers a "revolution" with no hesitation),[18] left-wing intellectual Muhammad 'Imara—who has edged closer to the Islamists while maintaining a critical attitude—emphatically affirms that "the Islamic state is a civil state," which, he adds, must be based on institutions and on consultation (*shûrâ*) and that the operative decision-making process requires that its authority be civil in nature.[19] For him, the civil state must administer majority preferences through the categories of "right or wrong" (and not through those of "faith or of its rejection"), in full recognition of the plurality of religions and political ideas.[20]

Some of the leaders of the Muslim Brotherhood, like Abdel Moneim Abul Futuh in Egypt or Rached Ghannouchi (who has already appealed for full acceptance of all the implications of the turn to democracy),[21] echo the position taken by the Moroccan movement al-Adl Wal-Ihsân (Justice and Excellence, known for its firm opposition to any form of compromise with the power structure); the priority of this movement, as Sheikh Yassine's daughter Nadia Yassine explains it, is to found a democratic republic (as opposed to the monarchy). The movement is now on record as preferring a "civil state," according to its spokesman Fathallah Arsalane,[22] a statement that confirms my argument that Islamist leaders seek to distance themselves from the notion of "secularism," seen in the Arab world as shorthand for Westernization, while steering clear of the idea of the "Islamic state," stigmatized by its cumbersome baggage of negative connotation. The Iranian experience has created the widespread impression that an "Islamic state" would be a kind of theocracy run by a clergy-like apparatus similar to Iran's Shiite hierarchy. The perception is so widespread that Islamists have been compelled to revise their terminology and define their concepts more precisely. When referring to recent experience, they more often—like Nadia Yassine—prefer the Turkish model to an Iranian-style revolution.[23]

Islamists are not the only ones looking for new formulations that will allow them to escape from the polarized opposition between secularism and Islamism. Even the perceived secular Jordan's Prince al-Hassan bin Talal has moved the debate toward what he labels an Islamic "middle way" (*wisatiyya*), a "civil society" (*mujtama' madanî*), and the state that represents it by virtue of democratic rules.[24]

The shift in terminology and semantics is no mere trifle; it reveals four lessons that must be singled out and studied. The first concerns what has just been said about historical experience: Islamists—like all involved in political movements—evolve in response to real events, reconsidering their doctrinal positions and strategies as they go. Of late, the leaders of such movements have come to know the West better, moving beyond the colonial relationship, and have been able to reconsider their perceptions, and often their prejudices, with regard to the objectives and ultimately the institutionalization of secularism. Though the term "secularism" has remained taboo, the quest of these leaders for new formulae and for inventive articulation between religion and power indicates significant development in their thought.

The second lesson can be drawn from developments in the "Islamic law and jurisprudence (*fiqh*)" approach over the past fifty years, a process resulting from the impact of social and political transformations in society. Conversely though, developments in legal thought have driven a renewal of vision and made it possible to devise new strategies. As the youthful academic Halim Rane of Australia's Griffith University has pointed out, Muslim scholars and intellectuals, Islamist or not, are increasingly turning to the legal fundamentals (*usûl al-fiqh*) of higher principles (*maqâsid ash-sharî'a*), thus limiting the approach that draws on the rules and structures laid down by the traditional schools of jurisprudence (*madhâhib fiqhiyya*). The shift has touched off a renewal of thought and has opened up previously unexplored prospects, particularly concerning democracy, the nature of the state, and the objectives of sociopolitical projects in Muslim majority countries:[25] a subject I have dealt with at length in my book *Radical Reform: Islamic Ethics and Liberation*.[26] In it I explain that "radical" reform of the way texts are approached must be couched in the light of ethical goals, going beyond the literality of rules, obligations, and prohibitions. The open method I describe is not new, of course, but today it is being revived and has made it possible for Muslim thinkers and scholars the world over to reconsider their approach, and for numerous organizations, whether Islamist or not, to rethink their outlook and their strategy of engagement in Muslim majority societies.

The third lesson is a crucial one: by accepting the idea of a "civil state," thinkers and activists (even Islamists) have explicitly endorsed the existence of two distinct authorities: one political, the other religious. The distinction is a critical one, in that it defines relations with the democratic process. Al-Adl Wal-Ihsân, the Moroccan Islamist movement, unambiguously states that administration of the affairs of state is a matter of *ijtihâd* (autonomous human legal reasoning) and cannot be a "divine right," as understood by some thinkers, scholars, and Islamist activists when they refer to "*al-hâkimiyya.*"[27] The distinction between the two authorities, which I hold to be present from Islam's earliest beginnings, is key to understanding what the role of the state should be in Muslim majority countries and what contours the democratic model might adopt, free of the narrow authority of religious scholars. The Iranian model has been a source of disappointment for citizens as well as for activists; the Arab world in its majority aspires to true democracy. Reference to the shari'a remains; the concept of secularism is avoided, but the aim is to find a coherent embodiment and a viable model for Muslim majority societies. The question was stated head on (a first!) in Casablanca, in the course of a debate entitled "What Secularism for Muslim Countries" with the Moroccan thinker Abdelali El-Amrani,[28] positions taken in which aroused reservations and touched off critical reaction. Subsequently, the young Egyptian professor and research scholar Heba Raouf Ezzat has spoken of the need to work toward an "Islamic democratic secularism."[29] In her opinion, a new juxtaposition of the religious and political domains should be created, all the while taking into account the tradition and history of Muslim majority societies and in full respect of people's choices and the consequences of those choices. This is no debate over concepts, but a fundamental reexamination of the relationship between religion and the state. The fact that both collective intelligence and common culture rest upon religion cannot be used to justify control over public affairs and/or political power. The Iranian model, with its religious hierarchy and the notion of infallibility connected with the institution of *Velayat-e faqih* has displayed its limitations (and the danger of confounding categories). The Islamic Republic has not stood the test of democratic transparency, has not shown that it can heed the voice of the people. All things considered, the Turkish model appears to have won the day, with the reservations noted. Between the two experiences, debate is now under way, with new positions being developed almost daily. At minimum, the question has been placed on the agenda.

The fourth and last lesson derives from the preceding three. Evolving thought, the wealth of accumulated historical experience, the renewal of Muslim legal thinking, and criticism of the confusion of the authorities have combined to elicit the question of the relation between Islam and the state in terms of applied ethics. Here, the interface between ethics (inspired by religion, collective intelligence, and culture) and the administration of state affairs must be articulated. Here, religion is no longer posited as a closed, irretrievably separate framework that imposes itself upon the political domain (which has never been the case with Islam), but as a corpus of principles and objectives capable of orienting and inspiring political action. Respect for the popular will and the mandates of elected representatives; the promotion of equality, justice, and education; the fight against corruption, cronyism, and illegitimate rule: all must bow before a structure of "political ethics." Islam, as the religion of the majority in these societies, has a part to play in defining aims and establishing priorities with a view to cleansing the political sphere. Under no circumstances must the expression of civil society be stifled; elected representatives must hear its demands, and the field of politics itself must be open to constant ethical questioning: the essence of good governance (*al-hukm ar-râshid*).

If one of the clear-cut conditions of democracy is the protection of the freedom and of the prerogatives of the state or of the elected government, another would seem to be the development of an ethics to be applied to the exercise of power. Absent these two conditions, both in Muslim majority societies and in the West (as Jürgen Habermas has intuited), the risk is great that democracies will be incomplete or purely formal. Under the sole authority of religion, the state is oppressed and oppressive; without ethics, it will be corroded from within by corruption, cronyism, and/or the pressure of financial and economic interest groups and (most undemocratically) the multinational corporations that exploit the state for their own ends, just as religion may have done or still be doing: the former by virtue of their lobbies and their money, the latter by virtue of their monopoly on heaven and dogma.

## In the Name of Ethics: Imagining an Alternative

The root causes and salient features of the crisis of democracy in the West must be analyzed and duly noted. It is impossible to evaluate the uprisings that together make up the Arab awakening without taking the time to develop a critical analysis of the state of contemporary democracies.[30] First, it must be acknowledged that today's states and democratically elected governments find themselves, structurally, in a position of virtual subservience to the economic sphere, which possesses its own imperatives, its institutions, and its multinationals where egalitarian, democratic, and/or transparent administrative practices are not enforced. The doctrine of free markets appears to be assuming the form of a new religion in the very heart of the secularized order. In this sense, separating the powers of state and religion does not mean that the problem of reconciling the democratic state's relations with the other national and transnational power centers of the day has been solved. Take the economy, finance, and the media,[31] which wield such power—and on occasion new authority—over state entities that they threaten to undermine the very foundations of democracy that they need and claim to defend.

The most recent global crises, particularly that of 2008, have demonstrated—assuming proof was still needed—that states are so inextricably linked to the private activities of the financial sector that citizens are forced to pay for the foolishness, avarice, and dishonest practices of the major private and semi-private banks, which have consulted no one yet mobilize immense media resources to insist on the imperative need for government intervention. Despite soaring public debt, democratic states have bailed out rich but undemocratically administered banks. Nothing really new here: these events reflect the essence of the neo-liberal capitalist system and its management of the system's cyclical crises. For all that, the frequency and intensity of the crises are sapping the very underpinnings of democracy. Suffice it to observe the fragility and the debt load of the American federal government, or the threat of bankruptcy that hangs over European countries like Greece, Portugal, Spain, and Italy.

As if that were not enough, economic globalization has given birth to a new ideology: the "end of ideologies."[32] Following the collapse of communism in the former Soviet Union and Eastern Europe in 1989, all traditional political parties of the right and the left have rallied to defend the virtues of the market economy. No serious ideology dared question liberal economic fundamentals; political debates were reduced to discussing the degree of freedom to be granted to the state or the private sector, administration of business priorities and disputes—neither always clear-cut nor germane—over economic and social policies. Ours, it is said, is an age of ideological consensus. In addition to the statement, like the consensus it refers to, being particularly tendentious and misleading, it hides the fact that the "end of ideology" claim is itself highly ideological, stemming as it does from a construct that pretends to confirm its vision and its relevance by the absence of direct challenge from all emerging economic forces (China, India, and Brazil in particular) and that seeks to marginalize all voices that might oppose the dominant order, North and South, in South America, Africa, Asia, and in many Muslim majority countries.

Democracy is in crisis. Its proponents avoid the real issues and seize the occasions generated by political and media power centers as pretexts to achieve their electoral and populist ends. The "shock doctrine" as described by Naomi Klein[33] inflicts psychological and emotional stress on the population (just as do terrorism and the "war on terror") to justify policies that are a threat to freedom at home (surveillance, the curtailment of citizens' rights) and war abroad (in the manner of the United States and the United Kingdom). If that is insufficient, it whips up fear of immigration,[34] social insecurity, and/ or the new "Islamic" (and not just "Islamist") threat. As political and media diversion strategies, these measures necessarily impact political life and the democratic debate in contemporary society. The ideology of fear and the politics of emotion are by definition antidemocratic.[35] The return of nationalistic, identity-based populism, mass xenophobia, structural racism, and policies that limit freedoms undermine the foundations of democracy and of human equality, nationally and internationally. Money now moves faster and more freely than people. Yet some people (generally white, middle- or upper-class, from the North) travel much more easily than others who are no less human and no less innocent, but who tend to be black, Arab, poor, or from the countries of the Global South.

The goal of the ideology of the "end of ideologies" is to convince us that reality is what we are told it is, that these are the facts, that no ideological choice, no political commitment is needed or wanted: we must deal with the state of the world as a physician deals with the human body. Descriptive objectivity must prevail over an individual's ideological convictions or political ideals. Ideological instrumentalization clothes itself in the garb of the purest scientific observation. The emotions of peoples are played upon; the facts presented to them are nonpolitical and objective: the arrangement is as clever as it is effective and, above all, dangerous. When human choices are presented as immutable natural laws, or even as dogmas, democracy is betrayed. Were not secularism and democracy supposed to distinguish between the two authorities? The time of new religions that dare not speak their name has come.

Crisis indicators for democracy exist and should be of primary concern to citizens. The need for citizens continuously to demand their rights and the maintenance of a victim's mentality (as in the case of immigrants, blacks, Arabs, Muslims, and others who feel the state or the political and economic "system"[36] has singled them out for abusive treatment) eventually erodes the individual's sense of responsibility: people are left with the feeling that everything is due to them, with no equivalent discipline or commitment on their part. Increasingly superficial civic education leads to falling voter turnout on election day, not to mention the media/political spectaculars that have come to resemble wrestling matches between public figures, and the celebration of candidates verging on personality cults. Citizens show less and less interest in public affairs and local political issues, even though these issues are of direct concern to them. Ours is an era of passivity, in which the "ethics of citizenship" I have repeatedly invoked have fallen into abeyance.[37] Protest movements have indeed broken out, short-term and massive outbursts of indignation (such as the Arab uprisings or the protests of the "indignant" in Spain, Greece, Israel, or the United States). But their very short-term vision (being against the dictator) and mass character might reveal an absence of long-term democratic commitment. Responsibility and rights are to be found where democratic structures are being built by the population and by civil society, and not merely in mass protest against government policies.

As popular movements take to the streets to demand democratization, Arab and Muslim majority societies must take stock of today's crises and find a way to propose other solutions. They would be well advised to call upon their history, their collective memory, and their intellectual, religious, and cultural references in their attempt to construct alternatives. As against the simplistic and ultimately dangerous rhetoric criticized earlier in this book ("Arabs and Muslims have at last become just like us; now they are making our values, and the universalism that we in the West represent, their own"),[38] new dynamics of mobilization must emerge from within the youthful and energetic populations of the Global South. There is also hope for the industrialized societies of the North fraught today with crisis and lacking real perspectives for the future.

Far from the timeworn and politically exploited confrontation between secularists and Islamists, attention must now be turned to the role of civil society, of institutions and intellectuals, as well as the prerogatives of the state in building the future. A genuine democratization movement in the Global South must, as its top priority, focus both on broadening access to education and on its content. Another theme that demands political commitment to reform is women's place in public life—their rights and their autonomy. Issues such as the role of the media, the status of journalists, and freedom of expression, exposition, criticism, and protest are far more important than endless wrangling over symbols and the phrasing of constitutional articles. The debate over religion and culture as sources of inspiration for collective ethics (and psychology), not to mention social and political models, must remain wide open, for these factors function as the life breath and the heartbeat of any democratic project that arises from the population concerned, from society itself, and from a nation's founding narrative. Yet the debate cannot become such an obsession that today's challenges can no longer be faced with serenity.

These are the ways in which Muslim majority societies can become reconciled with what they are and can become forces for progress in an age of economic and cultural globalization. They must enjoy not only a taste for liberty and democracy but also an acute sense of their own genius; they must have the confidence that they can find solutions, to point to another way and to surmount the crises that are sapping the strength of contemporary societies. In response to sharp differences over pluralism, multiculturalism, and inter-communal harmony, can another way of conceptualizing religious and cultural pluralism be found—such as India, for example, has long experienced? Do Islam and Muslims in general—whose societies were so long models of pluralism, as seen in the Arab, Asiatic, and Ottoman legacy—still have something to offer? Do the cultures and the ethnic groups of the Global South have anything to teach us? Such questions cry out for answers. Islam as a religious and cultural reference is not a closed system and must never be presented as such: it puts forward general rules and defines the objectives that guide ethical considerations, but the shape and substance of these considerations must be developed and evolved in practice, over time.

## The Social and Political Spheres

These reflections on the civil character of the state (*dawla madaniyya*) and on the role of religious and cultural references (as ethical framework or as a reminder of the ultimate goals that should inform action) must lead to the formulation of clear positions.[39] Neither Sunni nor Shiite Islam advocates theocracy:[40] there is no power "in the name of God" and no exercise of power "by divine right" (whether political or human). The idea of human infallibility is foreign to Islam, being introduced much later, mainly by Shiite theological-legal schools, or by Islamists, with the highly debatable interpretation of *al-hakimiyya lillah* ("Power belongs to God").[41] The Qur'an, as well as the life (*sîra*) and the traditions (*ahâdîth*) of the Prophet of Islam teach us that he himself distinguished between the divine and the human; he admitted that he was subject to errors in worldly affairs and was protected from them only when receiving and transmitting the divine message.[42]

The two authorities are exercised according to distinct rules and modalities. Relations between them must be conceptualized and organized in full respect for the distinct prerogatives of each. The idea of an "Islamic state" in which the religious sphere would impose its authority upon that of the state, or control it, is not only dangerous; it is contrary to Islam. Far from slogans, the optimum articulation between the two must be sought: the reference to religion must remain an ethical orientation, one that sets out a framework and objectives, but without intervening in the work of regulation that defines state authority, itself granted and legitimized by the delegation of power from a country's citizens. Possession of an ethical system makes it possible to avoid divorce between the administration of political power and awareness of its limits, the rules of transparency and service, and its goals. In other words, it would guard against other potential forces of influence taking the place of religion and imposing a logic remote from the rules of democratic procedure: commercial and/or financial lobbies, powerful multinational corporations, private institutions, or the media. The issue, then, is to elaborate and implement principles of good governance for a society in a given place and at a given time.

Management of such divergent forces is far from simple, nor can it ever be achieved once and for all. The relationship between applied ethics and power, and between ethics and politics, must be constantly studied and reevaluated, for spheres of influence and manipulation have expanded, becoming as numerous as they are complex. The culture of sloganeering (grown more invasive as the confrontation of ideas has become more superficial) must be cast aside; new social and political models adapted to our time must be constructed. The societies of the East and the West, those of the North and the Global South, must commit themselves to reform, whether to provide answers to the crises dogging modern democracies or to progress toward the pluralism evident in the ongoing popular uprisings in the Middle East and North Africa. In Iran, the struggle that pits conservatives against reformers within the regime reflects the same concerns. The rejection of the institution of infallibility (*Velayat-e faqih*) embedded in the Shiite Islamic Republic founded by Khomeini points in the same direction: no one should be granted superhuman prerogatives in administering the authority of the state, which can only be the expression of a negotiated and regulated human delegation of powers. The Iranian reformists, on this particular point, are close to the fundamental concept of political authority as defined in Sunni Islam: neither religious dogma nor the doctrinal infallibility of the hierarchy must ever be imposed, either from above or from below.

The role of the state in the administration of public affairs must be defined by a framework, a formal (or informal) constitution, which in turn can only be designed by human beings. It is impossible to understand, let alone literally enforce the slogan "the Qur'an is our Constitution," put forward by the Muslim Brotherhood: the Qur'an contains no specific constitutional articles, and above all, humans must establish fundamental laws according to particular times and contexts, using their understanding, their rational and critical faculties (collective *ijtihâd*), and their contradictory views. Such is the task that societies on the path to emancipation must take up, all the while avoiding pointless disputation. The function of the civil state, with a government elected and empowered to administer it for a limited term, requires a clear framework and precise objectives. A society, a community of citizens, rests above all on the absolute and indisputable equality of those who make it up, in their full dignity, their obligations, and their rights.

There can be no ambiguity about the ethical orientation that Islam provides: "We have conferred dignity on human beings"[43]—a principle that applies to all humans, women and men, rich and poor, black and white, Muslim or not. It is the primary, fundamental principle of social justice that, in practice, rests on two prerequisites: equal rights and equal opportunities. As John Rawls points out in his work on justice,[44] the two types of equality are not identical; equal rights are of no avail if equal opportunities are not accepted and ensured. The first steps along the path to this goal are education, social equality between women and men (equal rights, equal opportunities, equal pay for equal skill, etc.), the protection of freedoms (religious or philosophical, freedom of speech and/or criticism); they apply equally to all citizens, be they Muslims, of another faith, or of no faith. The principle of "no compulsion in religion"[45] must inform the state, as must human rights, which must apply to all without distinction. At the heart of social reality, the management of religious pluralism is strengthened by the internal dynamics of religions themselves. They can only exist and flourish—and even spread—in a space free of constraint, through the strength of coherence and persuasion, never by imposition or prohibition.

A genuine, tangible process of reform, democratization, and liberation cannot take place without a broad-based social movement that mobilizes civil society as well as public and private institutions. It is precisely here that the reference to Islam assumes, in Muslim majority societies, an immediate, imperative, and constructive meaning. The first priority of any social movement must be to gain access to education for all: a short- and long-term social investment. On this question, the philosophy of Islam could not be clearer: human beings can reach their full stature only through intellectual, spiritual, social, and professional education.[46] It is an inviolable individual right. And yet, the state of education in Arab and Muslim majority societies is alarming, in both form and substance. There, young people suffer from poverty and illiteracy rates that may affect more than half of their number. School systems are run down; getting a job a hopeless task.

Implementation of the shari'a ("the path of faithfulness to the higher goals of Islam")[47] does not mean enforcing prohibitions and imposing a strict, timeless penal code, as it is often understood by some literalist Islamists or as it is perceived in the West. No, the sharî'a must be seen above all as a call for social justice, for respect of the rights of children, women, and men to education, housing, and employment, as well as personal fulfillment and well-being. Far from being reduced to a disputed article in a constitution, reference to the sharî'a must be placed in a much broader context. Given the extreme sensitivity of Muslim populations, it must be expressed in terms that are accurate and practical. The sharî'a is not a rigid, sanctified legal structure. Quite the contrary: it corresponds with a spiritual, social, political, and economic dynamic that reaches toward higher goals associated with a certain idea of humankind. It requires us to envisage, produce, and implement a philosophy of social and legal action. Formalist arguments over this Islamic reference are reductive, dangerous, and counterproductive: instead of stimulating the state to action, instead of liberating popular energies, such arguments harden positions of restrictive understanding, which inevitably miss their goals and lose their sense of priorities. "Secularists" and "Islamists," right- and left-wing parties should—if nothing else—agree on the four social priorities of the day: draw up a program of public (and private) education; provide guidance and counseling for young people arriving in the job market (the majority in their societies); help women gain an education and autonomy; launch campaigns against the endemic poverty and corruption that have undermined their societies from within.

A Muslim majority country that wishes to reconcile itself with its heritage, with the animating spirit of its culture, will also find in Islam's sources and in the history of its many civilizations a multitude of texts and examples showing the priority accorded to learning, the importance of knowledge and education that make up the bedrock of human dignity. The same holds true for the question of women: there can be no future unless women are educated and empowered (with or without Islam, but not forcibly against it.)[48] Sociological and demographic studies have proven—assuming proof is really necessary—that the education and involvement of women in society are the keys to social stability, to the natural regulation of births, and to releasing pent-up social and economic capital. The answer cannot be, as happened under Ben Ali, to use the question of women's status for political ends, or to make do with purely formal reforms that change only the legal structure (as with Morocco's al-mudâwana).[49] What must be changed are mind-sets, perceptions, behaviors. Democratization demands such a commitment, which should be a national cause.

The same is true of poverty. Imposition of zakât (the purifying social tax) and the establishment of awqâf (the plural of waqf: inalienable religious endowments for works of public benefit) are, in the first case, an Islamic obligation, or, in the second case, strongly recommended. But the philosophy that underlies these two practices corresponds exactly to contemporary findings in social and economic development studies: solidarity must be organized in terms of the rights of the poor (and not of charity from the rich), who must be helped to gain autonomy (and not reduced to perpetual dependence).[50] Several interesting projects in Africa, the Middle East, and Asia have demonstrated how Islamic religious prescriptions and recommendations can be applied in a modern, intelligent way, but it must be acknowledged that the full potential of these instruments of solidarity and justice has yet to be realized. So sensitive has the Muslim conscience remained to the duty of solidarity that by relying on these two Islamic references alone, hundreds of millions of dollars could be generated on the special occasions that punctuate the social calendar, such as Friday prayers,[51] the month of fasting, or the two annual feast days.

Unfortunately, distribution of *zakât* and the setting of priorities in the establishment of religious endowments (*awqâf*) are often haphazardly administered, whether by public agencies or private organizations—proof positive that concern for the poor is not a priority, either for the states concerned or for society in general. Yet in the Global South, any democratization process that does not place this challenge at the center of the reform process will prove to be defective and unbalanced, and it is bound in the long run to fail. Muslim majorities should take advantage of the immense capacity for mobilization inherent in their own religious references—especially where solidarity is concerned—to set up development programs adapted to their own national realities. The vital importance of the struggle against corruption, poverty, and the marginalization of women, which would free them of the shackles of literalism and cultural backwardness and from poverty, cannot be overemphasized. How sad it would be if ultimately the "Arab awakening" amounted to nothing more than the uprising of a leisure class of young people who enjoy access to the Internet and to social networks, who demand political freedom, but who have forgotten the poor and the downtrodden in their own societies who also claim one basic freedom: that of living (and not just surviving) over that of speech.

The democratization and the emancipation of Middle Eastern and North African societies will depend on the mobilization of civil society. Getting rid of a dictator is not enough: a broad-based social and political movement must come to the fore. The active participation of the citizens, of civil society as a whole, of nongovernmental organizations, of intellectuals, and of the media is the precondition for ensuring that the dynamic of democratization preserves its independence. Close examination of the uprisings that have so far taken place has revealed a discrepancy: the people rose up together, cutting across ideological, religious, class, or gender boundaries. But their role appears to have ended with the fall of the dictator and of his regime. It is as though once the regime had fallen, decisions were taken somewhere else: between former regime officials (a few), new faces, and (mainly) members of the military. This configuration is fraught with problems and leaves little room for optimism about the future. Aware of the possibility that their victory was being stolen from them, the people of Tunisia and Egypt repeatedly took to the streets. It was clearly not enough. In Libya, former cabinet ministers and close collaborators of Ghaddafi, whom they literally betrayed, are still leading the country. In every case, civil society, which should have taken a central role once the question of reform and democracy had been broached, has been shunted off to the side, and then silenced. The uprisings, to say the least, have not yet engendered revolutions.

The political structures that emerge from changing social dynamics must of course be considered. At stake in the confrontation between proponents of the complete emancipation of state structures and those who prefer not to see militaries (through which the United States and Europe have acted as overseers and protectors of the established order) entirely shunted aside is precisely the question of which political model will prevail: respective positions must be made clear in order to manage the complexities of the present day. Instead of being presented as an obstacle to dealing with pluralism, the Islamic reference can become—in Muslim majority societies—an inspiration and a rallying point. It possesses an ample potential to give a section of civil society a voice in the ongoing debate and restore people to their rightful place.

Above and beyond the formal—and formalist—dichotomy between Islamic *shûrâ* and democracy,[52] I have repeatedly pointed out that democracy is characterized by five inalienable principles that are not only not in contradiction with Islam but are in fundamental conformity with it: the rule of law, equality for all citizens, universal suffrage, accountability, and the separation of powers (executive, legislative, and judiciary). These are principles that must be located within the context of the civil state. The role of the Islamic reference is that of ethical orientation, in the name of faithfulness to the overarching objectives of justice, equality, freedom, and dignity. The key consideration is to distinguish the authority of the state from the authority of religion, and not to separate politics and ethics.

This approach demands clarity from the political actors of the future: recognition of equal rights for all citizens, acceptance of religious pluralism (beyond the monotheism of the "People of the Book"), and full participation for atheist or agnostic philosophical currents and political forces. Pluralism enshrines this recognition as a right, alongside freedom of conscience, of worship (or lack of same), and of expression for all. The victory of minds and consciences can be achieved only through a robust exchange of ideas and arguments. These principles must be seen as universal, exclusive to none. Each society must find the political model that fits its history, its culture, and its collective psychology.[53] Only then can the Islamic reference, which has shaped the identity of peoples, of their memories, and aspirations, take on its full meaning and point the way toward new avenues to be explored with regard to the structure and administration of the state and its institutions. Throughout history, the powerful have always felt the need to limit the scope of possibility to their own experience and their own successes. But that is to forget that history has not come to an end; that every dominant civilization—Egyptian, Indian, Ottoman, or Western—progresses and regresses, as Ibn Khaldun noted in the fourteenth century, in a cyclical pattern of birth, zenith, and on occasion disappearance in perfect temporality.

Muslim majority societies find themselves at the center of the tension between principles, objectives, and the search for applicable models. Given their references, and in recognition that nothing in Islam contradicts the Universal Declaration of Human Rights, there is no reason that Muslims should not be able to act as full participants in the debate, to present themselves as a value added, especially on questions of ethics, and of the duties and inalienable principles of political action. Military establishments should stay where they belong and not meddle—playing the role of religion—in public affairs. Too often in North Africa and the Middle East this kind of distortion has been used to justify either secularist or Islamist regimes, which cannot in either case be confused with democracy. The horizons of possibility are very broad indeed: though foreign powers, former regime collaborators, or the military may attempt to seize control of them, the Arab awakening has opened up new perspectives. A return to the past may well not be possible. Civil societies must break free from their passivity; they must discard the crippling notion that everything has been decided at the highest level, by dark forces, by the CIA, Israel, or someone else. This paranoia is the worst colonialism because it is the most effective. If the popular uprisings hope to transform themselves into true revolutions with all their inherent promise of deep and radical reform, their first task is to rid themselves of the intellectual and psychological bonds of colonialism.

The citizens of the Middle East and North Africa, women and men alike, possess all they need to construct a social and political ethics adapted to our times, rejecting none of the complexity of the world. In so doing, they must pay close attention to the achievements and the crises of Western society while at the same time exploring the original spirit of their own references and historical experience. There is no need to alienate themselves; no need to betray the principles of their religion and their culture to embrace modernity: this equation is wrong, dangerous, and ideologically fraught. Reinvesting Islamic terminology and its rich semantic universe may well, for example, create new possibilities for stimulating people who will feel at one with their values, their referential universe, and their hopes. The psychological barrier to overcome is not a simple one. Peoples and nations will have to recover their self-confidence and learn to trust their own capacities, their heritage, and their aspirations. Just as there can be no individual citizenship without a sense of belonging to a nation, there can be no collective consciousness without a sense of belonging to a common, legitimate, and consistent universe of reference. The particular genius and the energy of peoples have been forged by such feelings, by such hopes.

If the sharî'a is to be pervaded by and founded upon the vision of the *higher goals* of dignity, justice, freedom, and religious, political, and cultural pluralism; if *jihad* is seen as the effort of resisting racism, corruption, and dictatorship, allied with a commitment to the reform of the individual's being and of society in the light of these finalities, then and only then will Muslim majority societies be able to throw off their shackles and cast out their demons. Crucial to their success will be a mastery of the tools needed for self-rediscovery, and for exactly delineating what has defined Arab and Muslim majority nations through history and in their multiple identities. Though it is a key element in the process, the Islamic reference is not the only one: factors such as language, culture, and historical experience are no less essential.

See how far we have come from the empty conflict between secularism and Islamism. The terms of the debate are wrong; time has come to invert them, by a process of reappropriation and reconciliation. All those involved must contribute; they must put aside simplistic solutions and put an end to the controversies that bring smiles to the faces of former colonial rulers and to the great powers of the day. The spectacle of Arab countries acting against themselves may indeed provide great satisfaction to those who intend to keep them in a position of ideological, political, and economic dependence—and what better dependence could there be than self-alienation? Blaming the West will change nothing. If free critical intelligence has fallen into disarray, none but the Arab countries themselves are responsible.

## Economic Considerations

The economic aspects of the new social and political configuration, both before and after the Arab awakening, have already been discussed. It is now time to examine them more closely: not only the most obvious elements, such as the management of oil and gas resources, but also the presence of new and powerful actors like China, India, Brazil, and even Russia, not to mention influential institutions like the World Bank and the International Monetary Fund (IMF).

What does contemporary Muslim thought have to offer the Arab countries—and Muslim majority societies—in terms of ethical and economic alternatives? Despite appearances, it must be admitted that the economic field continues to be given short shrift in contemporary Islamic thought. In several previous works I have discussed the issues of Islamic economic ethics and the notions of "Islamic economy" and "Islamic finance," which are often presented as alternatives to the global capitalist economic order based on interest and speculation.[54] My criticism—meant as constructive—drew on several distinct categories, but its two central postulates dealt with the philosophy of "Islamic economy" itself. In point of fact, the "Islamic" alternatives put forward essentially set out to prove that it is possible to compete with the dominant capitalist system and to obtain similar results and profits while changing only the vocabulary and the techniques used in transactions. It is much more a technical, administrative, and structural approach than a critique of the prevailing order, its goals, principles, and priorities.[55]

To begin with, so-called Islamic economy and finance are, today, nothing but devices to adapt to the dominant system by creating "spaces" and "windows of opportunity" where procedures can be changed without either disturbing or attempting to transform the global order.[56] The wealthier Muslim majority countries—starting with the oil-rich monarchies—could exert a powerful impact were they to invest in research and to implement more ethical procedures, but they show scant interest in the question (of Islamic economy, finance, and more generally, ethics), and when they do, they seem much more anxious to prove their concern for, and the "Islamic" legitimacy of, their management practices.

One undeniable fact remains: in the contemporary Muslim conscience, ethics and the economy must be reconciled. It is possible to err, as I suggest in these pages, in defining the strategies and goals of what is now called "Islamic economy and finance," but it cannot be denied that among Muslims there is a will to resist the excesses of the neo-liberal economic order. From ordinary citizens to Muslim scholars (*ulama*), there is a widespread feeling that the prevailing economic order fundamentally contradicts the ethical values expressed by religion. It is from this intuition, this breeding ground of awareness and resistance, that efforts to develop strategies to transform and renew the regional and global economic order must begin. The basic precepts and the goals of today's economic order must be called into question. If the reference to Islam is to play a role in setting an ethical course, it will do so not by the application of technique, but by recalling immutable founding principles. From the earliest days, Islamic tradition has influenced and guided economic activity because it is clearly linked with the exercise of political power.[57] The objectives of economic activity form the first consideration. By way of synthesis of the basic positions produced by the classical Muslim tradition in the economic field down through the centuries, it can be said to have established three priorities: respect for the dignity of the individual and of labor; definition of the conditions of fair and equitable trade; respect for the rights of the poor.[58] The prohibition of interest and of speculation must be understood in the light of these imperatives, since both practices contradict, in one way or another, the general goals outlined earlier.

In applying this referential template, the entire economic model, regionally and globally, must be brought under close scrutiny. It encompasses such realities as the obsession with conquering new markets in the name of growth and development; the laws of the so-called free market that systematically favor the wealthy; the internal logic of a system built upon debt (applied to countries and individuals alike); the free, uncontrolled, and undemocratic management of multinationals that possess more power than most states; parallel economies and tax havens: all are in blatant contradiction of ethical concerns. It should come as no surprise that as the Arab awakening unfolds, France and the United Kingdom (like the United States in Iraq before them) stand poised to seize control of Libya's oil wealth. The same countries seem to be in far less of a hurry over Syria and Yemen, which are not as richly endowed. What moral scruples, currently missing from the global order, could prevent them? In the global economic order, not only is it commonplace, but also *logical*—as defined by the superior logic of the system—to exploit, despoil, and deceive. Any other attitude, though it might be more moral, would necessarily be *illogical*. It is no less logical for US president Barack Obama to simultaneously express support for the ousting of dictators who have become his new enemies (like so many in the past, from Noriega to Bin Laden) and to lend support to (and thereby a modicum of control over) the economies of the newly liberated countries with the assistance of the World Bank and the IMF.

Choices are limited; the countries whose populations have taken to the streets have little opportunity to break free from the dominant economic order, which in itself sets objective limits to the uprisings. The strategies of wielding power through the economy, of seizing control of hydrocarbons, and of establishing alliances with political forces are all well known: nothing new to report. This being the case, analysis of the respective motivations and positions of the different players involved is imperative. The support of the United States and Europe for the uprisings in Tunisia, Egypt, and Libya,[59] their complacent attitude with regard to Syria and Yemen, and their support for the petro-monarchies of Bahrain, Saudi Arabia, and Qatar, among others, respond to objective necessity. Much the same can be said for the positions of Russia and China: their opposition to intervention in Libya and their support of Bashar al-Assad serve their best interests. In all cases, and for all involved, democratization is an entirely secondary concern; the aim is always—cynically and systematically—to assess the probabilities of gaining economic and/or strategic control, or at minimum to limit loss of influence. By the same token, Arab and Muslim majority countries must envision their emancipation in the context of current economic upheaval and of the eastward shift of the global economy's center of gravity toward Asia, and specifically toward China and India.

Paradoxically, the emergence of a new multipolar order and its accompanying crisis could be an opportunity to promote a more ethical approach. The Arab world's longtime obsession with the "West," with Europe and the United States, has had a disastrous impact on its self-perception, its self-confidence, and its trust in its capacity to offer another, more credible view of the world. Islam has for so long been relegated to the status of the West's "Other"—formally colonized, then dominated, but always lagging behind—that Muslim intelligence, as it observes itself in this negative mirror, has been left with one of two options: either to merge with the dominant ideology or to bind itself with the shackles of rejection and otherness. Both can lead only to failure and alienation. But Asia, South America, and Africa have had no such relationship with Islam and Muslims.

Now the time has come, as the historic center of gravity is shifting, for Muslim majority societies to come forward, to look upon themselves as forces of renewal and of initiative in the new multipolar world. To prove Samuel Huntington's "clash of civilizations" theory wrong it is not necessary to prove that "Islam" and the "West" are not in conflict.[60] It does mean integrating the two into a concert of civilizations (another of Huntington's insights) in which emergent countries can help extricate Muslim majority societies from the system imposed by the West, with its order, its debt, and its crises. Put slightly differently, the multipolar nature of the new global economic order need not lead to a clash of "other civilizations" with the dominant civilization of the West; instead, it should lead to the end of Western domination and to its progressive marginalization, first economically and then, as a matter of natural evolution, politically.

The time has come also for the North African and Middle Eastern conscience to free itself from the "dominant" figure of the West and to conceive of itself as belonging to another order, to another world. Will that world be a more moral one? Will Chinese capitalism be more ethical than its American counterpart? Not at all. What might lend ethics a greater weight in economic affairs is not the morality of economic actors but their diversity. At a recent lecture given by Ahmet Davutoğlu at the invitation of *Foreign Policy* magazine,[61] which I attended, the Turkish foreign minister argued that in today's era of economic globalization there are issues that coincide with the world's global interest: they include management of the economic crisis, the question of ecology, emigration/immigration, and poverty. In times like these, Mr. Davutoğlu suggested, any cabinet minister of a given country is also a "minister of the planet." Each of the great issues he enumerated is, in fact, directly connected with ethics, with the ethical management of the world economy, and with hard questions about ultimate objectives: what must be done to eradicate corruption, to respect human dignity, to protect nature, and to end famine—currently ravaging Somalia and many other African countries.

I have, on several other occasions, dealt at length with the principles, modalities, and objectives of applied Islamic ethics in economy and finance. Much remains to be accomplished and much must be studied in both fields from the standpoint of priorities, higher goals, and techniques to be applied[62] in recognition of the plurality of contexts and of shifts in the world order. Our moment is a critical one. Having galvanized people, the Arab awakening must now inspire hope. Yet the most difficult task awaits: political emancipation must guarantee economic autonomy; the old priorities must be inverted. To repeat: the key issues are to fight against corruption, to reassert control over the wealth of nations, to manage mineral resources autonomously, and most crucially, to adjust MENA's place in the world's economic geography by turning southward and eastward. Though such a shift is still far away, the first economic consequences of the uprisings indicate that a strategic realignment is under way, one that looks very much like the last attempt by the United States and Europe to protect their privileges in the region a little longer. Though control is still being exerted through economic measures and sometimes through the agency of the military, an era is coming to an end. Even as they celebrate the uprisings, peoples and civil societies must grasp the occasion to draw up a strategy for their economic emancipation by a top-to-toe reordering of economic priorities in the light of imperative higher goals.

Applied ethics cannot be reduced to an assessment of whether the technique of a transaction is licit or illicit (*halal* or *harâm*). It is a matter of the highest ethics to begin by reclaiming the wealth of the land and the nation: oil, gas, enterprises of both the private and public sectors. Society must fight against corruption, bribery, tax havens, and parallel economies. The choice of investment also stems from ethical reform: instead of spending billions on useless arms contracts, it is essential to address the vital necessities of the day: health, education and social services, housing, employment, poverty, and ecological opportunities. Ethical concerns extend as well to changing the way international emigration and immigration is perceived: double punishment cannot be inflicted on the victims of a world that drives them into exile—the survival instinct at work—instead of attempting to correct the root causes. Good governance, political and economic reform, the fight against cronyism (and always, against corruption) are essential in regulating the migrations touched off by economic imbalance—unless the victims are to be criminalized, as happens today. East and West, immigrants, refugees, and undocumented persons are often treated in an immoral and unacceptable manner. The same treatment applies to the poverty that afflicts millions of children, women, and men, and so glaringly persists in Africa and the Middle East.

There can be no political liberation in the Arab world without economic emancipation, just as there can be no political justice without economic equity: the old Marxist adage, later adopted by South American liberation theology,[63] has lost none of its truth. It was an insight shared by the pioneers of political Islam in their initial institutional practices, before religious literalism, confusion over priorities, and/or ideological subversion transformed or perverted their vision, goals, and commitments. The Arab awakening has raised these questions once more as the world experiences rapid and radical change against a backdrop of growing turbulence. It must be seen in the context of the global political and economic order. Only then can events be understood as they unfold. It is also the essential condition for grasping the complexity of reality, and the necessity of setting political and economic priorities from the perspective of ethical finalities. In the light refracted through this prism, the popular uprisings must become part and parcel of a global ethics of liberation.[64]

## Culture and Meaning

Culture is an essential element. As people rise up across the Middle East and North Africa, the diversity of their cultures is not only the means but also the ultimate goal of their liberation and their freedom. Though imperialism was primarily political and economic, it was also cultural; it imposed ways of life, habits, perceptions, and values that rarely respected the societies under its domination, that seized control of minds, a true colonization of human intelligence.

Globalization extends to culture, often leading, in the societies of the Global South, to self-dispossession. Genuine liberation, the march toward dignity and democracy, requires a "cultural uprising" in all dimensions of its popular, artistic, intellectual, and religious expressions. I have pointed to the importance of culture and the arts in undertaking the task of reappropriation:[65] the tools of thought and tradition must be used to lend shape and substance to the sense of belonging that alone can guarantee the well-being of individuals. Such is the function of applied ethics. If there is no culture without religion, and no religion without culture, as suggested, and if, finally, culture is not religion, the issue must be explored; the complex questions of values, meaning, spirituality, tradition, and the arts—the factors that give form to history, memory, nations, and identities, that transmit well-being and freedom, or fail to—must be faced squarely.

Arab and Muslim majority societies are riven by religious and cultural tensions that have at times torn them apart. The role of the religious reference is constantly being discussed; its relations with tradition and with Arabic—or other national languages—have triggered passionate debates and set ruling elites and intellectuals at loggerheads. Close examination and study of these experiences leads but to one sole conclusion: we are dealing with a complex, deeply rooted malaise. Its dimensions are manifold: cultural, religious, linguistic, and therefore, a fortiori, strongly identity-related. It cuts across all social sectors, all classes, and all trends of thought, from secularists to Islamists and from atheists to believers, observant or not. The attraction-repulsion complex vis-à-vis the West is not new; it existed even before the colonial period.[66] It has created an ambiguous relationship in which imaginations are fascinated and attracted by the now-global Western culture, while the same force of attraction is rejected by the analytical, cultural, and ethical conscience and then experienced as self-dispossession, colonization, and on occasion, as the violence of cultural rape.[67] The aspirations and contradictions that have arisen must be acknowledged, as they can be enlisted as a driving force for liberation movement, as François Burgat reminds us,[68] or become obstacles that paralyze societies by trapping them in sterile confrontations that perpetuate the identity crisis rather than solving it.

Much has been written, quite justifiably, about the new "Internet culture" of the young cyber-dissidents of Tunisia and Egypt, not to mention the rest of the Middle East and North Africa. Their mastery of the tools of communication and their ability to express themselves have earned them praise. To the West, they conveyed the reassuring impression that they were speaking the same language as "we" were, that they shared "our" values and "our" hopes. No one can deny their extraordinary progress as communicators: the younger Arab generation succeeded in conveying a message, both at home and abroad, that traditional political forces had failed to do over a half-century of political involvement. The power and effectiveness that flow from mastery of new technology cannot be underestimated: the "Internet culture" is also the expression of genuine power. Still, the precise nature of its power raises questions about how deep the roots really are of the mass protest movements in the Middle East and North Africa. Are young people reclaiming themselves and their freedom through the use of modern means of communication, or are the means of communication stripping Arab young people of their identity? The question is imperative, for a political liberation movement accompanied by cultural ill-being (in addition to the potential for economic manipulation) would be bound in the long run to fail. Full respect for the memory and the psychology of people, attentiveness to their aspirations, and reconciling them with themselves are historical imperatives. The "Arab problem" was never simply one of the violent dictatorships that succeeded political decolonization; it has always lain in the perpetuation of an alienating and paralyzing, if not destructive, intellectual colonization.

The process of reclaiming the self is one of reconciliation with meaning. Cultures, along with the religions that shape and nurture them, are value systems, sets of traditions and habits clustered around one or several languages, producing meaning: for the self, for the here and now, for the community, for life. Cultures are never merely intellectual constructs. They take form through the collective intelligence and memory, through a commonly held psychology and emotions, through spiritual and artistic communion. The

Arab awakening cannot afford to overlook these, the fundamental dimensions of freedom and of the liberation of individuals and societies. The Islamic reference—my immediate concern—is of crucial importance and cries out for special attention for, like all religious references, it can have, in particular historical circumstances, a positive, liberating function or become a reactionary, dogmatic, and authoritarian instrument, an instrument of oppression. Its examination must be preceded by political and economic analysis, by systematic reference to studies in anthropology, cultures, and religions.

As far as Islam is concerned, Arab and Muslim majority societies are seriously lacking in spirituality. There is not a deficit of "religion" but of spiritual life. It can be encountered among Islamists, as well as among secularists and ordinary citizens. Religion refers to the framework, to the structure of ritual, to the rights and obligations of believers; as such, it lies at the heart of social and political debate. In the classical Islamic tradition, framework, reference, and practices can—like all religions and spiritual traditions—be best seen in the light of their relation to meaning (here, to the Divine), to a conception of life and death, to the life of the heart and mind. Contemporary Islamic discourse, however, has too often lost its substance—of meaning, of understanding ultimate goals and the state of the heart. Increasingly, it has been reduced to reactivity, preoccupied with the moral protection of the faithful, based on the reiteration of norms, rituals, and, above all, prohibitions. But spirituality is not faith without religion; it is the quest for meaning and peace of heart as the essence of religion. Viewed in this light, Muslim majority societies are profoundly bereft of serenity, coherence, and peace. The time has come for a spiritual and religious emancipation.

The decline of Islamic civilization, followed by colonialism, have left their mark, as has the experience of political and cultural resistance. The way in which religion and the Islamic reference are understood was gradually adapted to the requirements of resistance: for both traditional Muslim scholars (*ulama*) and Islamist movements (which often began with mystical aspirations), moral norms, rules pertaining to food, dress and strict observance of ritual have come increasingly important as means of self-assertion, in direct proportion to the danger of cultural colonialism and alienation perceived and experienced in Arab societies. Caught up in political resistance, Islamist movements have gradually focused their attention on questions of form, setting aside the spiritual core of religious practice. Between the rhetoric of traditional religious authorities and institutions and that of the Islamists, whether narrowly rigorous in outlook or hypnotized by political liberation, ordinary citizens are offered few answers to their spiritual pursuit of meaning, faith, the heart, and peace. Add to the picture the claims of Arab secularists that have imported Western perceptions and misunderstandings about secularism and its institutionalization; they confuse these with the absence of religion and/or disregard for it, and likewise reject the spiritual sphere that may be connected to it.[69]

A yawning void has opened up; mystical (*Sufi*) movements have reemerged, some of them respectful of norms, some fraudulent, in what is often an approximate answer to popular aspirations. The Sufi movements or circles are diverse and often provide a kind of exile from worldly affairs, in contrast to ritualistic traditionalism or to Islamist activism. Focus upon yourself, they urge, upon your heart and inner peace; stay far away from pointless social and political controversy. A specific feature of mystical circles is that they bring together—though in physically separate groups—educated elites in quest of meaning as well as ordinary citizens, including the poorest, who feel a need for reassurance that verges on superstition. Their teachings are, more often than not, general and idealistic, far removed from the complexities of reality; politically, they sometimes voice passive or explicit support for ruling regimes, even dictatorships.[70]

Furthermore, a substantial number of Sufi circles yield to the double temptation of the cult of the personality of the sheikh or guide (*murshid*) and the infantilization of the initiates (*murîd*): the latter may be highly educated, hold high rank in the social hierarchy, yet at the same time place their hearts, minds, and even their lives in the hands of a guide who, it is claimed, represents the ultimate path to fulfillment. This culture of disempowerment strangely echoes the fashions of the day: a combination of withdrawal from the world and living in a kind of existential confusion between emotional outpouring (the spectacle of effusiveness toward and reverence for Sufi elders can be disturbing, disquieting and dangerous) and a demanding spiritual initiation. Such initiation should be liberating, open the door to autonomy through mastery of the ego, and lead to coherence between the private and public life. But what emerge instead are parallel lives: a so-called Sufi spirituality allied to egocentric, greedy, self-interested, and occasionally immoral social (and political) behavior. Arab elites and middle classes find such behavior to their advantage, as do socially fragile sectors of the population.

Between the overbearing ritualism of official religious institutions and the obsessive politicization of Islamist leaders, the thirst for meaning, which finds its expression in cultural and religious references, seeks for ways to express itself. Mysticism sometimes provides the solution. But careful thought should be given to the real-life impact of such phenomena as they relate to the crisis of spirituality and therefore of religion. In every case, the teachings propounded do not encourage the autonomy, well-being, and confidence of human beings in their everyday individual and social lives. In their formalism and concentration upon norms, the traditional institutions that represent or teach Islam reproduce a double culture of prohibition and guilt. The religious reference is transformed into a mirror in which the believers must see and judge their own deficiencies. Such rhetoric can generate nothing more than unease. The Islamist approach, which seeks to free society from foreign influence, has in the long run brought forth a culture of reaction, differentiation, and frequently of judgment: Who is a Muslim, what is Islamic legitimacy? It sometimes casts itself as victim, even in the way it asserts itself against opposition. Social and political activism prevails over spiritual considerations; the struggle for power has sometimes eclipsed the quest for meaning.

By way of response to this void, the majority of mystical movements and circles have called upon their initiates to direct their attention inward, toward themselves, their hearts, their worship, and their inner peace. Around them have arisen a culture of isolation, social and political passivity, and loss of responsibility, as though spirituality were somehow necessarily opposed to action. Still, a large number of Sufi circles do speak out on social and political issues, and actually encourage their followers to speak out and to become actively involved in society. Between the culture of prohibition and guilt and that of reaction and victimization, between abandonment of responsibility and isolationism, what options remain to the Arab world to reconcile itself with its cultural, religious, and spiritual heritage? What must be done to propound a culture of well-being, autonomy, and responsibility?

This is what I mean by rediscovering and reclaiming the spirituality that permeates Eastern cultures and that lies at the heart of the Jewish, Christian, and Islamic traditions, a consideration that today's social and political uprisings can ill afford to neglect. For there can be no viable democracy, no pluralism in any society without the well-being of the individuals, the citizens, and the religious communities that comprise it—with or without God.

Cultural emancipation is imperative and will require a holistic approach. As a first step, self-representation must be reformed through education. In the Middle East and North Africa, this first step is still remote. If the discourse of religion is to be reconciled with spirituality, cultural fulfillment can only be achieved through celebration of and respect for the languages, memories, and heritage of all, and with positive integration of minority ethnic affiliations and dialects. Along with the West, Africa, the Islamic Orient, and Asia have fallen into the trap of some of the negative effects of globalization, including divisive, exclusivist, sectarian, even deadly[71] claims to culture and identity. The same claims are omnipresent in the Arab world as well. Hence the importance of cultural policies, which must be developed in tandem with social policy, drawn from the common ground that determines the sense of national belonging.

Culture lends meaning a horizon. Everything in the heritage of culture and tradition that gives meaning is worthy of celebration. To achieve cultural liberation means calling into question all possible forms of parallel and/or secondary alienation: economic dispossession is devastating, just as cultural imperialism can be. Spirituality, understood as a point of recall, a quest for meaning in and through itself, individually and collectively, is an act of liberation.[72] Yet it must be part of an open, constructive involvement that, acting from within society and in full respect of the pluralism that characterizes the societies of the Middle East and North Africa, will determine the ultimate goals of the cultures whose substance constitutes the narrative of each nation.

To assert culture, memory, and identity is to assert that they are meaningful, to affirm that they are capable of addressing the challenges of the day. To assert one's self is to become a subject, to take full responsibility for one's heart, body, and mind, as well as for one's fellows, one's society, and for nature itself. The imperative of coherence is incontrovertible, the very condition of genuine well-being and freedom. Western societies are today taking stock of the deficiencies that afflict them, that undermine the principles of democracy by maintaining a culture of fear and insecurity. Insecurity of mind is the negative image of peace of heart. Arab societies are undergoing a similar crisis, in a different way perhaps, but with equal intensity. They suffer from a malaise of incoherence, and no amount of reform, or of political freedom, will resolve the feeling of unease that has sapped the foundations of East and West alike.

There is no lack of obstacles to be overcome in the Middle East and North Africa. Both the political and economic difficulties are well known, as is the strength of the people's cultural and religious references; the potential for spiritual and ethical opening is palpable. What remains is to find the means for their multiform expression. I have suggested what energy, what well-being could result from a relationship with religion founded on meaning, self-liberation, autonomy, and responsibility; a relationship with the world based on and grounded in a confident, lucid relationship with self; a deep spiritual sense that is at once intellectual and active, independent and cooperative, demanding and positive, humble and ambitious. It is time to remind ourselves that in the profoundest of Islamic teachings, believers do not rise to pray during the night in order to find themselves and forget the world; they do this to find themselves, but so as to give meaning to the day and to reform the world. The Arab world and Muslim majority societies stand in need of an awakening that is responsible, free of illusions, self-critical, and resolutely positive, just as they stand in need of creativity and imagination.

Reconciliation with self, liberation from intellectual and cultural colonialism, not to mention the emergence of an "Arab subject" can only take place when new life is breathed into our relationship with meaning and with ultimate goals, only when imagination, art, literature, painting, and music are reclaimed. It is the same with science, along with knowledge and the ways in which women and men express themselves and their imaginations, their hurts and desires, their grief and their hopes. The Arab world is in the throes of another crisis: the crisis of a fettered imagination from which it is struggling to escape, and that has a powerful impact on its very well-being. By this token, the Arab awakening must do more than overthrow dictators. It must break the bonds with which decades of abdication have shackled the order of science, knowledge, esthetics, art, and beauty in general.

Arabs today must find reconciliation with their deepest spirituality, and not only with the wealth of their Arab identity: this much is clear. Alongside the act of political and economic liberation, this reconciliation represents the only true promise of well-being, autonomy, and peace. Reform of educational and cultural policies will take time—and will demand personal investment from the young. Mastery of the new Internet tools alone will not suffice; it is essential to study history, to put down roots in an environment of personal meaning, to gain greater familiarity with both the natural and social sciences, to cultivate art, language, literature, painting, music, and taste in general. When measured against these challenges, the political liberation that today hovers in the distance seems almost derisory and hardly likely to produce the hoped-for results. Part of why it is so difficult for Arab and Muslim majority societies to break out of the political and economic impasses that have characterized them for so long may be the impasses in education and culture. Because these deficiencies are themselves the source of policies that not only neglected but actually dismantled both traditional and modern systems of knowledge transmission, we are confronted with a vicious circle that must absolutely be broken. We can hope that the Arab awakening will provide an opportunity for escape by opening up much broader prospects for liberation and creativity than the constitutional and structural tinkering we are witnessing today.

Can the African continent and the Islamic Orient together find an original role to play in today's multipolar world? Can they put forward forceful
proposals and offer contributions that do more than merely produce the same
results with changed means and/or methods? Can they advocate another way;
can they, starting from their own references, call into question the finalities of
the existing world order? The applied ethics approach is one way. It calls for
a renewed, deepened, and more sophisticated understanding of the spiritual,
social, political, economic, cultural, and, ultimately, humanist teachings of
Islam, and of local and national cultures; for new educational methods and
new ways of teaching. But the imperative of consistency must be carried further still, and searching questions must be asked about the way we live. Day-
to-day corruption, the obsession with productivity, indifference to ecology
and unrelenting consumerism are Arab realities that undermine—in a kind of
collective unconsciousness—even the practice of religion. Everywhere there
is permanent disregard for the law and social rules (from ordinary citizens to
civil servants to despots), a widening gap between a minority of the extremely
wealthy and an increasingly poor majority, widespread neglect of the natural environment, and last, thoughtless consumption[73] that gives little heed to
local production even when it offers alternatives both healthier and more economically equitable. It is no longer possible to blame the West for this variety of colonialism; responsibility now lies directly in the hands of Arab and
Muslim majority societies themselves. It is to be hoped that the young people
who are today awakening will prove more sensitive to the requirements of
true political, intellectual, and cultural liberation than they are fascinated by
the material goods of the West.

The alternative media—new television networks, the Internet, social networks—offer an extraordinary opportunity; yet by creating illusions they may
be setting a trap. While diffusing an abundance of information that can help
change the way things are done, they cannot ensure the kind of communication that puts people at ease. Within the global neo-liberal capitalist order
the alternative media may well be seen as means for quantitative management
and structural reform, but their very nature renders them incapable of achieving the kind of qualitative transformation that I have been discussing—they
may even prevent it. It is impossible to achieve wide-ranging reform, let alone
offer alternatives by relying on the same tools and maintaining the same world
outlook. Here lies the danger underlined earlier.[74] The youthful activists and
cyber-dissidents who so effectively mobilized now find themselves at a crossroads. By contributing to the liberation of their respective countries they have
brought themselves face to face with a fundamental dilemma: Should they

simply reproduce the same thing, apply existing models (all of which are in crisis), or must they—beginning with themselves, their history, and the people's hopes—develop the capacity and the tools to produce something new? Do these educated young Arabs, the intellectual elite, know who they are and where they come from, in order to know what they want and where they are heading? No one can doubt their intellectual and cultural potential. But has that potential been realized? Is there a genuine desire to realize it? Has their mastery of technique outrun their autonomy, their creativity in setting out goals, as is so frequently the case? These are questions of substance: central, critical, imperative, and urgent.

When liberation and freedom are at issue, it is entirely legitimate to ask searching questions about the kind of freedom called for by Arab youth— not only in political and economic terms, but in intellectual terms as well. For in the final analysis, the imperative is one of intellectual resistance— *intellectual jihad*, in the deepest sense—that lends the notions of liberation and identity a qualitatively different substance and a new density of meaning. The man-made, portable prisons constructed of prohibition, guilt, infantilization, and disempowerment must be destroyed; only then can Arabs recover the original spirit of their culture that will provide meaning, energy, creativity, and hope within their pluralistic societies. Having functioned as the agents of peaceful uprising, they must now work to bring into being a multidimensional culture of dignity and peace. It is not merely a question of diminishing hostility between in human beings and or states, but of seeing peace as essential to quality of life, to well-being, and to the sense of belonging, in conformity with the new parameters adopted in the "human development index."[75] Measuring life expectancy, educational levels, and living standards is not enough, however; there are higher requirements, those of self-reconciliation, the rediscovery of the past and of tradition, and above all, the imperative of exploring and reviving the full potential of language, culture, art, and religion—and of all that is subsumed by collective intelligence, psychology, and imagination, by faith, by the heart, and in the hopes and dreams of individuals and peoples.

Abû Hâmid al-Ghazali (1058–1111) wrote his seminal masterpiece *The Revival of Religious Sciences*[76] in a time of crisis and uncertainty. He felt the need to return to essentials, to reassert the priority of knowledge and to focus on meaning and goals. Muslim majority societies are (like many others) going through a similar crisis: liberation and pacification can be achieved only through a process of cultural, ethical, economic, and political reconciliation. Ideas and "ideologies" must once again be generated. A human society without ideology is like an animal without instincts: knowing neither how to live or how to survive, it will die.

## With the West

The task cannot be taken up in isolation. The relationship with the West is crucial and involves a number of major issues. I have highlighted the difficulties that have appeared in recent history, the complexity of ideological and political relations, and, above all, the phenomenon of attraction/repulsion that can be observed both among politicians and intellectuals and among ordinary citizens. If the Arab uprisings are to be meaningful, if they are to herald a new era, they must renew this relationship.

Historically and ideologically, the "West versus Islam" dichotomy has been constructed through a process both fraught and complex. To this day, it shapes perceptions in both the East and the West. There can be no substitute for frankness: a constant and implicit (and often explicit) feature of the relationship has been the imbalance of power and, as Malaysian thinker Chandra Muzaffar correctly notes, brute force.[77] The question of justice and peace between civilizations and ideologies, of power and force, must be confronted directly. If the Arab uprisings have demonstrated nothing else, they have made this clear. The United States and Europe, their governments, and their intellectuals, continue to view the Arab world and Muslim majority societies as former colonies, as historical (and financial) debtor nations, as countries that must be kept in a state of ideological and economic dependence in order to protect the vital interests of the North. It is well and good to talk of a multipolar world, of the pluralism of civilizations, cultures, and religions, to celebrate equality and peace, but it must be acknowledged that the terms of the relationship are as unequal as they are unfair—not only economically, but also ideologically and symbolically—and that they have kept the Global South and the Islamic Orient in a state of dependency and domination. Nothing in the uprisings being witnessed today appears to challenge this reality in any meaningful way.

The presence of the United States and Europe casts a shadow over the debate on political and economic issues whose outcome will determine the future of every country in the Arab world and in Muslim majority societies, dictatorships or not. These issues, ranging from the role of the state and of the military, or of international institutions like the World Bank and the International Monetary Fund, hark back in one way or another to the relationship with the West, to the question of independence, and of how the wealth of nations is to be managed. The stakes are too high for Western countries—the same countries that have been setting ideological priorities, controlling mineral resources and economic policies in the East—to allow genuine, autonomous democracies to emerge. Western power will neither easily nor happily be challenged. What may bring the West to revise its relationship with the Arab and Muslim majority world will be a shift in the center of gravity of the world economic order. Time will pass before this can come about.

Judging by the way the Arab uprisings have unfolded in Tunisia, Libya, or Bahrain, the day is indeed far off. Yet there is no alternative. Relationships must change, and they will, in the medium or long term. The arrival of new political and economic forces makes this inevitable, not only because of the different interests now involved, but also because of the very nature of these forces. China, India, Russia, Brazil, South Africa, or Turkey's relations with the Arab world and with Islam are quite different from those of the West. This is not to say that relations are uniformly fine; this is evident in the repression of the Uighurs in China's Xinjiang province in 2009, the conflict in Chechnya (not to mention ongoing internal problems in Russia) along with Russia's ruthless decades-long policy of repression,[78] and the massacre of Gujarati Muslims by Hindu nationalists in India in 2002.[79] There is no room for idealizing: several of the emerging powers are not democratic at all (China), while others are experiencing severe deficiencies of democracy (India, Russia) which are conducive to repressive or discriminatory domestic policies, often against Muslims. These realities have little impact, however, on the way these countries approach Middle East issues. The need for sharper focus on Islam's relations with the East and the Far East in the coming decades will undoubtedly have major consequences for its relations with the West. Nor can Japan's recent and deepening interest in Islam and the Eastern question be overlooked. The facts are there for all to see: no longer is the American-European prism the only valid one. Intellectuals and the media in China, India, Russia, and Japan (and in the Western hemisphere, Latin America) understand the Middle East, its sense of itself, and its aspirations quite differently from the West. The clouds of upheaval are gathering on the horizon.

For the time being, the West's main concern is to protect its economic and geostrategic interests by maintaining access to oil and raw materials, and exploiting them through multinationals and public or private sector enterprises. In the short run, its basic interests are safe. The West will deal with the issues of equality and justice in the Middle East and North Africa only when it is compelled to do so. Its own ideological, social, and economic crises, along with the rise of the countries of the Global South and East have thrown its hegemony into question, creating problems that cannot be avoided forever. Also, domestic matters in the United States and Europe—issues of identity, national belonging, and immigration—are shaking the West from within. The question of relations with Islam is everywhere evident, manifested as fear, rejection, and above all, widespread suspicion.

On this precise point, as I have noted earlier, the case of the late Edward Said is as emblematic as it is revealing. His scholarly work on the negative representation of the other, on the way imperialism and power politics have impinged on the construction of the otherness of "Islam" and of "Muslims" is seminal. For all that, the autonomous voices of Western Muslims expressing their aspirations from within Western society are hardly audible. Edward Said was an Arab thinker of Christian background who described himself as a secularist and an atheist. His critique of the ideological construction of the figure of the "Muslim" and of the "Orient" as the "other" is, I believe, legitimate, but Said embodies an external perspective that, however critical, does not conceptualize the other from within. Resistance to economic and cultural imperialism can never, he claims, be rooted in a religious substrate. As a consequence, his relationship to the dynamics at work in this "Orient," and that constitute it—as well as the complex, plural voices of Islam that can be heard there—remains particularly biased.[80] However, in spite of his sharply critical views, his work has been widely accepted—and his critique academically "integrated"—in the West. Relying as he did on a rational and secular methodology, he could be seen as "one of us," critical of "our" construction of the "Other," even though he himself came culturally—but not religiously—from the Other's universe, which added weight to his legitimacy.

True deconstruction of representations cannot be completed (nor can it be possible) until Western academic circles and the media allow for more objective—and less ideologically biased—analysis of the diversity of approaches and discourse coming from Arab and Muslim majority societies, and from Western Muslim voices. This is unlikely to happen soon, especially bearing in mind the Rand Corporation's document on the creation of "moderate Muslim" networks. The description of "moderate Muslims"[81] and of what they should represent is startling, to say the least. "Muslims have to do that [discredit the radicals' ideology] for themselves. What we can do is level the playing field by empowering the moderates."[82] Such moderate Muslims are those who will henceforth speak from within, and institutions like Rand will give them an audience and legitimacy. At stake here is not only a religious posture, but also a broader ideological and political mind-set: once identified, it suggests, religiously liberal "Muslim moderates" should, in political and economic terms, be the natural allies of Western liberalism.[83]

Beyond the Arab awakening, the way to deal with Muslim apirations is the question whose answer will impinge on the West's future relations with the Middle East, Africa, and with Muslims in general. The aspirations of peoples for greater freedom, justice, and democratization echo fundamental Western values, but they find expression in distinct cultural and religious references that the West can neither continue to ignore or delegitimize. People are rising up, bringing with them as they do their stories, their memories, their being, and their faith. They must be heard in the coherence of their resistance and their hopes. It is here, perhaps, that Western Muslims may be able to play a meaningful role, by helping the West make an ideological shift in its relations with Africa, the Middle East, and with Islam as civilization and religion. Yet they are still suspect: of not being entirely American or European (often seen as "too Muslim"). Populist political parties—from the US Tea Party to the European extreme right wing—intentionally fuel controversy and confusion, depicting the presence of Muslims as a problem, failing to distinguish between such issues as immigration, the "clash of civilizations," and the "otherness" of Islam. To the attentive observer, there is some similarity between the American and European approach to religious and political issues in the Middle East and North Africa, and their relations with their own citizens of Muslim faith. The similarity is particularly striking in two areas: the legitimacy of Muslim representation and the Israel-Palestine conflict.

In the West, the Muslim voices that are heard, valued, and granted legitimacy are the same as those cherished by the United States and the European countries in North Africa and the Middle East. Once again, it is not so much a question of strictly religious legitimacy as of ideological positions on the political and economic level. Tensions are running high, and they illustrate to what extent the presence of Muslims in the West is seen as a source of problems and of conflict, generating fear and mistrust. Existing problems are compounded by globalization and the loss of former national and cultural markers, a situation in which populists, extreme right-wing parties, and xenophobes can prosper. Yet it is only a matter of time: Western citizens of Muslim faith—practicing or not, and accepting the secular framework—are settling down in Western society, becoming an integral part of it, and acquiring the tools they need to gain intellectual, social, and political autonomy. In a nutshell, they are Westerners and are developing a deep-seated sense of belonging to their respective societies, which does not prevent them from being potentially (though not always actually) critical of the dominant ideology. Most are believers, whether observant or not, democratic, and secular (in the normative sense of respecting the secularized framework of their society). With their cultural references and their memory, they belong in full to the Western environment; they are at home with the tools of intellectual, ideological, and political criticism. At the West's very core, they mirror the aspirations of the young people who drove the Arab awakening forward with their calls for dignity, equality, and justice.

The West has changed. Many of its citizens are the people it once encountered in Africa or in the Islamic Orient. They are now a part of its existence, its self-definition, and its future. The memories of the Global South and of the East, along with those of Islam, are now also Western memories. These are the facts, though awakening to the reality can be traumatic for politicians, intellectuals, and societies in general. The West is going through an internal upheaval—really one among many—and the Arab awakening, beyond the necessity of dealing with its political and economic consequences, is shaking its former habits. It will now have to deal with the forces of openness, dynamism, and youth that, like Western Muslims, see no contradiction among Islam, pluralism, and democracy, but that also reject domination, resist alienation, and demand to be treated with respect, as equals. Far from the "clash of civilizations," they are resetting the terms of debate over power, justice, and ideological, political, and economic equality. Their voices echo those of Western Muslims, who oppose the instrumentalization of Islam and stand against "Islamizing" socioeconomic issues, discrimination, inequality in education, social marginalization by class or by place of residence, and violence. The "West versus Islam" dichotomy, which has breathed life into so many fantasies and justified so many ideologically dubious and misleading political and economic decisions, is dying today. It is dying a slow and painful death, but a certain death. It will be replaced by a new paradigm originating from within but also an outcome of the eastward shift in the economic and social center of gravity.

The Israel-Palestine conflict is pivotal. Both the success of the democratization process and the revival of the Middle East depend on a just solution. However much freedom is secured in Tunisia or Egypt, or the liberation of this people or that is celebrated, nothing will be brought to an ultimate conclusion if the rights of the Palestinians are not at last acknowledged and respected. This conflict is so central that there can be no hope for genuine evolution toward democracy in the Arab world unless a solution is found. Israel is, after all, quite happy with the dictatorial neighbors who guarantee its security, as in the case of Mubarak in Egypt. Whether in alliance (as with Mubarak, for whom Israel asked US support) or in verbal opposition (as with Syria, which it does not want to see destabilized), Israeli policy has been to establish relations that either guarantee its safety or justify a constant state of alert. Israeli governments have long known that the surrounding Arab populations are mainly hostile to them. Democracy in the countries of the Middle East would lead to increased rejection, greater instability, less control. The ongoing demonstrations in Egypt and the attack on the Israeli embassy on September 10, 2011, tend to validate this hypothesis.[84] But those attacks actually imperil the essence of the Egyptian uprising and could compromise the future of the democratization process, as their natural consequence would be to strengthen military control over order and security.

It seems obvious that a more comprehensive approach to regional issues is called for. The question of Israel is central, as it was when Iraq was invaded in 2003, as John J. Mearsheimer and Stephen M. Walt have disclosed, illustrating the influence of American Zionist lobby groups in the lead-up to the war.[85] No Israeli government can possibly remain a passive observer of events in the Middle East and North Africa. Israel's strategic interests in Libya have already been cited; the same holds true for Egypt, Syria, and Lebanon, as well as developments involving Iran, Jordan, and the petro-monarchies. The United States and Europe would do well to review their regional strategies: unflagging support for Israel's aggressive policies could well be detrimental to them. The days of such strategies may well be numbered.

Against all appearances, and despite its financial and military might, Israel finds itself in substantial political, economic, and ideological difficulty. Extreme right-wing minority parties now wield the balance of power; they impose policies favorable to illegal settlement and promote harsh treatment of Palestinians in the Occupied Territories. Israel's rhetoric has locked it into an escalation of security policies and war. Its strangulation of the Palestinian people, and its continuing military operations, are shocking, not only because they are so disproportionate, but also because of the irrationality that is used to justify them.[86] Israel's own "movement of the indignant" has highlighted the divisions that riddle Israeli society (the cost of living, social policies, unemployment, and the unequal treatment of citizens).[87] The divisions perpetuated by brandishing the "outside threat" can no longer stem the tide of social protest. Ideologically, the meaning and the very substance of the Zionist project are being called into question as the founding generation vanishes and repressive policies become more violent and more visible. The symbolic defeat in Lebanon (summer 2006) and the shocking, internationally censured attack on Gaza (December 2008–January 2009) can be seen as ideological and political turning points.

The crisis is deep. The West is still struggling to take the full measure of tensions in the region, attempting to grasp the need to reconsider its Middle East policy, for relations are intricate, with Zionist lobbies very active in both the United States and Europe. At the same time, a multitude of new parameters make policy change inevitable, and will continue to do so. The assertive presence of China, India, Russia, Brazil, South Africa, and Turkey will be a determining factor, as it undercuts the rhetoric that postulates Israel as an ally of Western values and of democratization to come. The facts have changed; the plurality of voices and the diversity of viewpoints are actively undermining former alliances and upsetting the old balance of power.

Vigilance is in order. The future will not necessarily be easier, freer, or more democratic. The new actors arriving on the scene are indeed powerful; they may help overturn the old paradigm, but their own policies of occupation cannot be passed over in silence. At an international conference on peace featuring the Dalai Lama in which I participated, he interrupted his disquisition on compassion for a few brief seconds to remind the audience of the true nature of the Chinese regime: that it is antidemocratic, militarized, and oppressive to minorities, in particular the Tibetans.[88] The Middle East and North Africa may hope for a shift in the world balance of power that would not be so one-sidedly favorable to Israel, but in their quest for democracy, the MENA countries must find their own, independent path toward freedom, equality, and justice for women and men. There will be no springtime, no long-term success for the Arab awakening if the Palestinians do not achieve independence and freedom, and the rights that accompany them. This is what the West must grasp in a constructive manner, and understand in point of fact.

In this sense, Western Muslims have a critical role: they can, and must, act as a bridge between the aspirations of young people in Arab society and the positive experience of young American and European citizens. Their presence in civil society, on campus, in politics, in the arts and the media is apt rapidly to modify perspectives in the West. Societies change; so do sensibilities. The process will take time, but few would deny that history is accelerating in front of our eyes. Western women and men with roots in Africa, Turkey, Asia, and the Middle East are emerging as vital protagonists in the transformation of representation, and of the balance between the East, the South, the West, and the Far East.

The Arab awakening, in spite of the questions and the unknowns, has opened a horizon of opportunity that will be difficult to keep under total control. The opening of new multilateral spaces for communication, exchange, and debate between Western Muslims and those in the Global South, the Islamic East, or Asia will prove vital for the revival of thought, for a critical approach to tradition, and for the formulation of ethical, ideological, political, and economic priorities for the future. The specificity of experience cannot be minimized; on the contrary, the potential for the expression of pluralism and diversity in full respect of specific histories and human rights must be recognized.

The contemporary Muslim conscience cannot avoid becoming involved in this critical undertaking: every experience, East or West, South or North, must make its contribution. Beyond rising up against despots, the task is to chart a new vision of justice, equality, the empowerment of women, and the struggle against corruption and poverty. It is, beginning with personal and collective memory and its references, to give substance to the idea of the dignity of all people that can arise from the melding of historical experience in all its variety with the essence of a universally shared idea of what it means to be human.

# *Conclusion*

THE ARAB WORLD has shaken itself out of its lethargy. After decades of the status quo, apparent resignation, and silence, millions of women and men have taken to the streets, answering the call of the younger generation and particularly of bloggers and cyber-dissidents, these expert users of the Internet, social networks, and alternative means of mass mobilization. Such terms as "Arab spring," "revolution," or "unexpected revival" have been used for these uprisings. Yet after analysis of the facts, things appear to be less unexpected, less "extraordinary" than at first glance.

In or around 2003, a new dynamic arose in the Middle East, emulating the mass mobilization strategies based on the Internet that had been so effective in Eastern Europe, particularly those that led to the fall of Slobodan Milošević in October 2000. The United States and the European countries (as well as the dictators themselves) were well aware of the training seminars in nonviolent mobilization inspired by the experience of Serbia's Srdja Popović, and his theory of the three key concepts: "unity, passive resistance, and nonviolent action." Centers like the Albert Einstein Institution and Freedom House, as well as many firms from the private sector, such as Google and Yahoo, participated in, organized, and/or funded such sessions in the United States, Europe, or the Middle East. Few would argue that these are realities.

But conspiracy theory is a trap that must be avoided. No, not everything had been "plotted"! I have attempted to show that such an approach would not only be reductive; it would, above all, be mistaken, counterproductive, and crippling. The United States, like Europe, needed to reevaluate its strategies in the Middle East and North Africa. For a host of political, economic, and geostrategic reasons, unconditional support for the region's aging dictatorial regimes was becoming impossible. Instead, the Western powers provided arm's-length support, observed, and ultimately welcomed the uprisings in Tunisia and Egypt, all the while maintaining close ties with former officials or collaborators with the repressive regimes, as well as with their military establishments, which have continued to play a key role. The tensions and difficulties that have appeared after the departure of the dictators should be sufficient to convince us that nothing has been decisively gained, that the uprisings have not yet blossomed into "springs" or "revolutions." Protest movements in Syria, Yemen, and Bahrain, as well as the dynamics unleashed in Morocco, Jordan, and even Saudi Arabia, prove that mass movements cannot be totally controlled, that the determination of the crowd remains a variable that is impossible to predict.

Entire peoples have come to realize that they had the power to oust tyrants nonviolently, that dictatorship had nothing to do with some form of historical determinism. The Arab Awakening has broken through a barrier; suddenly the field of possibilities has expanded. It is to this phenomenon that we must turn our attention, with optimism but without naivety. The issues are many; wide-ranging upheavals are under way. More than a few of the protagonists have praised the example of Turkey; true enough, that country has opened up new perspectives. Undeniably it has made progress, but this has fostered legitimate questions and oft-justified criticisms. What kind of alternative can Turkey really offer today? The military may well be losing ground (which is certainly favorable to the prospects for greater democracy), but the country's economic and geostrategic choices are surprising, and sometimes even baffling if not contradictory. The government tends carefully to its interests and is not without contradictions. Once more, we must remain vigilant, and carry on in-depth analysis.[1]

The job of civil society is to launch genuine debate on political, economic, and cultural emancipation, and to avoid superficial and unproductive polarization. The endless controversies between "secularists" and "Islamists" over constitutional articles or the structure of the state apparatus can offer no solution to today's problems. They harden positions and create diversions. More dangerously, they allow opposing sides to sidestep self-criticism: the mere presence of their opponents, rather than the quality of their programmatic proposals, ends up justifying their political involvement.

The quality of current debate indicates that Arab societies are rushing headlong into blind alleys. The world has changed. The Arab world and Muslim majority societies not only need political uprisings; they need a thoroughgoing intellectual revolution that will open the door to economic change, and to spiritual, religious, cultural, and artistic liberation—and to the empowerment of women. What is needed is a global approach. Nothing is served by focusing on political and structural upheavals at the expense of other, more vital matters.

I have sought, in these pages, to highlight a few of the challenges and to expand the horizon beyond the confrontations being witnessed today, which I consider to be as barren as they are simple-minded. Will it at last be possible to move beyond the superficial confrontation over secularism, while putting an end to the essentialist visions of Islam that are often kept in place by Arab societies, and by Muslims themselves? The "civil state," democracy, and pluralism can only become concrete realities in the Middle East when peoples and governments focus on the ethics of good governance. The fight against corruption, the demand for transparency, limiting the powers of military establishments and stimulating the emergence of an active, dynamic civil society are the preconditions of success.

I have underlined such issues as education, social and political work, new economic prospects as well as cultural and artistic alternatives. The Arab world must confront its historical demons, tackle its infirmities and its contradictions: when it turns to the task, the awakening will truly have begun. The younger generations have shown that they can master modern technology; they have also shown that they are courageous enough to commit themselves to ideals. Their energy must be saluted, then channeled into concrete action in support of public education, women's rights, social justice, the fight against corruption, and veritable democratization in society. The eastward shift of economic power is, in itself, yet another invitation to reconsider the place of Africa and the Islamic Orient on the global chessboard. For all that, the Arab awakening will prove to have been nothing but smoke and mirrors if the international economic order is not called into question.

Whatever the theories about pre-planned uprisings, Africans, Arabs, and Muslims in general would do well to become better acquainted with their own history, traditions, and values. They enjoy a unique opportunity to reclaim their identity and to reconcile themselves with their memory. It would be an understatement to say that my optimism has been shaken when I analyze the events that have followed the fall of the dictators. Still, there remains a horizon of possibilities to be experienced, laid claim to, and exploited. If the reference to Islam is to make sense, it must be couched as an invitation to reclaim meaning instead of transforming the religion into a real or symbolic instrument designed to induce guilt and justify oppression, if not to reduce women and men to infantile status. Islam must be conceptualized from within the abundance of cultures that have, as value systems, been long giving shape to the collective identities, tastes, powers of imagination, art, and ethical goals, and which peoples must once again explore, exploit, and develop. Primary responsibility for the success or failure of this enterprise lies with the Arab and Muslim majority world. It fully possesses the tools it needs to make its dreams a reality; it alone holds the reins of its destiny.

Does this mean that nothing can be expected or demanded of the West? I have endeavored to show that the emergence of China, India, Japan, Russia, Turkey, and the countries of Latin America is now confronting the United States and Europe with major political and economic challenges. I would venture further still: the "West versus Islam" dichotomy, with all its constructs, representations, and oppositions is fading away before our eyes. In only a few decades or generations—two or three at most—it will have lost its meaning. Will the Arab world be able to carry out the intellectual transformation that is now demanded of it? The Arab Awakening may help; so may the increasingly active presence of Western Muslims who could become factors of internal stability in the pluralistic societies of the West, as well as bridges to Africa and the East. In this sense, they bear an immense responsibility. The same responsibility will, in the long run, help decide the outcome of the awakening, and the fate of the Global South.

A cautious optimist, I have tried to avoid the extremes of emotional effervescence and unfounded suspicion. Instead, I have attempted to marshal and to study the facts, to analyze them, and to suggest what the future may hold. Though aware of the difficulties and the issues involved, I am confident of the potential and the power of peoples and their aspirations. Nothing is settled; nothing is final. Everything is possible. There is no room for shortcuts; it takes time for uprisings to engender revolutions; it takes lucidity for an awakening of the masses to bloom into enlightened, collective self-awareness. After the dictators, after the high emotions and the confrontations, now is the time to build, to contribute.

Now too is the time to define priorities, to determine the human, humanistic, and ethical goals to be pursued. History expects Arab and Muslim majority societies to be equal to the task, to meet the challenges inherent in the complexity of the world. From good governance to economic justice, from pluralism to women's rights, from rejecting corruption to rejecting poverty, from accepting universal values to defending singularity, daunting tasks lie ahead. Facing eastward after facing westward for so long will not alter the reality of the crisis. For all that, it is now essential to turn inward, to engage in self-criticism, to know our strengths and weaknesses, to yield nothing to doubt and to offer everything to hope. Beyond the question of East and West lie freedom, autonomy, courage, and determination. In them lies awakening—and revolution.

# *Acknowledgments*

I HAD TO take a step back, try to understand, refrain from going too fast. I also had to put things into perspective, to assess or question years of reflection, debate, and commitment about Arab and Muslim majority societies but also about the West. This suggests how difficult it would be to thank all the women and men who have in one way or another contributed to the production of this book. They are far too many to be mentioned by name.

During the weeks of study and writing, I delved into that fast-unfolding history, which seemed to upset so many habits and certainties: this required bringing together exact facts, in-depth analysis, and cautious conclusions. The challenge was intellectually stimulating, but highly risky. I would more particularly like to thank all the women and men who over the past months have nurtured my thinking and helped me fine-tune my analyses and broaden my horizon through readings, meetings, debates, and lectures.

My Tunisian friends Ahmad and Ridwan, along with so many others, allowed me to follow the events in Tunisia very closely. Then there was the spark lit by my daughter Maryam, who was present daily on Liberation Square (midân at-Tahrîr) and who was involved throughout the Egyptian uprising. She was often joined by Moussa, her brother, my son. This was a historical moment that my family experienced live, always with hope, often with doubt, and sometimes with fear. Those young people are the future and must be thanked for their strength.

At Oxford, my colleagues at the Middle East Centre, Eugene Rogan (who re-thought the title with Felicity Bryan, my agent), Walter Armbrust, Avi Shlaim, and Michael Willis contributed directly or indirectly. So did Kalypso Nicolaïdis at the European Studies Centre. I wish to express my gratitude to them all, without of course forgetting the earnest, constant, warm commitment of my (so efficient) assistant Caroline Davis, and of Julia Cook who so pleasantly manages the Centre.

The discussions and debates with colleagues at Qatar's Faculty of Islamic Studies, Basma Abdelgafar, Jasser Auda, Saif El Din, Khaled El Husseiny, also provided different critical, stimulating perspectives from within. My exchanges with the Arab world have been numerous and constant: here again, unfortunately, it is impossible to mention everyone who helped me develop my thought. My debt is huge. I do not forget my meetings and debates with Alain Gresh, Catherine Samary, Michel Collon, and the memories of dynamic exchanges with François Burgat, John Esposito, and Sami al-Arian. Directly or indirectly, this book owes a lot to their respective contributions. I would also like to mention the competent presence of my new assistant in Paris, Jennifer, and of course Cynthia and Helen, who each in their way helped this book come to light. Claude and Fred have translated the book from French, with competence and brotherhood. I do not forget Muna, Shelina, and all the members of the European Muslim Network that I have had the honor pf presiding over for some years.

The editing and improvement of the manuscript owe a lot to Claude, Cynthia, Fred, Helen, Olivier, and Iman. I would literally not have made it without their dedication, presence, and vigilant contribution. Thank you very much, from the bottom of my heart.

This book was mostly written in Morocco and in the Ramadan period. I have often repeated that Morocco is one of my adoptive countries. Without mentioning names (except, at least, for Hossein and his family) to avoid hurting anyone, I here wish to repeat how much I love that country and the numerous sisters, brothers, and friends who accompany me in one way or another and to whose heart and intelligence this book owes a lot.

To my mother, Wafa; to my sister Arwa; to my brothers, Aymen, Bilal, Yasser, and Hani; to my father's memory; to my parents in-law, Cosette and Georges; to each heart in my family, Iman, Maryam, Sami, Moussa, and Najma, I wish to express my love, my respect, and my deep, infinite thanks. Before God, and in conscience, I try to be worthy of all that you offer me. Thank you for everything. Everything. May the Light and His peace be with you, always.

# Appendices

## 1 Good Muslim, Bad Muslim

The dust from the collapse of the Twin Towers had hardly settled when the fevered search began for "moderate Muslims," people who would provide answers, who would distance themselves from the outrage and condemn the violent acts of "Muslim extremists," "fundamentalists" and "Islamists." Two distinct categories of Muslims rapidly emerged: the "good" and the "bad," the self-described "moderates," "liberals" and "secularists" versus the "fundamentalists," the "extremists" and the "Islamists."

The categories were nothing new. The literature produced by the colonial authorities (under the British, French and Dutch regimes) and by the Orientalists in the late 19th and early 20th centuries tended to depict Muslims in the same binary manner. "Good" Muslims were those who either collaborated with the colonial enterprise or accepted the values and customs of the dominant power. The rest, the "bad" Muslims, those who "resisted" religiously, culturally or politically, were systematically denigrated, dismissed as the "other," repressed as a "danger."

Times have changed, but the old mind-sets, frames of reference and simplistic or reductive portrayals continue to cast a shadow over today's intellectual, political and media climate. But what exactly are we talking about? Moderate religious practices? Political positions? A relationship with violence? Or with the West?

Underlying today's debate over Islam and Muslims is a confusion of categories. Islam, it is claimed, draws no distinction between religion and politics, thus it is permissible to use the most general descriptive terms without distinguishing religious conceptions and practices from political programs and actions.

To adopt a simplistic perception of the "Muslim world" means to brush aside the most elementary descriptive and analytical principles that would ordinarily apply to fields as diverse as theology and law on the one hand, and social sciences and politics on the other. Given the complexity of the subject, we must begin by ordering our priorities: first, by putting the question in religious terms. Can we speak of moderation as opposed to excess in the way Muslims practice their religion? How are we to categorize the diverse trends that co-exist within Islam? What are we to make of the political repercussions of the former and the latter? On a global level, what can the differing and frequently conflicting perceptions of the "West" among Muslims teach us? The order and the nature of the questions we ask will then determine what we mean when we say "moderate Muslims."

The theme of moderation in religious practice has been a constant in Islamic literature since the very beginning. In the Qur'an and the Prophetic tradition that accompanies it, Muslim women and men are called upon to exercise moderation in all aspects of their religious life. "God desires ease for you, and desires not hardship." the Qur'an reminds us, and Mohammad confirms: "Make things easy, do not make them difficult." Often cited is the example of easing the obligation to fast during the month of Ramadan for travelers, as a way of cautioning believers against excess. Such methods, from the very beginning, have been employed by the majority of scholars to describe the Muslims as the "community of Moderation."

Early on, two interpretations of religious practice sprang up: that which applied teachings to the letter without taking either context or easing into account (*ahl al-'azîma*) and that (*ahl ar-rukhas*) which considered not only these factors but also the need for flexibility in the social context of the day, not to mention instances of need (*hâja*) and/or necessity (*darûra*). The overwhelming majority of scholars and of Muslims around the world (whether Sunni or Shia, irrespective of legal school) have promoted and followed the path of moderation and flexibility in the practice of their religion. While strictly devoted to fundamental principles they have brought forward adaptations in keeping with the environment and the times.

We can locate the initial misconception of the notion of moderation at this level. In Western societies where the practice and day-to-day visibility of religion is close to zero (even in the United States, where religion as a reference is relatively strong), to speak of prayer, fasting, religiously grounded moral obligations and dress codes is seen as verging on excess. Seen from this viewpoint, moderate Muslims are those who adopt no distinctive dress, who consume alcohol and practice their religion "as we do ours," that is, not really, or by making it invisible. But histories and references are not identical; the notion of moderation must always be studied from within each system of reference.

We cannot deny that among the diverse currents within the Muslim world (literalist, traditionalist, reformist, rationalist, mystical and purely political) dogmatic and excessive interpretations can be found. It is precisely within the literalist, traditionalist and politicized currents that we find the most closed-minded interpretations, which will generate legal opinions that take into consideration neither social nor historical context with regard to religious practice and to culture, human relations, women or relations with "non-Muslims." Some groups attempt to discourage Muslims from interacting with Christians, Jews or Atheists, and even advise hostility or rejection. Several of these minority groups criticize other Muslim tendencies, going so far as to call into question the Islamic character of their beliefs and practices. More troubling still, and making categorization even more hazardous, is the tendency for some reformist, rationalist or mystic groups to develop—internally—the same dogmatic attitude toward their coreligionists, casting doubt on their legitimacy in the most categorical and exclusivist fashion. Moderation, as we can see, is multidimensional, and is not expressed only with reference to the West or to "non-Muslims." It is of vital importance that we recognize the diversity of Islamic interpretation, for only in this way can the inter-communal dialogue we so badly need today begin.

Closer analysis of the political positions of these diverse groups further complicates the task of understanding. Who and what are we talking about exactly? The question of political moderation is an entirely subjective one. Afghanistan provides an excellent example: the same people who, two decades ago, were hailed as "freedom fighters" against Soviet invaders are today described as "terrorists" when they resist the Anglo-American occupation. If everyone can agree in condemning the terrorist acts against civilians in the United States, Rabat, Bali, Amman, Madrid or London, how are we to describe the resistance movements in Iraq, Afghanistan or Palestine against foreign occupation considered or perceived as illegal? Are members of the resistance "extremists," while the "moderates" are those who accept the presence of American and British forces? Who decides, based on what criteria?

I have had personal experience with shifting definitions. When in 2003 I was received at the State Department, it was as an "open" and "moderate" Muslim. Less than one year later, under the Bush administration, my criticism of American policy in Iraq and Palestine (where I recognize the legitimacy of the resistance without in any way condoning attacks against civilians and non-combatants) transformed me into a potential "supporter of terrorism" and I was forbidden entry into the United States. Six years later, the terrorism-related accusations have been dropped. The Obama administration has decided that my opinions are not dangerous and that I may be useful in the critical debate about Islam: I am now allowed to travel to the United States.

Not only is political "moderation" an ill-defined concept, but also confusion between the religious and the political spheres make analysis even more problematic. People are quick—far too quick—to assume that because a woman or a man is religiously "liberal" with regard to Islamic practice, she or he will hold equally "liberal" political views. Nothing could be farther from the truth. The cases are legion, of political personalities, intellectuals and civil society militants who are indeed Muslims with extremely liberal conceptions and practices, when such practices are not entirely absent, but who publicly support the most hard-line of dictatorial regimes. Moderation in religion cannot be correlated with its political equivalent. In Western-generated analysis there is a tendency to conflate these two categories. Close, detailed study is imperative in order to arrive at a precise assessment of existing religious and political trends.

Relations with the "West" offer an interesting standard by which to evaluate the political and religious stances of contemporary Muslims. While violent extremist groups view their relations with the West only in terms of opposition couched in religious, political, cultural and economic conceptual language, the overwhelming majority of the world's Muslims—particularly Western Muslims—recognize the achievements of Western societies while claiming the right to determine for themselves the parameters of their identity, their practices and their spiritual convictions. Seen from this perspective, criticism and rejection of the West are linked with the refusal to accept political, economic and cultural domination.

Religion frequently provides a natural vector for mobilization in majority Muslim societies, but the object of criticism is overwhelmingly the political and economic domination of the West, and the incoherence of its support for the most venal and corrupt regimes. But, even within Islamist ranks, strictly religious discourse is predominantly moderate with regard to the West, from Malaysia to Morocco by way of the current government of Turkey, whose objective is to join the European Union. The zone of tension and latent conflict is not defined by religion, and has nothing to do either with Islam or with "moderate Muslims." It is a nexus of interconnected political issues that must be addressed as such.

It is possible, in the West, to define moderate Muslims as those who are invisible, or look just like us, or even as those who accept the terms of their subjection. But reasoning and conclusions of this kind cannot help us to understand the dynamics at work in Muslim majority societies and Muslim communities in the West. For they are as multifaceted as they are complex: there exists a strictly religious debate (couched in the language of philosophy, of Islamic jurisprudence and the fundamentals of faith) over the notion of moderation (*wasatiyya*) that must be grasped in full. By so doing we will be able to identify the contentious issues in the intra-communal debates between diverse trends and schools of thought, as well as the exclusivist and occasionally dogmatic leanings in what appear to be the most open of hearts. Using this approach, we will be able to approach political questions with far less prejudice and/or naivety. Once we have condemned the violent extremist groups that murder civilians and innocents, we must move forward, and place their political positions in context so as not to oversimplify our analysis with statements such as: the "moderates" are the people who support us or who resemble us, while all the rest are fundamentalists or Islamist extremists. Such judgments are, when all is said and done, ideological in nature and lead only to confusion that prohibits us from grasping their essentially political and economic nature.

This is what the rhetoric of the "clash of civilizations" conceals from us, as it sets up religious and cultural oppositions between constructed entities, while conveying none of the aspirations to justice and freedom that find their expression in the two universes of reference. Yet these are precisely the terms in which the voices of those who defend religious moderation (to which the immense majority of Muslims subscribe) must be heard. They must be heard in a far more "radical" way in order to grasp the similarity of ethical values, as against the profoundly asymmetric political and economic nature of power. It is of vital necessity that they be heard, and explain that religious moderation can well join forces with a radical political language that, while non-violent and democratic, stands firm against all forms of domination, exploitation and oppression.

## 2  *On Tunisia, Algeria and Niger…*

Only a dictator could claim that the rioting in the streets of Tunisia is the result of "foreign meddling" and "unpardonable" acts akin to "terrorism." The Tunisian regime, that incorruptible paragon of democracy, has spoken. Its Western allies express concern, of course, but condemnation has been slow in coming. Police and troops have used live ammunition against civilians; dozens have been killed. Not enough, it seems, to move Western governments. Their ally in Tunis must enjoy special privileges from the International Community to be able to deal as it pleases with opposition—or with any attempt to resist its dictatorial and oppressive ways.

Tunisia is no democracy; it is a dictatorship that practices political assassination and torture; that thrives on widespread corruption. It is our duty to support its people, and particularly the country's youth, as they take to the streets to demand freedom, respect and protection of human rights. The time has come—it's not too late!—to bring an end to this self-styled "modern" masquerade of democracy and progress designed to fool tourists and the gullible. The time has come—its not too late!—to call out to an awakening people: we are with you; we are not fooled! Tunisians, you are right to revolt! The silent onlookers, those whose only concern is to protect their political or economic interests, will be left with their shame. Whether the uprising ends in success or failure, its principles—resistance to the dictatorship and exposing its supporters (dictators, democrats and/or hypocrites)—will not disappear.

In Algeria, calm appears to be returning to the streets, but the people's demands have lost none of their legitimacy. Where has the country's oil wealth gone? Who are the corrupt individuals who line the pockets of their business cronies with fraudulent profits and illegal commissions while poverty spreads, unemployment soars and the entire system is collapsing upon a population that is already fighting for its life. Algeria, like its president, is suffering from disease: a closed system, systemic corruption, rampant lies and manipulation. The streets have spoken, and will speak again. Whether in the coming days or the coming weeks, they must be heard. The time has come— it's not too late!

Horrifying news from Niger: two young French citizens kidnapped and murdered in cold blood. Condemnation of these repugnant acts must be clear, decisive and unequivocal. Such things must not happen; extremist groups that are either manipulated or manipulators (whether of religion and its principles, or of any other cause) must be opposed and fought. As I stated at the International Symposium of French-speaking Muslims (CIMEF) in July 2010, I reiterate today that nothing can justify the murder of innocents (or any other similar act) be it in the name of Islam or of any other political ideology.

At the same time that we restate our condemnation in the strongest possible terms, we must also express with identical clarity our reservations about French and African government strategies for dealing with the threat of violent extremist groups and networks. Last summer I met three African military men who told me of their pangs of conscience, their concern and even the anguish they have suffered as a result of orders they have been forced to carry out, of the methods they have been obliged to use against these networks in the Sahel, where distinguishing extremists from bandits or looters is impossible. These orders are: take no prisoners; liquidate all the members of a group once it has been identified and located, whether or not it is armed or combat-ready. One of the officers confided in me that when he informed his superiors that he had located a small group, not prepared for combat, which included two women, the answer was immediate: "Liquidate all of them. Take no prisoners!" Why? How can such killing be justified? Another officer revealed that he had found the corpse of an individual captured on an earlier expedition and subsequently set free among the dead several weeks later. As strategies go, it is strange, pitiless and above all incomprehensible. The French army is well aware of these tactics; in an atmosphere of folly and futility, hunting down the kidnappers led inevitably to the death of their two captives.

But the killings in Niger cannot be viewed, nor condemned, in isolation. France's Sahel strategy must be exposed for what it is. The reign of terror, strategic confusion (is France fighting terrorism, banditry or corruption?), summary executions, non-respect of human life and of prisoners, and improvised military action cannot provide security either to Africans (Malians, Nigerians, etc.) or to French expatriates. Once again, by attempting to rescue two hostages "African style" France is fooling itself in Africa. Once again. But many African countries are also fooling themselves. It is high time to develop a coherent strategy for fighting violent extremists; to respect the basic principles of dignity and international law; not to believe that what is happening in the Sahel, far from the cameras, can be hidden by media silence. Innocent people have paid a high price. This must end. The time has come—it's not too late!

Our sympathy goes to the families of the victims in Tunisia, in Algeria and in France: we stand shoulder to shoulder with the oppressed, with the innocent victims. Always.


## 3 Revolution in Tunisia

All honor and praise to the people of Tunisia! Their resistance and non-violent civic revolutionary action, their determination and sacrifice, has shaken the dictatorship to its foundations. President Ben Ali has fled—he and his close collaborators should have been put on trial—and the country's prime minister (a long time Ben Ali's support) has taken the helm... but for how much longer? What we are witnessing is the first stage; the stakes are high, the situation fraught with danger. Anything can happen: an attempt by the regime to play for time or to manipulate the people's demands (with a sham "new" government), shadowy maneuvers by internal or outside forces. Vigilance is essential; there is no place for naivety; we must remain alert, and beware of hasty expedients. Tunisia's informal citizens' revolution has revealed an extraordinary power, but the new counter-power's strength can also become a weakness if confronted with political forces that will attempt to use the constitution, international political alignments or profit from a cooling-off period simply to reshuffle the deck. We must be equally vigilant about the role of the army. The people may be offered the appearance of freedom minus the dictator, followed by a new clampdown on Tunisian political life. Let us indeed hail this first victory—but be aware that the outcome is far from settled.

The people of Tunisia have taken to the streets in a spirit of non-violence, and have said "No!" The end of the dictatorship has come. We must salute it, respect it, and commit ourselves to supporting it. Without bending. We must pay close attention to all the new voices promising their "support;" voices that were perfectly silent under Ben Ali yet today present themselves as "democrats" without a past. Likewise, we must draw up a balance sheet of the individual and international accomplices who would like nothing more, now that non-violent resistance has triumphed, than for us to forget their treachery, lies and hypocrisy. Lives have been lost; men and women have been tortured, suffered exile and humiliation: these are the people we must stand shoulder to shoulder with. Their sacrifices, their suffering and their tears have not been in vain. The lesson is a beautiful one; the historical moment, a great one: a people have overthrown their dictator. Now, that people must have done with his system, his lackeys and his partners in crime.

As Tunisia's extraordinary revolution unfolds in all its dignity and massive participation, images of a possible dream fill our hearts and our hopes: that the Arab peoples oppressed by dictatorship rise up and with the same massive, non-violent determination, overthrow the autocrats that rule them and liberate their countries. At last! What a beautiful example: an uprising of the people and of the heart! If only all peoples could muster the strength of their example, of this alertness, of their nonviolent, revolutionary resistance: the historic definition of liberation itself.

## 4 *From Shame into Light*

We knew the transition would be hard. Members of the regime are still trying to salvage it, or simply to save their lives. Victory is not yet at hand. The Tunisian people, along with the intellectuals, politicians and the commanders of the armed forces must attempt to display determination, moderation and patience. Nothing will be easy. Expelling a dictator is a first step; dismantling and suppressing an authoritarian system based on cronyism and corruption is the next. The process will be a long one; we must remain vigilant. The revolution in Tunisia may be co-opted, confiscated or manipulated by individuals or groups with obscure and anti-democratic aims.

The transitional government that has just assumed control is no more than a fig leaf, to be rejected out of hand. The appointment of a member of the "old" regime as Interior Minister tells us all we need to know about how the "new" regime intends to operate. The alternative must be pluralist and non-partisan—but it must also be radically new, to make ready for elections in six months.

Unsurprisingly, we have heard the voices of new converts to "democracy" in Tunisia. Today they praise "the people's courage" and its "extraordinary movement" for freedom. They are popping up right and left, in political and intellectual circles: the same people who declared as recently as two years ago on French television that "in the name of secularism" the Tunisian regime was right to be undemocratic. But today they rush to sign appeals to democracy and moderation.

The French media, which find it so difficult to hear the voices of France's former colonies, continue to turn to these self-same accomplices of the collapsing regime, to explain Tunisia to the French. With or without Ben Ali, the only legitimate voices of the Maghreb, whether for the best families of Paris or the majority of media outlets, continue to be those of the colonized and the sell-outs. To their lasting shame.

Why do the media not listen to the voices of other intellectuals or journalists, people like Moncef Marzouki, a man of great integrity, in their struggle for true democracy in Tunisia? Hundreds of men and women, of all political persuasions, have refused to bow their heads. It is they who must take the lead in building for Tunisia a future of dignity, transparency and freedom.

Determined women and men are now working to accelerate developments in Jordan and in Egypt, not to mention Algeria and Syria. The regimes in those countries are on a war footing, firmly opposed to even a hint of change from below. In all probability nothing will happen in the short term; but how deeply we hope that their peoples awaken and shake the very regimes that political leaders, opposition parties and intellectuals have not been able to reform or to overthrow. How deeply we desire to see similar broad-based, determined, non-violent popular movements arise in all the Arab countries—wherever dictators rule, in fact—and that their example opens the path to a brighter future.

Something has happened in Tunisia: we have witnessed a historical moment. A psychological and political barrier has been breached. Each one of us must now work to keep alive the movement toward the dignity and freedom of peoples. There will be a price to pay: inclusive, non-violent movements will mourn their dead. But in the long run the future, and with it the lives of women, men and the younger generation will be safeguarded. That future is our business. No matter where we are.

## 5  Tunisia and Africa: The New Realignment

No one can deny the sudden and unforeseen nature of the Tunisian uprising. Mohamed Bouazizi's self-immolation touched off a movement that quickly evolved from a popular uprising into a broad-based revolutionary upheaval. Years of suffocation and frustration gave the movement the energy and the strength to overthrow the dictator Ben Ali who, to everyone's surprise, fled his country very quickly indeed. Too quickly.

More and more sources are today pointing to the central and critical role played by the United States in managing the crisis from behind the scenes. Washington's involvement in Tunisia (like that of Israel, on an ongoing mutual basis) has long been a matter of record in such sensitive areas as security, information and geostrategy. Dictator Ben Ali was himself a product of the United States military and security apparatus. While France ensured cordial relations with Europe, the Tunisian dictatorial system depended on American support and close collaboration with Israel. All of this was well known; the West's guilty silence on the corrupt Ben Ali torture regime amounted to little more than safeguarding their multiple interests in the region. It mattered little that he killed, tortured or ruined his people as long as their regional security interests were protected. Nothing new, in other words.

The immediate American reaction to a rebellion that was as massive as it was unforeseen was startling; it was also well thought-out and cleverly handled. President Barack Obama early on hailed the courage of the Tunisian people while the European countries, led by France, kept silent, as if confounded by the rapid pace of events. Clearly Washington was well ahead of the other "Tunisia-friendly" governments. In fact, the American National Security Agency and the Joint Chiefs of Staff were able to manage the quickly evolving situation through the Tunisian Foreign Minister and the Commander in Chief of the country's armed forces. After several hours of turmoil and uncertainty, rapid action had become imperative. Two key decisions were made: to exile the dictator and to assign to the army the role of mediation and protection. President Ben Ali stepped into a trap: the Foreign Minister persuaded him to leave the country "for a short time" the better to return once the situation was under control. Ben Ali left Tunisia believing that France was his destination (which explains the early rumors). But his aircraft flew to Cyprus where the Americans negotiated the dictator's terms of exile: he would be kept in isolation, movement and public declarations prohibited, totally neutralized.

The American government stole a march on France and Europe. In so doing, it ensured that it would reap the underlying political and geostrategic benefits whose impact will be crucial in future. The rapidity of Ben Ali's carefully stage-managed exile made it possible to circumscribe the potential impact of the Tunisian uprising on its Arab neighbors. Over and above the unexpected nature of the movement, and despite inevitable unforeseen developments, the situation was kept—and is being kept—under relative control. The army, whose high command has been and continues to be an ally of the United States, has contrived to preserve a basically positive image while playing the key role of observer, mediator and guardian of the highest interests of the nation. This is a significant accomplishment, which could prove determinant depending on how the situation develops in coming days, particularly with regard to the ongoing opposition to the provisional government (where key ministries are occupied by former regime stalwarts) and the prospect of free elections six months hence. The success of the Obama administration's return to the North African, and more generally African scene is by no means accidental; nor does it have anything to do with humanitarian concerns.

From Ivory Coast to Sudan, via the Sahel and the southern Mediterranean, the African continent has emerged as a vital strategic zone in economic, geostrategic and security terms. European, and particularly French influence is currently facing a growing crisis of legitimacy in Africa as a result of the American and Chinese presence. These two newcomers appear to be allowing African leaders to take their distances from their difficult, centuries-long relationship with Europe, its memory and its interests.

The stakes are too high to be overlooked. Exploration for raw materials remains a key economic issue; the recent discovery of oil in the Sahel (Niger and Mali) is unlikely to satisfy the appetites of the Great Powers. Behind the region's governments, its "friendly regimes," its "election irregularities" and its social and military tensions, the United States and Europe—and now China, the new kid on the block—are locked in a bitter struggle for decisive political and economic influence. The specter of terrorism has arrived in the Sahel, justifying the presence of friendly western forces in the name of international security. American and French military bases, along with European and Israeli agents and experts are focused on the struggle against terrorism in the region.

The strategy of surveillance and armed intervention is brutal, implacable: the policy is to "kill all terrorists" while taking no prisoners (why?). All those who participated in the kidnapping of two young French nationals in Niger were eliminated even after the French government had announced the arrest of two of the hostage-takers before issuing a retraction. Raids are taking place week after week; deaths (of terrorists, bandits and smugglers) are announced, with no measurable progress in view. It is as though a permanent state of emergency were in force in order to justify heightened security concerns, the foreign military presence and political interference. All this in a region that has become economically attractive due to its substantial oil and gas reserves.

Clearly, extremist violence must be fought. But we must not be so naïve as to forget that such violence can function as pretext for protecting and promoting other interests. The dictator Ben Ali, it was claimed, held Islamism in check, which in turn justified Western support. Today the Sahel along with South Sudan has emerged as areas of critical economic and strategic importance. The threat of violent, extremist Islamism is being used to conceal suspicious intentions.

While the Tunisian people attempts to protect all that it has gained in its revolutionary upsurge, American, European, Chinese and Russian power are attempting to carve out a role in Africa. Nor can the influential role of Israel's intelligence services throughout North Africa, including Sudan (as detailed in Pierre Péan's journalistic investigation in Morocco, Algeria, Rwanda and Eritrea, and even in Ethiopia). What is at stake are economic, security and strategic military interests.

The Tunisian revolution is widely praised; the former dictator disgraced. But behind the scenes of the public and media theatre, political maneuvering and meddling are continuing apace. The American administration is following developments closely, and is close to events as they unfold in Tunisia. It will do whatever is necessary to protect its interests, and those of Israel and of its allies in Egypt, Jordan and throughout the Middle East. While the issues of Iran and Lebanon appear to have monopolized American and European media attention, we must not minimize the second U.S. front, that of African and regional policy at the risk of naively hailing a "Tunisian revolution" without taking strict account of what remains to be done to ensure its political independence and democratic transparency. And of smiling at the bright promised victory while other forces cynically count, in the shadows, the dividends of their newfound influence and windfall profits.

We need lucidity, that of active, positive realism, not the illusions of wistful dreamers and naïve sentimentalists.

## 6 Egypt: the Voice of the People and History

The Tunisian uprising has changed everything. We have reached a turning point: it is clear now that dictators can be peacefully overthrown! To do so takes courage, a mass movement, determination and hope; faith in God and/or in the future. Crushed by repression, the people have stood up to claim full human dignity. To assert their irrepressible right to be free.

The Tunisians have blazed the trail. In Algeria and Mauritania, then in Yemen and Egypt women, men and young people of all backgrounds have taken to the streets to express their anger and frustration, their intense desire to see their respective regimes fall. Sparks are flashing everywhere; demands being drafted; protests have occurred even in Syria where the government has announced a series of reforms should the people begin to consider mass action.

In Egypt, tensions have been growing over the last few days. After thirty years of unshared power—having imposed a state of emergency after the assassination of Anwar al-Sadat in 1981—Mubarak and his regime now face open and widespread defiance of his authoritarianism and bloody repression. The police and paramilitary force have beaten, arrested, tortured and fired on the crowd; hundreds are dead, thousands injured. It was to be expected: Egypt is not Tunisia, and its regime knows, when it comes to its alliances and its geopolitical situation, that it enjoys full Western support. Of course, the Obama administration and Europe are calling for the people to have the right to demonstrate but at the same time, support for the regime and the imperative of regional stability remain priorities that can neither be ignored nor minimized.

Nothing will take place in Egypt or in the region as a whole without the United-States (and indirectly Israel) attempting to control or, at minimum, to direct the developing situation. It is difficult to imagine that Washington will drop President Hosni Mubarak, but if resistance and calls for his overthrow grow strong enough, and appear to be gaining momentum, there is every reason to believe that they will be deeply involved in drawing up alternatives. American, European and Israeli strategists are already studying scenarios in which the Egyptian president loses control of the situation. His overthrow in the short term seems unlikely, but anything is still possible. Whatever the short-term outcome, Washington and Tel-Aviv prefer to play a "win-win"

game: either a weakened president (whose policies they could then determine), or a compliant regime that they will have set up behind the scenes.
Nothing has been settled; the process of democratization will be a long and
painful one, full of obstacles and pitfalls.

Egypt's rulers, like their Tunisian counterparts, have been brandishing the "Islamist threat," pointing to the "active presence" of the Muslim
Brotherhood among the demonstrators. Its members are the very people
who were first arrested in an attempt to convince the public that they were
behind the popular upheaval. No one can deny that the organization, illegal today, remains a significant factor in the opposition movement. But it is
not taking a leading role, and does not represent the majority of those confronting the Mubarak regime. While we must scrutinize and remain critical
of certain of the Brotherhood's positions, as well as those of other legal and
non-violent Islamist groups, these organizations have abjured violence and
have developed new policies on democracy, women and civil society. Turkey
has demonstrated that Islamists have been able to deal with these issues in a
responsible way. Any democracy worthy of the name must allow all components of society that reject violence and accept democratic norms for all—
before and after elections—full freedom of expression, and participation in
the political debate and in elections.

For geopolitical and security reasons, not to mention the Israel-Palestine
conflict, it would appear that true and transparent democracy, free of corruption and manipulation, is not on the immediate agenda for Egypt. Everything
will be kept under control even if a more open regime than Mubarak's (which
is devoutly to be wished and supported) were to emerge. The people will
decide whether to keep up the fight for its rights and its dignity. From our
vantage point in the West, our obligation is to follow closely and lend our
support to popular movements in Africa, North Africa, the Middle East and
Asia as they reject dictatorship and repression and seek to live free. It is our
moral duty.

We must demand no less from our governments. Barack Obama was presented as an alternative to George W. Bush and his bellicose, neo-conservative
administration. Expectations were high that he would introduce new methods
and policies. That happened at the rhetorical level (and in a handful of spectacular cases) on both the domestic and international fronts, with his remark-
able speech in Cairo on June 4 2009, promising a new era. If the election
of Barack Obama made it possible to break down, symbolically, the ancient
barrier of racism in the United States—with the election of the first African-
American president (which has remained little more than symbolic)—, we

are still waiting for him to break down the barrier of American and European blindness toward the Arab world and toward the planet's Muslim-majority nations. Time has come to stand up for the principles of justice and liberty, of true democracy and respect for peoples rather than pay only lip-service to democratization and popular outrage while political systems remain hermetically sealed and collaboration with dictatorial regimes has become an open secret. Such would have been the true achievement of the Obama era: to respect peoples in deed and not simply by a change in tone, with fine words.

It may still be too soon. And yet! If we look closely at the world as a whole, and at Africa and the Middle East in particular, we see that the center of gravity in international relations is shifting. With apparent slowness, depending on electoral deadlines in the United States or in Europe, but at the same time with striking rapidity when measured against History and the transformation of societies. The rising powers of China and India, as well as Asia generally (not forgetting Latin America and the Global South) are now firm fixtures on the world's political and economic landscape. None of these powers bears the West's historic burden, nor do they entertain the same relations and prejudices toward the Arab world and the Muslim-majority societies. Their relations with Israel are far removed from those of the United States and the European countries. The West cannot continue to mislead itself without significant costs, it can no longer dig in its heels, cannot continue to choose its friends on the basis of geopolitical and economic alliances at the expense of the most elementary human principles. The continued shift of power and influence away from the United States and Europe is likely to increase their isolation, and that of Israel. This will happen not because the growing influence of the emerging powers, but because the governments of the United States, like those of Europe and Israel, have continually chosen to place their economic, security and strategic interests above their declared human principles. One day the wheel of History will turn; new forces will arise and overturn existing power relationships, reminding the mighty of yesterday that they should have used their power in a different way.

It will be a lesson that far too many leaders and governments, drunk on their power—whether dictatorial or democratic—will, unfortunately, learn too late.

## 7 *After Mubarak*

In the wake of mass demonstrations in Tunisia and the fall of its dictator two questions have monopolized the attention of Western media and obsessed analysts: would events there be repeated in other Arab countries, and what would be the role of the Islamists after the eventual collapse of dictatorships in those countries? Who would have thought that the Tunisian regime would collapse so quickly? Who could have predicted that Egypt would soon witness such unprecedented mass protests? A barrier has fallen; nothing will be the same again; it is quite likely that other countries will soon follow Egypt's lead, given its central and symbolic strategic and geopolitical situation.

What then of the Islamists whose presence has for decades justified the West's acceptance and support of the worst dictatorships in the Arab world? The same regimes that demonized their Islamist opponents, particularly Egypt's Muslim Brotherhood, which represents historically that country's first well-organized mass movement with the political influence to match. For more than sixty years the Brotherhood has been illegal while being tolerated; it has demonstrated a powerful capacity for mobilization in each relatively democratic election (trade unions, professional associations, municipalities, parliament, etc.) where it has been a participant. Are the Muslim Brothers the rising power in Egypt after Mubarak and, if so, what can be expected from such an organization?

In the West we have come to expect superficial and ideology-driven analyses of political Islam in general, and of the Muslim Brotherhood in particular. Islamism, however, is not simply a mosaic of widely differing trends and factions; these groups have also evolved over time and in response to historical shifts. The Muslim Brothers began in the 1930s and 1940s as an anti-colonialist, legalist, non-violent movement that claimed legitimacy for armed resistance in Palestine against Zionist designs in the period prior to WWII. Examination of the writings of Hassan al-Banna, founder of the Brotherhood, between 1930 and 1945 reveals three things: he opposed colonialism and strongly criticized the fascist regimes in Germany and Italy; he rejected the use of violence in Egypt even though he considered it legitimate in Palestine, in resistance to the Zionist Stern and Irgun terror gangs; the British parliamentary model represented the model closest to Islamic principles. His objective was to found an "Islamic state" based on gradual reform, beginning with popular education and broad-based social programs.

Hassan al-Banna was assassinated in 1949 by the Egyptian government on orders from the British occupiers. Following Nasser's 1952 revolution, the movement underwent violent repression. Several distinct trends emerged. Some of its members (who finally left the organization), radicalized by prison and torture, concluded that the state had to be overthrown at all costs, violently if need be. Others maintained the movement's original position of gradual reform. Many of its members were forced into exile: some in Saudi Arabia where they were influenced by its literalist ideology; others in Muslim majority societies, such as Turkey and Indonesia where a substantial variety of groups existed; still others settled in the West, where they came into direct contact with its democracy and its freedoms. Today's Muslim Brotherhood brings together these extremely diverse visions, to which must be added a generation gap: the leadership of the movement (those who belong to the founding generation are now very old) no longer fully represents the aspirations of its younger members who are much more open to the world, anxious to bring about internal reform, and fascinated by the Turkish example. Behind the unified, hierarchical façade contradictory influences are at work. No one can predict which way the movement is heading.

The Muslim Brotherhood is not leading the popular upsurge that is bringing down Mubarak, which is made up of young people, of women and men who have rejected dictatorship and are calling for Mubarak's departure and the end of his regime. The Muslim Brotherhood, and the Islamists in general, do not represent the majority. There can be no doubt that when and if Mubarak departs, they hope to participate in the democratic transition, but no one can predict which political faction will emerge in a dominant position, a fact that makes it impossible to determine the Islamic movement's priorities. Between the literalists and the partisans of the Turkish way anything can happen; the Brotherhood's political thinking has evolved considerably over the last twenty years.

Certainly neither the United States nor Europe, not to mention Israel, will allow the Egyptian people to make their dream of total democracy and freedom come true. Strategic and geopolitical considerations are such that the reform movement will be—and is already—closely monitored by American agencies in coordination with the army, which has played for time and assumed the crucial role of mediator. The Muslim Brotherhood leadership, by its decision to line up behind Mohammed El Baradei has clearly signaled that now it is not the time to expose itself by putting forward political demands that might frighten the West, not to mention the Egyptian people themselves. Caution is the watchword.

Respect for democratic principles demands that all political forces that reject violence, respect the rule of law and democratic principles (before and after elections) participate fully in the political process. The Muslim Brotherhood must be a full participant, and will surely be if a minimally democratic state can be established in Egypt (though no one can predict the intentions of the foreign powers). Neither repression nor torture has been able to eliminate the Brotherhood. On the contrary. Only democratic debate and the vigorous exchange of ideas have had and are having an impact on the development of the most problematic Islamist theses (of which there are several, from understanding of the *Shar'ia* to respect for freedom and defense of equality). Turkey's example should an inspiration to us. Whether or not we agree with the theses of a non-violent Islamist political group, only through the exchange of ideas, and not by torture and dictatorship can we find solutions that respect the people's will.

The West continues to use the "Islamist threat" to justify its passivity and its outright support of dictatorships. The Israeli government has called upon Washington to back the Mubarak regime against the popular will. Europe had adopted a wait-and-see attitude. Both positions are revealing: at the end of the day, lip service to democratic principles carries little weight against the defense of political, economic and geostrategic interests. The United States prefers dictatorships that guarantee access to oil, and allow the Israelis to continue their slow colonization to credible representatives of the people who could not allow them to continue. Pointing to the voices of "dangerous Islamists" to justify not having to hear the voices of the people is a short-sighted tactic, in addition to being illogical. The United States, under both the Bush and Obama administrations, has suffered heavy losses to its credibility in the Middle East; the same is true for Europe. If they do not reexamine their policies, they may soon see other Asian or South American powers interfering in their elaborate structure of strategic alliances. As for Israel, which has now positioned itself as the friend and protector of the Arab dictatorships, its government may well come to realize that those dictatorships are committed only to its policy of blind colonization. In the end, only democracies that embrace all legalist and non-violent political forces can bring about peace in the Middle East. Such a peace, however, must respect the dignity of the Palestinians and not prove to be empty words that open the door to rampant colonization that would rule out a viable Palestinian state.

## 8 Historical Responsibilities: Democracy Now!

Popular pressure is mounting with every passing day. The Egyptian people have defied their autocratic government for more than two weeks now, writing a new page in History as they do. The decisive moment is at hand. Should Mubarak's dictatorial regime fall, like that of Tunisia's Ben Ali before it, the potential consequences, regionally and internationally, will be immense. With the collapse of the Egyptian regime, given its vital economic, geopolitical and security position, everything suddenly becomes possible in the Arab world and the Middle East. World governments, beginning with those of the United States, Israel, Europe and the Arab countries, know it, can feel it and are maneuvering in the shadows, hoping to prolong the public face-off in the search for alternatives, to protect their interests and to prepare for the best—or the worst (or to attempt to infiltrate and control a mass movement that no state actor, no political party and no organization either initiated or been able to guide). Behind the smoke screen of fulsome praise for democracy, liberty and human rights, cold and cynical calculations are underway. From Washington to Tel-Aviv, from Cairo to Damascus, Sana'a, Algiers, Tripoli or Riyadh, the fundamental concern is the same: how best to control this movement, and if possible to turn it to advantage.

For who, at the end of the day, wants a genuine, independent, transparent democracy in Egypt or in the Arab world? Aside from the people themselves, and the voices of civil society, who really cares if the mass protests now shaking Egypt attain their objectives of freedom, dignity and true democracy? We hear Barack Obama, Angela Merkel, David Cameron and others admonish the people, as they explain the meaning of democracy and of popular choice. These are the very same leaders who, for decades, showed no scruples about coddling the worst of dictators, including Hosni Mubarak whom they call upon today to become more democratic. Who is naïve enough to believe their fine words and their crude attempts at political manipulation?

The voices that reach us from within Egyptian civil society and the ranks of the opposition now face historical choices. The regime's propaganda machine (its television, its attempts to divide the population) is working full time, and has succeeded in undermining solidarity and sowing division among the citizens of Egypt. The opposition must remain mobilized, non-violent and united in its demands, as reflected in the extraordinary images of Egyptian Copts and Muslims arm in arm on Cairo's Liberation Square. They must remain clear-eyed and courageous: liberation will not be as "easy" as it was in Tunisia; attempts to take over the revolutionary movement will be continuous and complex. The stakes are high: if the Egyptian people are able to overthrow an autocratic regime and bring about a minimum of true democracy, nothing will be the same, and the Arab world will witness the dawn of the new era to which all democrats aspire.

To get there, it is not enough to demand Mubarak's departure. His entire corrupt regime and the system based on cronyism, torture and systematic theft must be dismantled. The Mubarak family (including son Gamal, not to mention their many allies) fortune is thought to be worth tens of millions of dollars invested in banks, in wholly controlled or fictitious companies or markets. The women and men, the political and intellectual leaders, and the representatives of civil society or of the opposition (from the Left to Islamists like the Muslim Brotherhood) are now facing a moment of truth: either they agree to set up an opposition front that respects the people's will, or they attempt to take over the popular movement at the risk of dividing the revolution and leading it to certain defeat. Neither the Left, the trade unions nor the Muslim Brotherhood can claim the exclusive right to represent a mass movement much greater than any of them, and which they must serve. The future of the Arab world will depend on the intelligence of the opposition forces that make up the movement: should they fail they will have only themselves to blame. Some religious representatives (like the Mufti of Egypt) have come down on the wrong side of history by condemning the protests: if institutional Islam, the Islam that serves the State cannot (or lacks the courage to) oppose the government that employs it, it would have been better to remain silent and not attempt to politicize religion. The future will depend on the people's ability to create platforms that unite the voices of the pluralist opposition and work for democratic elections that will eventually judge the legitimacy of those who claim to represent the people.

The freedom loving citizens of the West face their own moment of truth. They can pretend to believe the rhetoric of their respective governments. They can continue to allow themselves to be manipulated, to imagine that the United States and the European countries fear revolution in the Arab world because they "sincerely" fear the Islamists might seize power and betray human rights, the rights of women, and more fundamentally, the very principles of democracy. Did the United States, Europe and the United Nations (with Israeli agreement) not organize the first free and fair elections in the Occupied Territories, accepting that the Islamist movement Hamas change its name on the electoral rolls, before going on to win as expected...only to punish and to stifle the Palestinian people for their historical error? Strategic relations between Western governments and Islamist movements have a long history, frequently involving alliances: their relations have always been determined by economic and geopolitical interests, and Western governments have never had the slightest hesitation at allying themselves with extremist groups.

Western citizens, however, must remain true to their principles and demand that their governments respect democratic principles and the people's choice. They must cease to close their eyes (consciously or not) to the selective demonization of opposition movements in the Arab world and in Muslim majority countries. Our responsibility as Westerners is immense: because we enjoy freedom, because we have access to information and to education, it is our duty to support legitimate popular demands without hypocrisy and without illusions. Populist, conservative and potentially radical opposition forces exist in all Eastern and Western societies; democratic principles require that we confront them in debate and by political means as long as they respect the rule of law, the principle of free elections and the democratic process (before and after elections). It is no longer acceptable for the "democracies of the North," in the name of security or of their economic and geopolitical interests, to countenance dictatorship, repression and torture. The Israeli government's recent appeal to the West to support the dictator Mubarak is nothing short of astonishing coming from the country that purports to be the sole democracy in the region, as if its security depended on being surrounded by dictators who suppress their own people. A country truly dedicated to security and regional stability does not conclude peace treaties with torturers, but with free peoples whose dignity is fully respected.

Since the great terrorist attacks of a decade ago, there have been attempts to launch debates or forums for "dialogue" or the "alliance of civilizations." In the light of real events in the Arab world, these efforts now stand revealed either as purely theoretical exercises or stratagems designed to draw attention away from real political issues. The world is changing; the Middle East is quaking. The West can go on repeating to the point of satiation that opposition forces in the Arab world are dangerous (because they are exclusively Islamist or radical) and that, implicitly, it would be justified to limit (or control) Arab and Muslim access to democracy. Or citizens in the West can stand shoulder to shoulder with peoples in their march toward freedom. The issue is one of human values and political ethics. As for the defense of "our" interests that often causes us to forget our principles, we would do well to remember that in the long term the respect of peoples and of their dignity is the only way to ensure the security of the West. Only when the peoples of the Global South are free and enjoy full access to their wealth can we correct the international imbalance that feeds forced migration and insecurity. Our futures are linked—and shared.

## 9  Emotions and Lucidity

The first stage of the revolution is over; the dictator has fled. The last days of his rule were curious, almost as though scripted for television: carefully thought out, in apparent disorder yet orderly, while guiding us, the spectators, to the only possible outcome. The young people, the demonstrators, all those who came out against the regime had adopted new forms of communication and mobilization—as did the power of the state. It would be wrong to think otherwise.

Former President Mubarak's statements often appeared at odds with reality. His resignation was expected; representatives of the regime announced it twice, on the eve of his second public declaration, and once again on the afternoon of his third speech. Yet each time the Rais confounded the forecasters. The people's feelings, the powerful emotions of the eighteen days resembled a gigantic yo-yo, complete with high hopes, deep despond, then even higher hopes that were again dashed, until final—and apparent—victory. Elementary psychology teaches that emotional shifts, particularly when experienced by large numbers of people, can influence analytical capacity and make it impossible to maintain critical distance. Media impact, instantaneous communication and widespread public excitement necessarily amplify the effect.

Now, it is time to pause, to think over all we have seen and what is ultimately at stake.

From a distance, the shifting position of the American government seemed to be following the same curve as the lack of control and the ignorance evident in high-level decision-making. "History is unfolding" said President Barack Obama a few hours before Hosni Mubarak announced that he was staying on. Once more the voice from Cairo dashed hopes of a rapid resolution in Washington. The American administration was out of its depth; its mastery of Egyptian affairs far from certain: it had no choice but to accept and to recognize the people's victory. Not intervening, simply watching, and finally—and wisely—taking the side of the people.

However, developments taking place behind closed doors may well have been far less random than they appeared. Emotions were powerful, poignant, vivid and intense, but the reality of conflicts and the high stakes they represent is far more circumscribed, measured and down-to-earth. The conflicts and tensions within the command structure of the Egyptian army are well known; its close relationship with the United States has never been a secret. The transition period that is now opening will prove to be more difficult and dangerous than the popular mobilization against the dictator Mubarak. Even greater vigilance, lucidity and courage will be called for.

The military command has announced the dissolution of parliament, suspended the Constitution, and promised elections in six months at the latest. The government, most of whose members are Mubarak appointees, continues to administer current affairs and supervise the transition. The regime has not fallen; the actors remain the same. As for the most optimistic observers, they will remain convinced that the main goal has been reached. But analysts— drawing on the lessons of history—will remain more skeptical. There is every reason to believe that Egypt's eighteen days, in addition to the coming period, have made it possible—and are still making it possible—to reframe the reform process, to re-evaluate the interests to be preserved and the objectives to be achieved; to satisfy the people's aspirations and emotions, while protecting existing alliances, geopolitical and economic interests.

We have been witness to two Revolutions, seen masses on the march, become aware of young people and of new forms of global communication. Media coverage that carried away people's sense of commitment functioned, literally, as a "blanket," as a deforming screen that obscured reality and masked key issues. All praise to the people of Tunisia, and of Egypt (whose bloggers have been working to raise public awareness for nearly three years). Their contribution to the awakening of their peoples has been incomparable. Their calls for liberty, and their mass demonstrations have brought about a break; have opened a path to freedom.

But we must remain alert. The powers that be are well aware of these developments. To all those who believe that the American administration miscalculated, demonstrated clumsiness or could not keep up with events, we suggest that they would do well to re-evaluate the situation in the light of what has happened and what may happen in the coming days. Egypt—like Tunisia—is still under tight control; the way in which power was successfully transferred points to a considerable grasp of communication (up to and including apparent errors in judgment exposed to the public in press conferences) and of the internal logic of the Arab world.

People must now be less emotional; the leaders of the opposition must be more vigilant and responsible. These leaders must shoulder the critical— and historical—responsibilities that are theirs as these lines are being written. Mobilization must always be an option. But now, the primary task for Arab civil society is to create opposition platforms that reflect the multiplicity of political voices and ideological aspirations. No longer is it possible to look on passively as the mass movement is diverted by lessened tensions, by the passage of time, by fulsome speeches and hackneyed declarations of principle. From where we stand, the same basic recommendations mist apply: stay alert, to not confuse political promises or pledges of support for emerging democracies after thirty years of propping up dying dictatorships, with hard cash.

Several years ago, I called for the emergence of a new "We," based on principles, values, demands for coherence and a sense of belonging to shared national ideals. Now a fresh page of history is opening before us, ours to inscribe with the concrete and practical objectives of this new "We." Together we must now commit ourselves, freed from potential emotional deafness, and nourished by a realistic knowledge of democratic demands, so that our governments—in the West as in the East—can no longer divide us, can no longer manipulate us, are no longer able to convince us of differences that simply do not exist in our daily lives, and to undermine our hopes to be fully human.

After all the joy and relief it is time for lucidity, time to set up common fronts based on resistance and on reason. Lucidity and perseverance must become the arms of our non-violent resistance. Neither Tunisia or Egypt is free or independent yet; mass mobilization in support of the revolutions unfolding before our very eyes must continue, inspiring a vision of more to come.

## 10  Freedom Friday

Today, more than ever, homage is due to the historical uprising of the Tunisian people. Millions of women and men overcame fear and faced down terror. The Egyptian people followed their example and brought down the despot. While the regimes may still be in place, an irreversible, uncontrollable movement has begun. North Africa and the Middle East will never again be the same. Whatever the schemes of military and the Western powers for political, geopolitical and economic control, a new dynamic has been created. Non-violent, determined and courageous mass movements have shown that anything is possible, that History is now forging ahead in the Arab and Muslim world. From now on, it will be impossible to silence the craving for freedom and to halt the onward march of liberation, even though setbacks and missteps may occur.

The people of Libya have now taken to the streets and, city after city, freed its country from the grip of the eccentric dictator of Tripoli. The despot's madness, as cunning as it is unpredictable, has not yet spoken its last. But it is clear that he too will fall; that Libya will be freed of the horrors of his long reign. He too stole, tortured, summarily eliminated, and lied. For more than forty years he cleverly manipulated, provoked and humiliated the Western powers. Today, his own people have courageously chosen to confront him empty-handed. It is a question of vital importance to salute them, encourage them, assist them and support them. There is little that can be done from outside. But the movement is gathering strength; we must do all we can to convince our own authorities to take a clear and forthright position. It will not come a moment too soon! For how dismal is the now-confirmed rev-elation of years of silence, hypocrisy and falsehood: the Orient now stands as a distorting mirror in which the craven policies of the United States, of Canada, of Europe and Australia are reflected. Today, the people in revolt are chanting not a word of reproach toward the West. It could do no better than shake itself out of its stupor, as the Arab world is now doing. Courageous self-criticism is worth far more than guilty silence. Wait not a moment longer!

In Yemen, Bahrain, and Iraq; in Morocco, Algeria, Iran, and Jordan... peo-ples are calling out their desire for freedom and dignity. Expressed in their Friday gatherings, the power of the people defies description; the symbol-ism is overwhelming, irresistible. Muslim women and Muslim men, praying together, give voice to the universal human aspiration for liberty, justice and dignity, for the power of sovereign people. For those who have, over the years, painted Muslims as impermeable to the ideals of liberty and democracy, and naturally inclined to violence—due to the very essence of Islam—the answer is clear-cut and unequivocal: tens of millions of Muslims, on these Fridays, have chosen the path of resistance, of sacrifice and of liberation in a spirit of non-violence, respect for life, without ever criticizing the West, its values and its betrayals. They have done so alongside Anglicans and Copts, alongside athe-ists, communists, and citizens of all beliefs and ideologies. What finer answer could there be to the simple-minded, racist analyses propagated by populist parties in the West? On Freedom Friday, with its massive crowds coming together to pray in the name of resistance and liberty, we witness, in real time, Islam—and of Muslims—joining forces with liberty, justice and democratic principles. That the first European leader to have greeted the resisting peoples and called upon the dictators to leave was the Turkish prime minister should serve as a caustic reminder of the value of the short-sighted and tendentious analyses of the "Muslim world" that have long infested Western diplomacy and intellectual life.

The movement must not end here. We must hope that the peoples con-tinue their onward march, that they completely free themselves from the yoke of the tyrants and complete their democratic revolution. The final word has not yet been spoken, either in Tunisia, Egypt or Libya or elsewhere, but the movement will surely prove stronger than those who are attempting to con-trol it. Therein lies its power. It is essential that all the components of the pluralist opposition seize this historic occasion to dialogue, to establish com-mon fronts representing civil society in order that army commanders do not turn the revolution to their advantage, or to the advantage of foreign political or economic powers. We must hope that governments pay heed. They must either implement thoroughgoing reform or leave the scene entirely, and make way for systems of government that respect the popular will, and that apply uncompromisingly the five basic and inalienable principles: the rule of law, equality of all citizens, universal suffrage, limited electoral terms and the separation of powers. This is the imperative, and the minimum acceptable: without corruption, insider privilege, and in full independence. We must hope that the movement continues to spread throughout North Africa and the Middle East...up to and including Israel, that Prime Minister Benjamin Netanyahu and his racist foreign minister Avigdor Lieberman also be overthrown and with them, the interminable policy of colonization and non-respect of the dignity of the Palestinians and the Arab citizens of Israel.

On Freedom Friday, everything is possible. Full of hope, with clear eyes, we must hail the march of the peoples and remind governments—whoever they may be, those of the tyrants or the shameless friends of those same tyrants—that nothing lasts forever, that despots and traitors can never be eternally shielded from their peoples, or from the judgment of history.

## *11 From bin Laden to the Arab spring*

Reactions during the first 48 hours after the announcement of Osama bin Laden's death have been indeed revealing. While the symbolic impact of the news touched off a media frenzy in the West, coverage was far more restrained in majority Muslim societies and throughout the Global South. It was as though we were witnessing, in real time, two distinct perspectives on the world.

The rhetoric of violent extremist organizations, be they al-Qaeda or others, never gained traction among the world's Muslims. With the exception of tiny groups functioning autonomously, we can conclude that terrorism has been a marginal phenomenon since September 11 2001. In fact, terrorists have killed more Muslims than Americans or Europeans, from Bali to Amman and from Morocco to Iraq, by way of Pakistan and Afghanistan.

The "celebration" of the execution of bin Laden raises a number of questions that—far from conspiracy theory—any thinking person is justified in asking. Far from any rejoicing, they represent the uncertainties that continue to trouble Muslim minds around the world—not to mention numerous Westerners. How can bin Laden have avoided detection in a place so close to Islamabad for more than five years? What precisely is the relationship between Pakistani and American intelligence services in the light of their contradictory versions of the event? Why was there no attempt to arrest him?

How are we to explain the absence of photographs, the disposal of his corpse into the sea (in pointed disregard for the Muslim rite his executioners publicly claimed to respect)?

Aside from such questions, and the legitimate doubts they express, the death of bin Laden, as an icon and symbol of terrorism, is all but a non-event for the world's Muslims. His vision and actions were neither widely emulated nor respected, as numerous surveys by Western governments and anti-terrorism experts have confirmed. We are dealing, above all, with a primarily American, and more broadly European event. The staging of the announcement, in the form of the American president's firm and carefully worded statement on live television, was designed to convey the impression of calm in the hour of victory over terrorism and over America's public enemy number one. There was no empty boasting. Barack Obama, who has in the past been sharply criticized for his apparent lack of strength and determination on national security issues as well as on the wars in Iraq and Afghanistan, has scored a powerful symbolic success that will have a strong impact on public opinion. Not only did he keep up pursuit of bin Laden, but in total secrecy commanded a sensitive and ultimately successful operation that seems sure to strengthen his image as a decisive president able to take action in the critical fields of national security, defense and patriotic pride. The only images available to date are those of the president micro-managing operations from his Washington office: a succession of cleverly calculated and skillfully conceived media dividends.

But we must go well beyond the flurry of exuberance that saw people celebrating in the streets of New York. What lies ahead for the Middle East, as it contemplates two contradictory realities: on the one hand, the massively popular peaceful revolutions taking place in the Arab world, and on the other, the death of the symbol of violent extremism, of a leader of tiny marginal and marginalized groups? There may well be terrorist reprisals; they must be anticipated and met with all necessary firmness. But the task will be to combat and to neutralize isolated acts of provocation that under no circumstances can be used to justify a philosophy of political action, the course adopted by the previous American government. It is time to treat violent extremism for what it is: the action of small groups that represent neither Islam nor Muslims, but deviant political postures that have lost all credibility in majority Muslim societies.

The elements of a new political philosophy defining the West's relationship with Islam and with the Muslims can only emerge from the crucible of the broad-based movement for justice, freedom, democracy and dignity now sweeping North Africa and the Middle East. The rebirth now underway in the East must first be understood as an appeal for critical self-examination by the West. Once the rejoicing at the elimination of bin Laden, the "symbol of the cancer of terrorism" is over, the West should move rapidly to review its regional policies. The American and European presence in Afghanistan and Iraq, coupled with the absence of a firm commitment to resolving the Israel-Palestine conflict, is an obstacle to any positive development. To this list must be added domestic issues such as discriminatory legislation that offends human dignity and personal liberty, the existence of Guantanamo and the use of torture: practices that amplify mistrust of the United States and its allies. Selective support for dictatorships in the Middle East or in the oil sheikhdoms should be rapidly reconsidered lest these policies raise legitimate questions about the West's true support for the democratization process in the Arab world.

The Muslim majority societies have a substantial responsibility for managing their own future. It cannot be stated strongly enough that the sirens of violence and extremism have never seduced the overwhelming majority of their peoples. More than ever, as the people awaken, it is essential that civil society (including intellectuals and political parties) remain mobilized and alert; that it expose corruption and the absence of the rule of law and of justice; that it develop a genuine strategy to create free and democratic societies, and that, in the end, it create the conditions for new political and economic relations with the West. For the old couple made up of Islam and the West is no longer young; the presence of new players from the Far East, starting with China, is even now resetting the parameters of the world economic order. The United States, like the countries of South America, like China and India by way of Turkey, know exactly what is taking place. It may well be that the Arab "spring" is, in reality, the autumn of the Arab world's relations with the West, and a new path to another, broader spring, bounded this time by East and West. Against this emerging geo-economic landscape, the announcement of bin Laden's death has all the force of a fading wind, of a random event.

## 12  Barack Obama: Words and Symbols

Almost two years after his June 2009 speech in Cairo, American president Barack Obama once more addressed the Arab populations of the Middle East and North Africa. This time, he was responding to two major events: the revolutionary upheavals that have shaken the region, and the death of Osama bin Laden. The election of a first "African American president" raised high hopes in majority Muslim countries, due less to Barack Obama's roots than to a perceived renewal of America's vision and policies after the dark years of the Bush regime. Where do these hopes stand today?

The current chief executive has proven himself an adept orator and a skilled manipulator of symbols. A change has clearly come about in the United States; the final page of a sinister era has been turned. But optimism has its limits; deeds must be measured against words. Candidate Obama promised to bring the lawlessness exemplified by Guantánamo to an end; to reform discriminatory legislation and to abolish the degrading practice of torture (legitimized in the name of the War on Terror); to wind down the wars in Iraq and in Afghanistan; to advance the Middle East peace process; and, ultimately, to inaugurate a new era in multi-polar international relations.

But, as we look beyond the words and symbols, we realize that little has changed. In fact, America's obsession with security has increased: Guantánamo remains a shameful reality, under new anti-terrorist legislation certain politically or religiously "sensitive" citizens face arbitrary and discriminatory treatment (from imprisonment to deportation based on mere suspicion), the wars in Iraq and Afghanistan drag on and the peace process is nothing but sound and fury signifying nothing. What then has changed, and what, in fact, must change?

Barack Obama's silence is as significant as his words, and reveals the true substance of his message. He faces two principal challenges: on the international front—the core of his speech—and in domestic politics (about which he has maintained total silence one year before the presidential election). Political considerations determined his timing. His speech came hard on the heels of the "legal" operation against Osama bin Laden in Pakistan.

The execution of the al-Qaeda chief revealed once more the breadth of the chasm that separates the American administration from Muslims in the United States and around the world. Compared with the Western media, which played the event as a victory over the "symbol of terrorism," reactions to bin Laden's death amongst Western and Eastern Muslims, not to mention in the Global South as a whole, were muted. The absence of images and of proof, the hasty disposal of the body at sea raised questions and reinforced doubts. Most of all, they underscored the gap in perceptions. For the al-Qaeda leader never commanded the respect of the masses, never galvanized the hearts of the Muslim peoples (with the exception of a minority of violent extremists). By its behavior the American government proved once again how poorly it understands Muslim hearts and minds. Barack Obama's announcement of the elimination of bin Laden may have been eloquent, but few Muslims heard it and fewer still appreciated it. The president's audience was strictly American. He demonstrated presidential resolve, readiness to act to protect his country and to make the hard and dangerous decisions incumbent upon a military leader. Often criticized for hesitation, his ratings shot up twelve points: a successful operation on the eve of an election year.

The time had thus come for a new message, pitched this time to Arabs, democrats, and Muslims in general. Mr. Obama had realized that he was not being understood, that he had failed to win over his target audience. But behind the American president's seductive image and fine words stands an administration concerned neither with principle nor troubled by its incoherent domestic and foreign policy. Promised American support for the pro-democracy movements in North Africa and the Middle East is marked by radically different approaches (between Libya and Syria, where the indispensable Bashar al-Assad, whose forces have opened fire on unarmed civilians, is expected with the wave of a magic wand to reform his despotic regime) or by guilty silence from its allies the petro-monarchies (such as Saudi-backed Bahrein) that repress and kill civilians and non-violent opponents. We heard a clear appeal to end the sufferings of the Palestinians and to recognize their rights. But the Obama government's policy for the last three years has been one of silence: silence during the Gaza massacre, and over the killing of dozens of unarmed civilians during the commemoration of the Nakba on May 15 2011. It is all well and good for Mr. Obama to pay lip service to the 1967 borders as a basis for negotiations between Israel and the Palestinians. But American inaction in the face of the ongoing Israeli policy of colonization and of "facts on the ground" reveals his position as not only as inconsistent, but inapplicable. Once again, words are employed to make Palestinians and Arabs dream, while Israel is given a free hand to implement its long-term strategy behind the media façade of tensions between the American and Israeli governments.

Guantánamo and torture are a fact of life in Barack Obama's America, where the basic rights of prisoners are systematically denied and where the blood of Iraqi and Afghan civilians appears to count for nothing. Less, certainly, than that of Libyan civilians. Why? Is American policy in North Africa and the Middle East driven exclusively by economic considerations? Everything points in that direction. Barack Obama's messages—spoken and unspoken—are unlikely to provide the Arab street with much reassurance. In his speech, the president emphasized the economic dimension of the Arab revolutions. There can be no true democratic process without economic stability and development, he argued. The formula is sound, the equation seductive. Barack Obama then went on to announce debt reduction, increased investment and American financial support to the region in collaboration with Europe, the World Bank and the International Monetary Fund. It would seem that the region's democratic opening is contingent on the opening up of lucrative new markets. The American administration and the multinational corporations it represents appear less committed to democracy, justice and freedom than they are to profit and to promoting the ideology of consumerism. Mr. Obama presented American economic support in terms of solidarity and generosity toward the peoples of the region, while uttering not a word about his country's decade-long record of neglect. Noteworthy too was his failure to mention new regional economic powers such as China, South America and Turkey. Do American and European strategists consider them as negligible factors? Most unlikely, now that we have learned to decode Barack Obama's silence. Regional economic benefits (in North Africa and the Middle East) may well prove more important than bringing democratic norms to political life. The emerging model promises superficial political independence with a handful of freedoms tied to greater economic dependence with all the restrictions it implies. Economic liberalism is liberal for only a select few. Barack Obama enjoys repeating that, "America has nothing against Islam and Muslims" while failing to add "as long as they, whether democrats or autocrats, do not stand in the way of our interests." A new face speaks the same old words. Only concrete action can be the motor for change. Muslims can hear perfectly well what is being said, and what is not being said. And in terms of a truly new policy, they are still waiting.

At the same time, Islam is emerging as an issue in the upcoming American elections. The Tea Party movement and their neo-con allies are warning against the dangers of Islam and the "Islamization" of America. Eighteen American states are currently adopting surrealist legislation that would prohibit the application of the *Shari'a*, which is invariably presented as the epitome of barbarity. No longer is extremist and violent Islam the target, but Islam as a religion. Building upon controversy, the movement is gaining strength; a noxious atmosphere is being created. From the Park 51 (so-called "Ground Zero") mosque to "Burn a Qur'an Day," from local initiatives against Muslim activities or the building of mosques, tensions are rising, based on the same arguments and slogans that have surfaced during recent years in Europe. Muslim baiting and Islamophobia have reared their ugly heads, and are being used to isolate a large segment of the American population on the basis of their religious beliefs (in addition to long-existing racism against African-Americans). The policy draws on the same mix of fear, suspicion and rejection used by

European populists like Geert Wilders who plays to full houses in the United States, confirming the new xenophobia's popular appeal.

Paradoxically, the election of Barack Obama has provided these movements with an opening to advance their agenda by discrediting him, his origins and even his religion (23 percent of Americans believe he is a crypto-Muslim; 42 percent think he is not a good Christian, for a total of 65 percent skeptical Americans). Criticism of the president has become more strident; rumor and innuendo are used to undermine his credibility. It is all well and good to assert that Islam is an American religion, but his administration, in its domestic policy, must do more than mouth pious wishes. It must confront the Islamophobes and their xenophobic allies with greater determination—and more egalitarian policies.

The president's fine words have produced scant results at the grass roots. The upcoming elections are unlikely to lead to any significant change. Yet firm action would certainly be the best way for Mr. Obama to position himself as the president of renewed hope, capable of winning on a just and reasonable platform in 2012. The stakes are high. On the question of rekindling relations with Islam and Muslims, international and domestic politics go hand in hand. President Obama can no longer limit himself to an intelligent (and unfailingly open) dialogue with Muslim leaders and intellectuals. On the streets of the Middle East, as in America's inner cities and recession-hit suburbs, ordinary Muslim citizens care little about his words and images. They continue to listen closely to the silences that reveal much more, and to certify the inaction that defines the critical inadequacy of Obama's policies over the last three years. Like all peoples, those of the Islamic world are aware of the high irony of awarding a Nobel Peace Prize to a man that talks much about peace but does nothing to bring it about.

Today's serious challenges cry out for concerted action. But the president's fine, well-written speech runs once more the risk of being badly understood or misunderstood, if it is even heard at all. In the name of democratic transparency, should we not be asking that it be accompanied by something resembling coherence?

## 13   *The Middle East: Independence and Dependency*

Some call it the "Arab Spring," others, the "Arab Revolutions"; still others, more cautious, use the neutral term "Arab uprisings." It remains difficult to ascertain, and to assess, what has happened and is actually happening in the Middle East. An irreversible shift is clearly underway but no one is able to pinpoint exactly what is going on in these mass protests or to predict their ultimate outcome.

There is every reason for hope and optimism in the Middle East and North Africa (MENA), and around the world. The Arab populations are on the march towards freedom, dignity, justice and democracy. They are determined to regain their historical political independence and have set their sights on modernity and democracy. "History is unfolding," says American president Barack Obama. Hundreds of political analysts have predicted a "happier future." This is good news; the Arab world is awakening.

We must first salute the courage and the determination of the people of Tunisia and Egypt who have been the first to challenge the dictators and their corrupt regimes. The dictators have fled; the way towards true and transparent democracy is now open. It is now time to implement the basic and immutable principles: rule of law, equal citizenship, universal suffrage, accountability and the separation of powers. Domestic debates have begun in both Tunisia and Egypt over the content of their respective constitutions, political parties, elections, etc. Never before, over the last century at least, has such positive social and political energy been so powerfully felt. We are witnessing what may well be the birth of true political independence, even though everything still remains fragile and uncertain.

We should be guardedly optimistic. These historical changes are not happening in a vacuum; they cannot be isolated from either economic realities or the geostrategic environment. The economic situation of both countries is serious; there can be no true democratic process without economic stability. But when we analyze events in the light of Western—and especially American and European—strategy, we are tempted to revise, or at east to suspend, our judgment. Political independence can only be achieved with economic reforms that lead not only to stability but also to economic independence.

However, we appear to be heading in the opposite direction: the new US and European involvement in MENA—putting aside decades of support for and complicity with the two dictatorships—will deepen Tunisia and Egypt's economic dependency. Before emerging as democracies, these two countries are to be viewed as markets with great profit potential. This has always been the case, but the role of the World Bank and the IMF in the post-revolutionary era is to set up a structure of ideological and economic dependency beneath a veneer of democratic freedoms. For the poor countries of the Global South, the adjective "liberal" does not mean the same thing as it does in the West, whether to describe "democracy" or "the economy:" the former might come close to "liberty," but the latter implies inevitable subjugation.

Are we witnessing unfinished political revolutions wedded to economic regression? Will the countries involved end up as "controlled" democracies? Or have they experienced uncompleted revolutions? These questions are reinforced when we analyze the situation in the region. The so-called international community praises Tunisia and Egypt, while the oppressed populations of Syria, Yemen and Bahrain seem almost forgotten. How are we to explain why the Libyan opposition (including so many new leaders who were previously among the strongest supporters of the dictator Ghaddafi) is receiving such unconditional assistance in removing the regime, as NATO forces daily bomb Tripoli? The mass protests and the blood being shed by the newly re-categorized Arabs do not have the same quality and value. Tunisia and Egypt, even with apparent democratic procedures in place, remain under economic and military control. Libyan oil resources are so vital that supporting a divided and nebulous opposition is a risk worth taking, even at the cost of breaking up the country. It appears that Syria, Bahrain and to a certain extent Yemen are so critical in geostrategic terms that their governments are free to kill civilians and unarmed protesters (three months passed before the UN managed to adopt a very timid resolution against the Syrian government). Not only is media coverage different (from CNN to al-Jazeera); political language proves quite elastic when it comes to changing regimes and advocating democracy.

The regional economic and geostrategic stakes are very high. New forms of dependency are being established and must be taken into account. True and effective political and economic reforms require, to provide autonomy and justice, a deep shift in relations between MENA and the United States and the European countries. There are new actors to be invited to participate in regional dynamics. Relying on South-South political and economic partnerships, the future must involve the active participation of the South American countries, Turkey, China, Malaysia and even India. There will be no effective "Arab spring" unless the centre of gravity of the international political and economic order can be shifted both southward and eastward. No one knows when such a shift might take place, but there are indications that it may already be underway. The regional uprising might well presage further upheavals, this time at the international level. The time has come for the Arabs to live up to these hopes and to do justice to their social, political, cultural and economic potential. They are rich; they need to be courageous and smart.

## *14 Revealing Syria*

Bashar al Assad is a dictator; his regime is a dictatorship. During the first days of repression, some voices attempted to exonerate him of responsibility for the torture and the killing of hundreds of civilian protesters, including many women and children. He was not to blame, they said, but some old torturers still in charge since his father's time. What a lie, what a distortion of the facts and the crude political reality! Then the truth began to unfold, day after day, through eyewitness accounts, images and reports. Human Rights Watch, and many other organizations, revealed (and are still revealing) the extent of the atrocities.

Young boys, aged no more than 9, 10 or 12, have been arrested and tortured, their nails pulled out, teeth broken, sexually abused and mutilated. What shame! In the streets, unarmed protesters have been shot down as they marched. Men, women, innocent people —portrayed by the regime as conspirators, terrorists, radical Islamists—were killed in cold blood; entire villages and cities have been "cleansed" of the "plague." On Monday June 20, Bashar al Assad gave an unbelievable speech promising "national dialogue," "reform" through "consultative meetings." Journalist Robert Fisk was right in describing the speech as "insulting both the living and the dead." Two days later, Bashar's army was marching toward the Turkish border where thousands of refugees were trying to escape the horror. Some have reached safety in Turkey; others are still on Syrian soil and fear the worst.

The so-called international community is almost silent, and/or paralyzed. The Tunisian and Egyptian uprisings received wide coverage, and help. Why is nothing being done in the Syrian case? The cruelty of the successive al-Assad regimes, of both the father Hafez and his son Bashar (with his brother Maher in command of the army's elite Fourth Division) is well documented. In Tunisia and Egypt, the revolutions were saluted; the "new era of democratization" brought hope to Western capitals. We even heard talk of "the Arab spring." Yet, this spring seems to have turned into winter in Syria (as well as in Bahrain). So many geopolitical and economic considerations have primacy over the people's freedom and the dignity. In the Arab world (and the Global South) democracy is a good thing as long as Western interests are protected. By the same token, in the Arab world (and the Global South), dictatorship is not a bad thing, as long as Western interests are protected. The so-called "Arab spring" reeks of cold calculation and profit. It has nothing to do with ethics and morality; everything to do with power and money.

Syria is a crucial and complex country. Beyond the Alawite minority's monopoly of power through a mixture of autocracy and terror, nobody can predict possible political alternatives. The opposition forces, from the Left to the Muslim Brotherhood, are not sympathetic to either the US or Israel. While Israel has long understood how it could benefit from the Syrian dictator as a useful enemy, it is concerned about a democratic regime that would give voice to the people's anger over the humiliation of the Palestinians and the ongoing colonization of Palestinian lands. As with Egypt, so also in Syria: Israel cannot tolerate democratic regimes in the Arab world and prefers to deal with merciless autocrats who can guarantee a controlled peace. There is also the Iranian factor; potential new alliances may emerge if a new regime comes to power in Syria. Bashar, following in his father's footsteps, agreed to play a contradictory role in the region, one that suited both the United States and Israel: he was the "bad guy" with whom they could keep talking and who accepted the status quo by (usefully) questioning the peace process—a complex and contradictory role, but a very useful one.

The Kurdish equation is critical in the region and may explain—among other factors—Turkish hesitations. If Bashar's regime collapses, new alliances and claims could be created that could be very difficult for Turkey and the role it wants to uphold regionally and internationally. Syria's allies, Russia and China, see in the current regime the channel through which they can access, and are accessing, the wealth and markets of the Middle East. Syria is a key factor in the region; if the "Arab Spring" takes hold in Damascus, it would generate concerns for several regional and foreign powers. There are many considerations, many challenges.

One thing seems clear, however. The Arab spring will only be a true spring if the Syrian regime collapses and paves the way for a truly democratic, non-corrupt political system. Such is the real path towards freedom and autonomy in the region. Tunisia and Egypt can still be controlled. The balance of power does not yet favor autonomy and free civil society. To achieve the first step toward that "spring," Bashar and his regime must be dumped... if not, the "spring" would be nothing but empty words while behind the scenes nothing would change. Syria is critical—and will be a revealing factor

Today, the Syrian people are the victims of both a cruel regime and very cynical political and economic calculations. Even if intervention is difficult, current international passivity is intolerable. We need to remember that there is no place for naivety in politics. Powers are driven by interests and it is the duty of the democratic forces—around the world, whatever their culture and

religion—to prove that, on the long run, dignity, freedom and democratization are not just fine words to manipulate but also policies to implement in
the interest of all. Oppressed people will never forget. History will always
remember.

## 15 Waiting for the "Israeli Spring"

From around the world, women and men supporting Palestinian rights have
been preparing to embark on a symbolic expedition. In the name of humanitarian ideals, they were taking direct political action: an international flotilla
was to head towards Gaza (where the people are still suffering under the most
adverse conditions because of the Israeli blockade) to express international
solidarity with the Palestinians. The Israeli government, from the Foreign
Ministry to Mossad and the secret intelligence services, tried its utmost to
stop the boats by pressuring the Greek government, sabotaging some of the
vessels and launching a media campaign that accused the non-violent activists of being extremists and radicals. To a large extent, and in the short run,
it has been successful: only a few boats of what should have been a large and
peaceful flotilla remain operational; the Greek government, because of its
new relationship with Israel, folded under pressure and prevented the boats
from sailing.

One year after the killing of nine non-violent (mainly Turkish) activists
in international waters, the Israeli government wants to avoid the shame but
is still not prepared to heed the international cry for justice. Israeli Prime
Minister Benjamin Netanyahu does not want to lose his dignity because of
potentially damaging media coverage, but he is not afraid of enforcing inhuman policies against the people of Gaza. Once more, the "international community" remains silent. More than two years after the massacre of more than
1200 civilians in Gaza, one year after the attack against unarmed civilians
on the Freedom Flotilla, and while we are witnessing the ongoing colonization of the Occupied Territories, the International Community remains
paralyzed. We celebrated the so-called "Arab Spring" while turning a blind
eye to the intolerable plight of the Palestinians. For more than 60 years they
have been offered fine words—but no justice. And so it goes: Israel remains
the same: deaf and obdurate. Can we look forward to an "Israeli spring" to
celebrate?

The Palestinians were advised to stop their armed resistance in order to get
the support of the West. They were told to implement internally a democratic
process and to accept the preconditions of the so-called peace process. They

have been invited to talk and to talk, again and again: they were promised "peace," for the fifth time, by 2005. Six years later, their situation is worse than they could ever have dreamed of. Divided, partly because the international community did not accept the people's choice in the "first free elections in the Occupied Territories," they have neither an independent State nor any hope of improvement. Israel is pushing ahead with its silent expansion: slowly, surely, knowingly, strategically.

Nothing, apparently, has changed except the Palestinian strategy. They know it is going to be a long process. In the light of the Arab uprisings, they are assessing the potential power of non-violent resistance. But it would be nearly impossible for them to launch an effective mass protest due to geographical and political realities. The situation in Gaza is desperate; the West Bank is starting to suffocate as well. But the Palestinians still resist with dignity and courage; they will not give up. We must pay tribute to their justified and legitimate resistance and call on the Israeli government to cease its oppressive policies and to listen. Meanwhile, the United States utter timid words while the European countries simply follow.

The global movement of non-violent resistance to Israel is gaining ground. The international flotilla was part of this strategy: peaceful activists were going to raise awareness around the world through the symbolic act of bringing supplies to the Palestinians and breaking the immoral blockade of Gaza. At the same time, they are promoting the call to boycott Israeli products, to disinvest from Israeli economic interests and to sanction Israeli policy. It is a non-violent, pacifist and worldwide movement that must build up more and more momentum. The only hope is, though international pressure, to impose on Israel a "domestic spring" of its own.

It is appalling to see Western countries fold under Israeli pressure and block legal and non-violent action against Israeli oppression of the Palestinians. The future seems dark and nobody can predict what is going to happen in the Middle East. The only certitude is that the Palestinians will not give up and will eventually get their rights. While some may ask, "what if non-violent resistance does not work?" our response should be: there is only one right decision in history and that is to resist oppression and colonization. The Palestinians know better than anyone else what are the means at their disposal. And as for us, we know the instruments of our international resistance: to speak out, to break the isolation of the Palestinians and to boycott Israeli products. It is a historical and essential struggle for the region—and for the world as well.

But there can be no doubt: soon spring will come.

## 16 On Libya and Syria

Ghaddafi's regime is collapsing. No one knows exactly when and in what state—alive or dead—he will be found. But the game is over. Libya is now turning a dark page of its recent history. The Libyan regime was brutal and merciless toward its opponents. Torture, and summary execution reflected Ghaddafi's eccentricity, madness and intelligence. The Libyan people thirsted for freedom; they followed in the footsteps of the Tunisians and the Egyptians. We must pay tribute to their courage, commitment and determination. No one would have thought Ghaddafi would leave before his death, for his behavior was so unpredictable that he would have repressed and killed without a thought for the consequences. The end of his rule was better than expected.

Yet, some critical questions must be asked. Contrary to Tunisia and Egypt with their non-violent mobilizations, in Libya the mass movement turned into an all-out civil war with heavy weapons being used by both sides. NATO, which first justified its involvement by claiming to protect civilians, helped the resistance win battles on the ground. We know that American and European intelligence agents militarily advised the opponents on the best strategy to overthrow Ghaddafi and his sons. This happened after France, followed by thirty countries, officially recognized the Transitional National Council as the legitimate representative of the new Libyan State. The Council, headed by former members of the regime, falsely announced three times that it had arrested Ghaddafi's sons. The question arises: how could such a curious Council be so quickly accepted and trusted while all the signs show it to be a very curious collection of people and visions?

Dark days might well be behind but who can predict sunny days ahead? Libya is a rich and strategic country. Foreign intervention is no accident. Who is going to control its wealth, how is it going to be used and/or divided among the Western transnational oil companies (instead of the Chinese government, which had contracts with Libya and was opposed to the war)? Can we hope for a true and transparent democratic process? Nothing is less predictable and assured, for it remains difficult to assess the level of autonomy of the opposition forces. Libya was controlled by an unpredictable dictator and might remain under control through a non-transparent pseudo-democracy. Our happiness at the fall of the dictator must not overcome our caution about what is being prepared for Libya. Our moral duty is to be on the side of those claiming freedom under a democratic regime exercising full control over the country's wealth. In Libya, the game is far from over.

And it is not over in Syria either. More than 2500 people have so far been killed by the Bashar al-Assad regime as it shows its true face. Among the victims are teenagers, women and even Palestinians refugees. By preventing international media from covering events and by stifling speech, the regime thought it would be able to repress in silence. With no Western allies, no NATO, no "international community," and no weapons, the Syrians continue to say "No! We will not give up," and day after day demonstrate and protest. Day after day they have been killed, their hands empty of weapons, innocent chest proudly thrust forward. It is our moral duty, as well, to tell our Western governments to stop paying lip service to democracy, not to wait six months before asking for Bashar al-Assad to leave. Six months of talking, with nothing to show for it. It would have been possible to isolate the country in an effective way with a military option. The Western powers did nothing and dismayingly, Venezuelan president Hugo Chavez called Bashar "a humanist, a brother."

We must pay tribute to the courage of our Syrian sisters and brothers in humanity. Their non-violent movement will prevail, but many more will die along the way. The non-violent Syrian movement is asking us, during this month of Ramadan, to pray for the missing and the dead on August 28. Let us pray and join with others of conscience, with faith or no faith, in remembering the fate of innocent people struggling for their freedom and dignity. Let us dignify ourselves as living human beings by supporting the dignity of their dead.

## 17  Hope and Disappointment in Libya

The situation in Libya is confused and quite disturbing. Ghaddafi has disappeared; nobody knows exactly what is happening in Tripoli. We seem to be witnessing the Iraqi scenario all over again: French, US, and British forces are helping the rebels both on the ground and in the air as they try to convince the world that their intention is to protect civilians and to free the country from "this monstrous dictator." We heard the same tune before, in 2003, when former ally and friend (during the 1980–1988 Iran-Iraq War), Saddam Hussein, suddenly became a tyrant with a sinister face in contrast to the purity of American policy. It was all about weapons of mass destruction, freedom, democracy, and civilization, we were told. All lies. A few years after the American economic blockade (enacted by President Bill Clinton) that was killing more than 500,000 innocent Iraqi civilians per year, the Bush administration was ready to launch a war and to kill again. In the name of geopolitical interests (driven by Israel and its American lobbies, as reported by journalist Robert Fisk) and oil resources. But we must remember that the war had begun even before George W. Bush took office.

The French newspaper *Libération* revealed, on September 1, 2011, the existence of a secret agreement between the French government and the Libyan Transitional National Council (TNC): after the war, 35 percent of the country's oil exports would be allocated to France. France, it seems, was playing in Libya the US game in Iraq. The war was fought for democracy, freedom and dignity inspired by the "Arab Spring," boasted French president Nicolas Sarkozy. The Libyan leader he had welcomed to Paris only eighteen months before had overnight become a satanic figure. It was France's moral duty to liberate the country from the "mad tyrant." Now we are hearing another version, a different truth that reveals far less glory and a much greater concern for business.

The role of French intellectual Bernard-Henri Levy, who acted as an impromptu foreign Minister for few days and helped to set up the TNC, is fascinating. Why indeed was he involved, with whom, and how? It was as though his mission was to merge French and Israeli interests in the region. Ghaddafi was an obstacle; to get rid of him was a great step forward for Israeli strategy not only in the Middle East but in Africa as well (French essayist Pierre Péan revealed in his book *Carnages: The secret wars of the great powers in Africa* the true extent of Israeli activity on the African Continent). Realpolitik; cynical logic.

It was impossible for the current American administration to be at the forefront of the Libyan intervention. The wars in Iraq and in Afghanistan and the domestic impact of the global economic downturn made it impossible to justify direct involvement, so France took the lead: a win-win scenario for both. Should we be surprised? There is little new in North Africa and even as the West pays lip service to the "Arab Spring," we must not forget decades of support for dictators.

Caution about the way things are going to be handled in the region is indicated. China, India and Russia have emerged as new actors, and beyond promoting democracy or not, the Middle East remains first and foremost a battlefield for economic interests. It is unlikely that these interests will be neglected in the name of a so-called new longing for Arab democracy. It is critical to be aware of such cynical calculations—and to hope that the Arab populations will take advantage of any opportunity to free themselves from foreign powers and to find their way towards political and economic independence.

It is equally critical not to go to the other extreme. These days, on the Internet, voices can be heard denying the very facts, so obsessed are they with criticizing the West and detecting an American plot behind every single event. Ghaddafi was, after all, a dictator and so is Bashar al-Assad. In other words, politics is not a simple matter of calling the enemy of my enemy my friend. By all means denounce the American and French game (and generally that of all the great powers from the West to China, India, Russia or Israel) when it means support for dictators to protect interests. But it would be wrong to support the despots at any price.

The only way forward is to oppose both the hypocritical position of the great powers and the unacceptable repression of the dictatorial regimes: neither idealization nor naivety. The Arab populations need support without our buying what is said in the West, China or Russia, or accepting blindly media coverage of recent events. To look forward to the fall of the Ghaddafi and al-Assad regimes requires a sharp mind in order not to be manipulated once again by governments that care nothing for human rights, freedom, equality and democracy.

In the final analysis, it is our duty as citizens to be vigilant: democratic rights cannot be given; they must be won. Our struggle is an intellectual, civic and political one and it should be launched—and will hopefully prevail—in the West, in Africa, in the Middle East and in Asia. It is an ongoing struggle that will demand all our intelligence, understanding, lucidity and dedication. Our hopes have rights; the first is that we must never forget to think.

## 18  Erdoğan visits Egypt, Tunisia and Libya

The visit of Turkish Prime Minister Recep Tayyip Erdoğan to the Middle East and North Africa (MENA) has been an immense popular success. Over the last three years his image has changed tremendously. His popularity and respect have increased for many different reasons: he has been elected and reelected and even his opponents—despite their criticisms—have acknowledged his competence and the effectiveness of his government; Turkey is improving both at home and abroad: less corruption, better management, less conflict and a strong economy (17th in the world today). After having tried hard to integrate into the European Union (EU)—and after facing ongoing European reluctance—the Prime Minister wasted little time in launching a multidimensional foreign policy directed towards the South (Africa, Latin America) and the East (China, India, Malaysia, etc.). The "zero-conflict" strategy promoted by Foreign Minister Ahmet Davutoğlu has had a visible and positive impact. On the domestic front, the new role assigned to the army has helped the current government strengthen Turkish democracy.

But it is not for these good reasons that Prime Minister Erdoğan's image has changed in the MENA. On January 29, 2009 in Davos, he stood up and left the room while debating with Israeli President Shimon Perez. Erdoğan was reacting to the massacre in Gaza and expressing his opposition and revulsion. The great majority of Arab governments had been silent; Mr. Erdoğan was perhaps the first and the only major political personality to translate the feelings of Arabs and Muslims into a symbolic and media act: the Israeli policy that killed innocent civilians was appalling and he dared to say it politely but powerfully. This was a turning point: the Turkish Prime Minister signaled that he was a truly independent leader listening to both the Turkish and the Arab streets (even though Turkey's extensive economic and diplomatic relations with Israel are an open secret).

One and a half years later, when the Israeli commandos attacked the Freedom Flotilla in international waters and killed nine Turkish peace activists, Mr. Erdoğan was once again quick to react: he asked for an official apology and has held the same position up to the present. Turkey then expelled the Israeli ambassador (and lower-rank diplomats) and suspended its substantial military ties with Israel, demonstrating that this was no longer a conflict of symbols but that he was ready for a diplomatic showdown. Arabs and Muslims looked on with amazement and admiration. Finally, in Cairo, he reminded his hosts that recognition of a Palestinian State at the United Nations General Assembly in September, "is an obligation not an option," adding to his symbolic and psychological power. Not only is Mr. Erdoğan a successful prime minister leading his country towards political transparency and economic autonomy, he is also the champion of the international Palestinian cause. He warns: "Israel cannot do whatever it wants in the Mediterranean Sea" as Turkey's navy "will step up its surveillance" in the area. The message could not be more explicit.

His visits to Egypt and in Tunisia must be seen against this overwhelmingly positive background and dramatically increased stature. We must also add that the Turkish Prime Minister was one of the first to pay tribute to the people who demonstrated again the dictators. Early on he called upon Ben Ali and Mubarak to quit and to accept the will of their people. From the very beginning, he has defended the rule of law, transparency and democracy and the Tunisian and Egyptian protesters heard his voice. Now, he is visiting MENA in full confidence: he was on the right side of History and he has remained consistent throughout the ongoing crisis. Palestinians deserve an independent and democratic State as much as the Tunisians, the Egyptians, the Libyans and all the Arab and Muslim majority countries. His call to both the secular and the Islamist trends to go beyond the current fruitless debates that separate them and to opt for a democratic civil State is very powerful and precisely to the point.

Recep Tayyip Erdoğan is intimately familiar with the substance of the current debate. Coming as he does from an Islamist tradition and dealing with secular resistances in Turkey, he knows that these debates are nothing but ideological traps. What is of prime importance today is to agree on basic democratic principles, to work for transparency and for the respect of the popular will while making sure popular uprisings cannot be hijacked by religious dogmatic trends, new secularist despots, or still-powerful militaries. It is high time to move on from useless ideological debates to effective policies and implementation: being a Muslim does not prevent us from being democrats and to combine ethics with politics in a pluralistic manner.

The Turkish prime minister knows that democracy will not be secured without economic stability. The United States, the European countries (with Cameron and Sarkozy visiting Libya), the World Bank and the International Monetary Fund (IMF) are competing to conquer markets and to exert control over future regional development. Mr. Erdoğan is visiting the region with an impressive delegation: 200 businessmen intent on improving economic ties and signing contracts (oil, telecommunications, transports, services, education, etc.). It is obvious that Turkey has ambitions and that it seeks a heightened international role. In a new multi-polar world such a role is to be welcomed. As we look at the global economic order, we are witnessing a shift towards the East. Not yet a guarantee of more democracy and international justice but hope at least for a better-balanced world. Turkey can and must play an important role if the Turkish Prime Minister and his government remain true to their principles both at home and abroad. Let us hope Tunisia, Egypt, Libya and other Arab and Muslim majority countries will study the Turkish example (its successes as well as its setbacks) and join in the dynamic. This would mean the emergence a pole of newly democratic countries helping to reconcile Muslims with confidence, autonomy, pluralism and success.

## 19  *Egypt in Danger*

The worst thing that could befall Egypt today is division such as we are witnessing between the country's Coptic and Muslim citizens. Against the same cruel dictatorship they stood united in Liberation Square (Midan Al Tahrir) demanding that former president Hosni Mubarak leave and his regime be removed. For political revolution to be achieved in Egypt, unity between the two main religious traditions (and of course all other Egyptians with or without religious and spiritual affiliations) is basic and imperative. All belong to the same nation; they share the same history, memories, culture and hopes. As a human being and as a Muslim, I must begin by expressing my deepest condolences to the victims of the bereaved families and my sympathy for the wounded, women and men. These attacks against peaceful protesters must be condemned.

What happened and why did it happen now? On September 30, a church was burned down in Aswan. The act of arson followed a statement by the governor, Mustafa Al Sayyed, claiming the church had been built without a permit. Demonstrations began in Aswan; Coptic leaders then decided to demonstrate peacefully in Cairo to underline that the issue was one of gravest national interest: there will be no future for Egypt if manipulations that seek to divide Muslims and Christians are tolerated. Their action was a call for unity in reaction to an attempt to divide. Such attempts are nothing new: both former presidents Anwar Sadat and Mubarak used the same strategy again and again over the last 40 years to justify their policies of repression: a clash would be fomented following which they would send in the troops and arrest people claiming they were preserving national unity and security.

Egypt's national television covered the events in the usual old way (followed, interestingly, by Al Jazeera): they claimed that the Copts had been manipulated from abroad, and that the protesters had stolen weapons and started shooting at the army, which had no choice but to react. But many other reports and alternative media coverage are telling us another story. The peaceful protesters, arriving at Maspero, were first attacked by unknown stone throwers; then two armoured personnel carriers drove straight into the crowd of demonstrators. The scene was chaotic, as protesters tried to flee. About two dozen people were killed.

These events took place at a particularly sensitive moment and have clearly benefited the army. The Copt protesters got it right as they chanted: "The people want the removal of the Field Marshal" referring to Mohammad Hussain Tantawi, the head of Egypt's ruling military Council. The same slogan was used against Mubarak and now, again, against the head of the army by Copts and Muslims in their demonstrations over the last months. Elections have been postponed; behind-the-scenes bargaining is in progress to protect the supporters of Mubarak's regime (army officers and politicians); nothing is transparent. It was the right time to fabricate such an attack and to split Egyptian citizens along religious lines. The Supreme Council of the Armed Forces (Scaf) looms in the shadows; the methods are still the same. The Cairo massacre shows that the Egyptian army is still a powerful force, and much smarter than some have thought.

## Calculated strategy

Its neutrality and peaceful attitude during the uprisings that began on January 25 was not a sign of support for citizens demanding justice and freedom. Beyond the divisions, and the different alliances within the armed forces, it was a calculated strategy of wait-and-see; a win-win situation. For Tantawi, the armed forces, as well as their domestic and foreign allies, Mubarak and the structure of the regime were not the point. They could well collapse and disappear while the army successfully continued to hold power. Over the last weeks the Scaf has been playing a very clever game, taking full advantage of all the potential divisions that afflict Egyptian civil society. The political parties are at odds, tensions between the secularists and the Islamists are permanent, and the absence of civil leadership is glaring: in these circumstances, the Scaf will contrive, one way or another, to protect its people and to gain decisive control over Egypt's political future. Democratic Egypt is indeed in danger.

What remains unclear is the nature of the relationship between the US (and the European countries) and the current military high command. US Secretary of State Hillary Clinton's statement is interesting, as it is implicitly accepting the official explanation: "the need [is] for the Egyptian government to ensure that the fundamental rights of all Egyptians are respected, including the rights of religious freedom, peaceful assembly..." The ambivalent position of the US is an additional factor showing that the path towards freedom will be long and hard: complete and transparent democracy appears remote. The role of civil society (encompassing all the citizens and their institutions, of whatever background) is more critical than ever. It is time to set up new alliances, new dynamics, and new objectives that will unite all Egyptians. To call for more demonstrations in Midan Al Tahrir will not be enough. What is needed today is a broad, united, positive and articulated political vision — not a fragile, divided and emotional opposition.

Published in *Gulf News*, October 15, 2011

## 20 Dead Without Trial. Again.

Once more there was to be no trial, no judgment. Over the last five years the scenario in the Arab world seems to be the same. Over and over again, the same confusion, the same dramatic end. Saddam Hussein, Usama bin Laden and Qaddafi were killed without a fair trial, no judge or jury brought down a verdict, in the most undignified manner. Saddam Hussein was hanged the day of the Muslim festival (after a parody of a trial) and his execution was filmed by mobile phone camera. Usama bin Laden was assassinated unarmed with no image to prove his fate. Qaddafi was caught alive, beaten and then executed, with hundreds of people around him taking pictures of his blood-covered face. They were laughing, shouting and even dancing while tearing at his hair and twisting his head to prove it was indeed he. One wonders at this pitiful sight where our humanity has gone. Qaddafi was a tyrant and a dictator, no doubt about it. But as a living human being he had the right to be judged and once dead, his body should have been protected and respected. The coverage of his capture and death and the comments made about him were inhumane, insane, revolting. I did not like Qaddafi; I hated the way his killers—near and far—behaved.

We now know part of the story. He was trying to escape from Sirte with a group of followers when NATO forces located and bombed them. The French forces leading the operation were able to stop the convoy and thereby help Qaddafi's opponents capture him. This was the image of the Libyan uprising: without NATO, the opposition to Qaddafi would not have succeeded. A critical question remains to be answered: what role will foreign influence play in Libya's future? How disturbing to see the Presidents and Prime Ministers, from Nicolas Sarkozy to Barack Obama and David Cameron—who were openly dealing with Qaddafi until last year—greet his death while trying to persuade the public that they had always supported democrats and democracy. In the intoxication of victory there is no shame in profaning the dead, no shame in lying to the living. Libya is under control, they say. But who is controlling Libya?

The National Transitory Council (NTC) cannot be trusted. It is led by a former minister in Qaddafi's regime thought to have had secret connections with American intelligence well before the rebellion. Other high-ranking members of the NTC were also involved in the previous regime, some from the army; some from the Libyan intelligence while others were even identified as extremists. However, it is quite clear that if the NTC received such quick support from the West and the United Nations, it is because the key actors were known to them and because they had received assurances that their interests would be protected. The presence of French, British, American and Turkish leaders in Tripoli, before even the capture of Qaddafi confirms that they were right.

The NTC seems today to have the situation under control—but numerous questions remain unanswered. So much contradictory information is coming from the NTC (about secret agreements with the West, the capture of certain individuals, and even its successes on the ground) and so much inhumane treatment has been witnessed during the fighting (especially against African immigrants), that there is every reason to question the future of Libya as a state founded on transparency and democratic values.

Qaddafi is dead. Libyan people have been shouting and celebrating. A page of a dark era has been turned. Yet the revolution is far from complete. A quick look at Iraq, Egypt or Syria is enough to convince us that powerful economic and geostrategic interests are at play, and that the countries involved are far from autonomous. Libya will be no exception: the United States and the European countries will not let the new regime use its oil resources to develop a dynamic of South-South solidarity in North Africa. Libya is now at a critical juncture; the coming months and years will show whether we have witnessed a revolution in the region or a cynical redistribution of alliances. So indebted are its new leaders to the West that it seems quite impossible to hope for a truly independent future. Such controlled democracies are far from democracies; the way towards complete and real liberation is still filled with challenges.

Watching the images of Qaddafi dead and mistreated was a sad experience. Reading the media coverage and listening to some Western and even Arab leaders celebrating his death and congratulating the Libyans was even more disturbing. Were they celebrating because the dictator was dead or because the road was henceforth open for new strategies of control to be implemented? What was supposed to be a march toward freedom today looks more and more like a path leading to future troubles and new kinds of servitude.

In Star (Turkey) October, 23 2011

## 21  *Playing with Islam*

Over the last few weeks the new Libyan leader, Mustapha Abd al-Jalil, chairman of the Transitory National Council (TNC), has been repeating, "Shari'a will be the main reference and will be implemented in Libya." Several of his references to Islamic legislation came in the presence of Western politicians and intellectuals like the pro-Israel French self-styled philosopher Bernard Henri Levy, who, surprisingly, did not react with any shock whatsoever. Surprising indeed! It was as if Mustapha Abd al-Jalil was determined to show that the "Libyan revolutionaries" were truly independent and not supported or protected by France, the United States, or the West. The "West" kept silent, though some media have asked pointed questions about whom the French, the Americans, and the British were supporting.

Given Libya's extremely complex political situation, Abd al-Jalil's statement was timely and very smart. He referred intentionally to concepts seen as very controversial in the West to make it clear to the Libyan people he was not a Western puppet. In a way that seemed weird to a Western ear, he spoke of "Shari'a" and "polygamy," knowing that for the emotionally wrought Libyan Muslims he was offering proof of his complete independence (such references are of course demonized in the West). For France, Britain and the United States it was a way to show the world that Libya was now "on its own;" time for NATO to allow the new Libya build its future by relying on its own traditions. The religious and political reference to Islam thus serves to appease the Muslims and lend traditional and religious legitimacy to the TNC while concealing the West's tri-dimensional—military, geopolitical and economic—penetration of Libya.

The Arab uprisings are showing that the peoples of the region are drawn to freedom, dignity and justice but are not prepared to betray their traditions and religious beliefs. The recent victory of Tunisia's Islamiist party, an-Nahda, in that country's constituent elections, underlines a historical reality: Islam remains an unavoidable reference for the Arabs and as such will be critical in building the future, especially through the democratic process by which peoples are now able to express their political demands, their concerns about identity and their economic hopes. The conservative parties that invoke Islam in one way or another (hence the Islamists as well) are gaining ground and achieving greater political legitimacy. They are operating on three distinct levels: acceptance of democratic rules, preservation of the nation's Islamic identity and readiness to open their markets to the dominant economic powers and the multinational corporations. The Turkish example has set a precedent: no one can deny that the AKP—coming from an Islamist background—is proving its leadership's success in these very three fields: they are religiously conservative, geopolitically prepared to deal with all the Western powers (including, until recently, Israel), and economically integrated into the dominant capitalist system. They have shown great openness (with the EU) and demonstrated considerable flexibility. The West can indeed do business with any Islamist party that evidences a similar willingness to adapt and to collaborate, from an-Nahda to the Muslim Brotherhood. Things are moving fast in the Middle East and North Africa (MENA); the new political strategies are based on new economic and geopolitical concerns, driven by the active presence of new state actors in the region: Brazil, Russia, India and China (BRIC). The West has no time to waste in the race to win Arab minds, hearts and money.

In these highly complex political and economic games, one issue stands out as crucial. The Western countries have shown in the past (with the petro-monarchies or in Afghanistan) that they have no major problem in dealing with political Islam to protect their interests. Given the presence of the BRIC's countries, they have no choice as the latter are ready to establish strong political and economic ties whatever the situation in the respective Arab countries. The key factor will be Israel. All the Islamist parties have taken strong position against the Zionist state (even Turkey recently), which is the reason for their broad popular support (including the current Iranian regime). The Islamists may well be ready to promote the democratic process and to participate fully in the dominant economic system (the great majority of the Islamist parties accept it today) but they remain quite explicit in their stance against Israel. Here lies the core of the acute tensions and contradictions in the United States and the European countries: they need to be involved in MENA but they cannot distance themselves from Israel. Meanwhile, the BRIC countries do not have the same historical alliance with Israel and they seem ready to challenge the Western bias towards the Middle East conflict.

The Islamic reference is at the heart of the debate in the Arab world. Political Islam is at the crossroad: it faces numerous challenges and must deal with conflicting interests. Only a comprehensive approach can give us a sense of what is at stake. Many trends—even some Islamist parties—are playing with Islam in an attempt to gain legitimacy. There can be no doubt that politics corrupts. Who, in the Arab countries, will be able to hold power while respecting the Islamic imperatives of dignity, justice and transparency—let alone truly supporting the just cause of Palestine?

Published in *Gulf News*, November 1, 2011

## 22 *"Arab Spring": One Success, Many Failures?*

Nobody can deny it: Tunisia is heading towards a better future. After the uprising and the people's rejection of any compromise with the old regime, elections were organized with a high level of transparency. The Islamist party won with more than 40 percent of votes cast and is now poised to play a leading role in the new government. The result—whether we agree with the Islamist political vision or not—shows that the country has freed itself and that the West is no longer controlling Tunisian internal political dynamics. We are witnessing the full achievement of the first Arab uprising: the dictatorship is over; we will never return to the past; Tunisia is free. A success— and an invitation to celebrate what many call the "Arab Spring."

Tunisia is the first—and may well remain the only one. Whichever way we turn in the Middle East and in North Africa, things seem less clear, less successful. In Egypt, the military is still in charge; despite the upcoming election, what we are witnessing looks more like military coup d'état every day. American officials raised the possibility in February when Mubarak left power; it seems they were right. The Americans may have let Mubarak drop but they were never far from the officers and their new power. The people gathered in Midan at-Tahrir were calling for more justice and freedom. Mubarak left and the military regime began to show signs of weakness. Ten months later, it is far from being overthrown. The country is under control and the Supreme Council of the Armed Forces (SCAF) has the upper hand over Egypt's destiny. American influence and presence are proving decisive. Even though, at the end of the process, a civilian such as Mohammed el-Baradei may be elected, the military apparatus would never allow the regime to move too far in the direction of transparency, freedom and democracy. (Try to guess where the Army would stand within the new political structure!). There has been no revolution in Egypt.

The National Transitory Council in Libya has announced it would establish "shari'a" and accept "polygamy," as if to tell the Libyan people that the country would be free of Western influence. Yet behind the scenes, after the NATO intervention, what passes for autonomy is more theoretical than real. The country's economic and the geostrategic relationships with the United States and Europe are an open secret. Qaddafi is dead, yet the country is far from free: a controlled democracy is better than a dictatorship, we are aptly told; still, it remains a democracy under foreign control.

Events seem to be following the same course in Syria, Yemen and even Bahrein. Each country has its own particularities, yet they share the same fate. Popular movements are saying, "enough is enough" to the dictators, but the dynamic has been redirected and the balance of power has shifted. It is not enough to say that the beautiful future will be unlike the ugly past; simply acknowledging the end of the dictators is not sufficient cause for happiness. The key question is that of true political autonomy and genuine freedom in the respective countries. Ultimately, as we analyze the events now unfolding, one legitimate question springs to mind: who will benefit from the Arab uprisings?

The Tunisian experience is perceived as a reference; no one can deny the democratic evolution that has actually brought "moderate Islamists" to power. But the example of Tunisia might play out more as hope, as a potentially misleading example, a distorting screen. The Tunisian "spring" might stop us from seeing other countries clearly. We think of the Arab spring as a movement, a domino effect, while instead it should be seen as a chess game. As you advance your pawn, your knight or your bishop against the dominant political and economic powers, you might sense victory. But the strategic centre of the board, centering on the king and queen, are under close control. Your temporary emotional victory might, in the long term, turn to failure, an unachieved revolution.

Published in *Star* (Turkey) November 22, 2011

## 23 *Egypt at a crossroads*

It is crucial for people to remain non-violent and to hold fast to the philosophy and the spirit of the first Tahrir protest | Tuesday November 29, 2011

These are critical days. Egyptians are gathering in Tahrir Square demanding that the military step down. They want a true and transparent democratic process within which civil society can find its legitimate place and role. It has become clear that this is not exactly the military's intention and vision. After accepting the prime minister's resignation, the ruling junta floated the name of Kamal Ganzouri, a 77-year-old former Hosni Mubarak lieutenant. The simple mention of such a candidate demonstrates how the military is trying to control the situation. Tantawi and his henchmen are simply not ready for, and not willing to support a true democratic transition. From behind the scenes they search for allies, and attempt to conclude agreements to protect themselves and maintain control over the state.

The people who are protesting in Tahrir Square need support. They clearly understand that Egypt is at the crossroads; if true liberation is on the agenda, it is here and now that things are going to be decided. To remove Mubarak was but a first step; now the protesters are facing the regime with its structure, its interests and even its allies. These days they are resisting the less visible and complex forces that lie at the heart of the Egyptian apparatus, domestically and internationally. In doing so, they are not only addressing domestic issues, but also face international challenges connected to the Middle East (the Israeli-Palestinian conflict, western and Asian interests, other popular movements, etc.). It is not going to be easy: after months of non-violent resistance (and the military's apparent restraint), we are now witnessing repression, arrests, torture and killings by both the police and the armed forces. They might apologise but something has changed. It is crucial for the people who continue to protest in Tahrir square to remain non-violent, to hold fast to the philosophy and the spirit of the first demonstrations: no weapons but assertiveness, courage and dignity.

Friday was advertised as the demonstration of "the last chance." We should remain more optimistic, and make an in-depth analysis of the situation in all its complexity. From behind the scenes the military is playing a dirty game that has nothing to do with a potentially democratic future. Some are arguing for patience; it is a transition period, they say. That is partially right—transitions take time, compromise and effort—but this is not exactly what is happening in Egypt. Calls for democracy are heard, promises are repeated (by the junta, announcing it will leave in June), and an election date is set, while negotiations and potential deals are made to share power and interests. The military is a big player; it is in touch with all the significant organisations and trends within Egyptian civil society. Among them is, of course, the Muslim Brotherhood. Tensions within the Islamist organisation are high: some of its leaders are close to the young generation and want to support the protesters by calling for a complete reform of the regime while others (the majority of the current leadership) want to secure their future role within society and are ready to deal with the armed forces to get out of the current situation. They have distanced themselves from the demonstrations and played an ambiguous role between the civil society and the army. On the other hand, it should not be forgotten that the Americans are not far from the negotiations. The Egyptian armed forces are an important ally and, although we hear American calls for the civilians to take over, the US position is far from being clear. A deal between the Army and the Muslim Brotherhood might prove an interesting outcome for the American government. Even more so if they can manage to convince a "civil figure" who can please the street and secure their interests, such as Mohammad ElBaradei, to assume office. The Egyptian spring looks more and more like a cold political calculation within which the people's hopes are secondary, if anything.

Egypt is not Tunisia. From early on, I was pessimistic about the Egyptians following in the footsteps of the Tunisians. They proved me wrong. But the current situation might prove me right again: appearances can be deceiving. There were protests, hopes were high and eventually Mubarak left; but we are far from the Tunisian example. It might be interesting to read the Egyptian situation in the light of what is happening in Syria, Yemen and Libya (where the secret negotiations between the National Transitional Council, the American and European governments give an insight into what is really going on) much more than the situation in Tunisia and even Morocco, where the Islamist party is certainly going to play a new role in the political landscape.

Contradictory forces—domestically and internationally—are playing for time; powerful interests are at stake. In the Middle East, the challenges are many, as are the conflicting interests. Genuine democracies in Egypt, Syria, Libya and Yemen are far from becoming a reality. In fact, genuine democracy is far from being the objective of many of the region's protagonists. The struggle will not be easy. Nevertheless, we should remain consistent and courageous in our support for the civilian populations who refuse to give up.

They are in the streets in Egypt, Syria and Yemen; they have been struggling in Libya. It is imperative to take their side. Innocent people have not been killed in vain: whatever the immediate result of such dirty, behind-the-scenes calculations, something is happening in the Arab world. Today, or tomorrow, there is not only a hope but also a historical truth: Arabs will find their way towards empowerment and freedom. The armed forces, the western or Asian powers, or the political puppets who might secure their immediate interests will not ultimately prevent people from winning their rights and dignity. It is a question of time, and courage. Courage is everywhere in the Arab streets these days.

Published in *Gulf News*, November 29, 2011

## 24 *Understanding the Middle East*

How are we to understand the situation in the Middle East? Things are moving so quickly and in so many different, if not contradictory, directions. The reality has always been complex, but interpreting it has become more and more difficult. The actors involved, the challenges and the interests in conflict are so numerous that one wonders that the result of the popular movements in the region and the political changes currently underway is impossible to foresee. On the one hand, intrinsic domestic dynamics have created a new balance of power, which is having a powerful impact on Egypt, Libya, Yemen and Syria, but also on Tunisia and Morocco. On the other hand foreign countries, such as the United States, Israel, the European countries, China, Russia and even Turkey and Qatar are involved in various ways and in different capacities, either attempting to further the new realities or to try to control them to the fullest of their capacity, according to their ideological, economic and political interests.

In Tunisia, Egypt, Yemen, Bahrain, Libya and Syria, millions of people have been calling for freedom and justice; the first results in Tunisia, Morocco (where some reforms have been granted in order to avoid uprisings) and Egypt are giving the Islamists the upper hand in the political arena. Some suggest that the popular movements have been hijacked, others claim it as the result of a true democratic process: in these Muslim majority countries, the Islamists remain the most popular force: a fact that must be accepted. Like it or not, the Islamists have a historical legitimacy as opponents who have paid a heavy price in opposing dictatorship: prison, torture, exile and executions have punctuated their history over more than half a century. But what is likely to happen in these countries; how will the great powers manage the new situation? It would be childish to think the United States, the European countries, China and Russia as well as Turkey are not involved, in one way or in another, in the discussions (and the political transactions) with the Islamists, the Army and their old allies. Israel will never be a passive spectator in the Middle East: its most powerful ally and staunch supporter, the United States, is working hard to gain some control over the situation. What is the nature of any potential agreement between both the Western and Eastern powers and the respective armies and the Islamists? It was known that these old demonized Islamist parties would win in Tunisia, Morocco and Egypt and nothing has been done to prevent them from emerging as the leading political forces. Why?

The Islamists have changed. They have always been very pragmatic (from Morocco to Egypt and Asia all the way through Palestine) and able to adapt to new political challenges. They know the balance of power is shifting in the Middle East and they deal with it accordingly. Yet they are facing contradictory expectations: they must remain faithful to the "Islamic credentials" that brought them to power and face foreign pressure that is testing their flexibility on respect for the democratic processes, their economic outlook and their attitude towards Israel. While the Turkish example is interesting, it cannot be a reference in the Middle East. It is not the same history, the actors are not the same, nor are the challenges. The Islamists in the Arab world, while happy to win successive elections, may well be entering a far more sensitive period of their history. They may lose the Islamic credibility they had as opposition forces or be obliged to change and adapt so much to the political context that the substance of their political program is abandoned, or reduced to the form of a less corrupt regime with formal Islamic features. Winning might be the beginning of loss.

What is happening in the Middle East is critical and complex, and it is clearly a turning point. From behind the scenes, Libya's future is being decided by potential new leaders and by the Western powers that supported military intervention. Transparency is far from being a reality: the so-called "humanitarian intervention" was motivated by geostrategic objectives that are now fully visible. What we knew, we are now witnessing. Nobody knows what the future of Syria will be: the population refuses to give up; thousands of civilians have been killed by the dictatorial regime. Israel, The United States, European countries and Iran have tried to avoid dealing with a regime change. There seems to be no alternative however. This is where the complexity of the Middle East is confusing with so many conflicting parameters. If the Syrian regime falls, its regional ally Iran would paradoxically become either a danger or an easier target as the balance of power and alliances shifts. The recent campaign against Iran must be read in this context. It started with the Saudis asking the American "to cut off the snake's head," followed by the alleged assassination attempt in the United States (we are ask to believe Iran wanted to kill the Saudi Ambassador in New York), and then using the attack on the UK embassy in order to create an international coalition against Iran. Iran, meanwhile, is operating on multiple levels and has a multidimensional strategy: to secure domestic support and to establish reliable ties in the region as well as internationally. The knot is tightening and the situation is increasingly worrisome for the current regime. Despite the lack of domestic freedom and transparency, Iran still has some allies and some powerful assets. Are we going to see internal democratic and popular forces mobilizing to change the regime or will it become a new war front? The picture is far from clear.

Whatever the future in a Middle East in the throes of political upheaval, the new political players will all be assessed by the "international community" on the basis of three criteria: what kind of economic system and rules do they accept; what is their position towards Israel; and, eventually, where do they stand in relation to the Shia-Sunni divide in the Muslim majority countries. Understanding the Middle East means keeping these three factors in mind. On some issues Islamists might be more flexible than anticipated (except for the Palestinian-Israeli conflict) while the geography of the Middle East is changing radically. Yet, inside or outside politics, Muslims should face the cruel reality: their main challenge is in their internal conflict and especially the Shia-Sunni divide (and unhealthy competition). This is one of the most critical questions of our time: one cannot blame one's enemies for being too strong when one is directly responsible for one's own weaknesses.

Published in *Star* (Turkey) December 6, 2011

## 25 Egypt: A Complex Equation

It is not easy to assess what is really happening in Egypt. After the first round election results, all hypotheses remain possible; the outcome is unpredictable. The two Islamist parties, Freedom and Justice representing the Muslim Brotherhood and Al Nour, representing the Salafists, have emerged as the main political forces in Egypt, giving rise to questions about the nature of the future state.

Things are moving rapidly and many elements are surprising, unclear and even unknown: it is difficult to identify not only the protagonists but also the new alliances that are taking shape at this historical turning point.

In less than six months, the Salafist movement has completely changed its ideological and religious position toward "democracy." Their leaders had been repeating for years that "democracy" was not Islamic, that it was even kufr (rejection of Islam), and that true Muslims should not take part in elections— or in politics at all—as the whole system is corrupt to its very foundations.

Then, suddenly, the Salafists set up a party, started to be active everywhere in the country, producing leaflets and booklets, calling the people to vote for them and, if not, at least for the Brotherhood. Their 180-degree turnabout was as quick as it was surprising and curious. How could they now declare to be Islamically legitimate what only yesterday they called kufr? How can they ask the people to vote for the Brotherhood who they constantly criticised, almost from the beginning, as being too far from "true Islam," too open to harmful innovations (bida), and, in a nutshell, too "westernised and modern?" Why are the Salafists changing so dramatically?

It is not the first time we have observed such changes among the more literalist and traditional Islamic organisations. In the mid-nineties in Afghanistan and Pakistan, the Taliban refused to consider political involvement; for them it was Islamically wrong. In less than eight months, they organised themselves into one of the main forces in Afghanistan and got involved politically.

We later learned that they had been pushed into that position under Saudi pressure (even though the Saudis considered the Taliban to be following a distorted Islamic school of thought) in response to American strategy in the region.

The Americans have never had a problem in dealing with the more literalist Islamist trends. On the ground, in Afghanistan, as today in Egypt, the Salafists are playing a contradictory game: they have adopted a completely new—for them—Islamic position, while in practice they work for the very interests (such as those of the US) that they reject and demonise in theory.

The same scenario may well be unfolding in Egypt today.

The problem with the Salafists and the traditionalists (such as the Taliban) is not only their interpretation of Islam (literalist, narrow-minded and often obdurate) but also the potential use that can be made of their presence in political terms. No one can deny they can be (and very often are) religiously sincere. At the same time, they are politically naive and easy to manipulate. This became clear in Afghanistan and may hold true in Egypt again.

The world is looking at the first-round election results, and concluding that the two Islamist parties account for almost 60 percent of the vote (as there should be a natural alliances between the two). That might be a completely wrong interpretation. It is possible that the Al Nour party may have another role to play in the Egyptian equation. Supported, ideologically and financially, by the Saudi government, it may emerge as one of the actors of America's Egypt strategy.

Al Nour would be a tool to weaken the Brotherhood's influence and power by forcing it into risky alliances. If the Brotherhood chooses to conclude a pact with the literalists it will very quickly lose its credibility and put itself at odds with its proclaimed reformist agenda. If it decides to avoid the Salafists, it would have no alternative but to consider an alliance with other political forces (which are very weak) and mainly the military, which remains very powerful.

The Brotherhood decided to contest only 40 percent of the electoral positions and not to contest the presidency. It announced it would be an active and key political force but would avoid exposing itself. This strategy was a way to appease the West and to avoid losing its credibility, as it would be acting in a more discreet mode.

The Brotherhood now finds itself in a very tricky, and for it, quite a dangerous, position. Al Nour may become the strongest enemy of the Brotherhood and the objective ally of the military. On the ground, the two Islamist parties invoke the same references and promote several common objectives; in reality they represent quite distinct political forces and visions.

Over the years, the Brotherhood has shown how pragmatic it can be: evolving with history, adapting its strategy and diversifying its contacts (Saudi Arabia, the US, the European countries, the emerging countries, etc). It seems it will not be possible for the Brotherhood to avoid dealing, one way or another, with the military.

There were rumours of an agreement but nothing was clear: now it seems such an agreement is quite unavoidable. This is what the US government, which is maintaining close links with the generals, is working for in order to keep some control over the situation.

A civilian face such as Mohammad Al Baradei (also close to the Americans contrary to what is said) might be democratically elected later, yet true power will be elsewhere.

Despite what we have witnessed over the last few weeks, it would be better to suspend judgement and remain cautious in our conclusions. Egypt is a critical country in the Middle East and neither Israel nor the US will remain passive onlookers when the Egyptians choose the Brotherhood, whose ideology is the same as Hamas's (when it comes to the Palestinian-Israeli conflict).

Some other regional actors, which do not really care about democracy, such as the monarchies, are playing a key role in neutralising the Islamist forces. And, in any event, these forces still have much to prove; no one knows whether they will keep their promises when in charge.

The way towards democracy in Egypt is far from transparent; we should avoid taking appearances for realities. Islamists might work against Islamists just as a democratic western government might support a non-democratic military apparatus. This is politics; we must remain vigilant even in our optimism. Religious or not, sincerity in politics is never enough.

Published in *Gulf News* December 15, 2011

## 26  Pondering over 2011

It was a strange year, full of unexpected events. The world is changing quickly. For centuries and decades there has been talk of the "world order," the "global economic system," the "relationships (clashes or alliances) between (organised and structured) civilizations." But are these ways of looking at and describing the world still relevant? Since 2008 the economic downturn has undermined the old order; it is impossible to tell if there is still a foundation, or even a shared economic paradigm, to which we can still refer. The traditional political power relationships seem scattered, while "the West," "Islam," or "Confucianism," as civilizations, seems to be under siege. The shared feeling is one of "doubt, fear and insecurity;" the common and natural reaction is to seek protection and reassurance in a sense of belonging. Some fall into a victim mentality, creating an "other" who epitomizes all threats, real and imagined. In the midst of apparent global chaos, to create one's universe, an "us" to belong to, brings comfort. Things could be summarized thus: in 2011, people have been searching for an "us," a space and a meaning they can connect with. People, East and West, North and South, have been driven by ill-defined hopes much more than by structured ideologies.

In March, the earthquake and the tsunami in Japan—which killed more than 15,000 people—reminded us that, beyond our narrow and nationalistic concerns, there are transnational realities that must be dealt with. Nuclear power stations are fragile; the energy they generate is potentially dangerous. The whole world is affected. The floods in Thailand and global warming (felt everywhere) are signs that beyond our specific identities, nations, our civilizations, we have common challenges that we must face together. Global chaos requires communication, synergy, and courageous, concerted political actions. But there is no sign of political courage on the horizon.

The global economic crisis has affected all countries. In some, governments fell without the citizens being consulted. New unelected technocrats have taken over in Greece and Italy and bond rating agencies are express opinions and make decisions that have an impact on the political life and destiny of each and every industrialized country. No President, no Prime Minister, no political party seems able to handle these new realities on their own: transnational dynamics are imposed on the United States, as much as on Russia, China or the emerging nations of South America and Asia. While people are looking for an "us" (something to belong to) the world is revealing our complete "interdependence": "us" is nothing without "you," "them"; the global us.

People in the streets of Spain, Greece, London, New York, etc., from the transnational *Occupy movement*, are calling for more justice, transparency and true democratic procedures. They feel alienated, disrespected; their social benefits and rights are slowly being eroded and lost. They do not see a future beyond the chaos and they realise that only few people and institutions are deciding their future far from any democratic process. What is the point to vote if neither the citizens nor the elected people have an effective say on the final decisions. Who then is guiding us?

The Western protests echoed the uprisings in MENA. In Tunisia, Egypt, Libya, Yemen, Bahrain and Syria people have been saying no to dictators. They call for social justice, dignity and democracy—the same democracy that is now being questioned, mistrusted and more and more often betrayed in the West. This is a transnational movement, some call it "an Arab spring," yet the awareness and the claims remain very nationalistic. Tunisians for Tunisia, Egyptians for Egypt, and so on and so forth: liberating national movements are creating this protective "us" for a while. But for a while only. Soon, in Libya, Egypt and Syria the regional and global challenges will be revealing the ultimate socioeconomic truth: to free a country is not enough; it is nothing, in fact, if the underlying economic power relationships are not challenged, reformed or simply rejected outright. A political so-called spring can lead to a cold economic winter. The streets of the South should listen carefully to those of the North and vice-versa: their "us" needs "them." A true liberating movement must merge the hopes of the former and the disillusionments of the latter in order to produce a realistic alternative.

2011 has revealed much. While the oppressed remain oppressed, and while the Palestinians are still forgotten, we must remain positive and full of energy. Peoples across the globe are saying "No;" they want to be treated with dignity. They might not know how to build a better future but the first step is to stand up and to speak out. Let us hope 2011 will prove to have been a year of transition: beyond the Occupy movement, the Arab awakening, confronting the global environmental and economic crises—we can only hope peoples will understand how interconnected their fates have become. Paradoxically, in our global world, there will be no freedom for one country if all countries fail to understand their mutual dependence. The South's dreams are connected to the North's resistant dynamics as much as the Japanese nuclear threat is related to our survival. Our world needs, beyond our scattered hopes, a new transnational ideology. Our narrow "us" needs a new global "us," for the sake of "our" unique humanity.

Published in *Gulf News* January 8, 2012

## 27 *The Salafi Equation*

As we observe political developments in both West and North Africa as well as in the Middle East, it is critical to take full account of the "Salafi equation," which may well prove to be one of the most significant religious and political challenges of the coming years. One year after the Arab awakening, Salafi organizations and political parties are playing an increasingly active role throughout the MENA region. The Saudi and Qatari Salafi organizations are very active domestically and internationally. They support other Salafi groups around the world, in West Africa (Senegal, Mali, Niger, Nigeria, etc.), in North Africa (Morocco, Algeria, Tunisia) as well as across the Middle East and Asia (Egypt, Lebanon, Indonesia, Malaysia, etc.) up to and including the European and American countries.

Their support is primarily ideological and financial, aimed at spreading a specific message of Islam with books, brochures, lectures and the building of mosques and institutions.

All Salafi organizations share a highly literalist approach to the scriptural sources, generally focusing on the visible dimensions of the Islamic references (rules and jurisprudence, fiqh) in daily life: licit or illicit behavior (halal and haram), dress codes, rituals, etc. The literalist Salafi approach is gaining ground in many countries (even in the West) and among young people as it promotes a simple black-and-white (halal-haram) understanding of Islam. Muslims, they argue, must isolate themselves from the corrupt surrounding societies, and avoid involvement in politics. This binary vision of the world (Muslims versus the others, the good versus the bad, protected religious purity versus corrupting political involvement) has shaped over the years a religious mindset based on isolation, defensiveness and sharp judgments (who is within Islam and who is a dangerous innovator, or even outside the faith). The great majority of Salafis have gone no further and a very tiny minority (in closed and marginalized networks), with the same binary mindset, has transformed the defensive attitude into assertively aggressive and sometimes violent political activity, styling themselves as jihadi Salafists (as-salafiyya al-jihadiyya). There are clearly no ideological and organizational links between the literalist Salafis and the jihadi Salafists but the latter have carried into the activist political realm the same mindset found among the literalists with regard to questions of behavior (adding to it the justification of violence towards non-Islamic and "corrupt" regimes).

But in recent years and months we have seen a change in Salafi literalist political involvement. Having for decades refused political participation—equating democracy with kufr (rejection of Islam)—they are now slowly engaging in politics. Afghanistan, in the nineties, was a crucial laboratory where the Taliban (traditionalists who were first opposed to political participation) became the main force of resistance to Russian domination, supported by both the Saudi and the US governments. Now we see, especially in Egypt and Tunisia, the rise of active and quite efficient literalist Salafi organizations and political parties which are playing a substantial role in structuring debates and reshaping the political balance within the respective countries.

The United States as well as the European countries have no problem in dealing with the type of Islamism promoted by the literalist Salafism found in many petromonarchies: these regimes might oppose democracy and pluralism, but they do not hinder the Western economic and geostrategic interests in the region and internationally. They even rely on the Western support to survive: this useful dependency is enough for the West to justify an objective alliance—with or without democracy.

The US administration and other European countries are fully aware that Salafi organizations, based in Saudi Arabia, in Qatar or elsewhere in the Middle East, are pouring millions into "liberated countries" and especially recently in Tunisia, Libya and Egypt (a RAND report has mentioned an impressive figure: 80 millions USD invested before the elections for Egypt alone). Why, one wonders, do the Western countries lend direct and indirect support to Islamist ideologies that are so obviously at odds with their own? After almost one century of active presence in the Middle East, and especially after World War I, successive American administrations and their European counterparts have better understood how they can manage and take advantage of their relationships with both the petromonarchies and the Salafi ideology they produce and propagate.

The benefits are threefold: 1. The petromonarchies and their Salafi ideology are first and foremost concerned with political power and religious credibility. They focus—in a conservative and rigid way—on political appearances and social and juridical details; but from an economic standpoint they are liberals, capitalists who care little about the Islamic ethical reference within the neo-liberal world economic order. Indeed, they are pushing it even further. 2. Promoting the Salafi trends within Muslim majority societies helps both to create divisions from within these societies and to prevent the potential reformist trends and movements critical of Western policies (reformist Islamists, leftists or even some traditional Sufi circles) from gaining immediate and natural religious credibility, and even a strong majority within their societies. Instead of being confrontational (which, on the contrary, would unite the Muslims), the most efficient strategy for the West is to divide the Muslims on religious grounds: in other words to transform the natural diversity among Muslims into an effective and useful tool for division. 3. The Salafi resurgence is creating trouble and tension within the Sunni tradition and between Sunni and Shiite Muslims as well, as the latter are considered as deviant by the literalists. The Sunni-Shiite fracture in the Middle East is a critical factor in the region especially in the light of Western and Israeli threats against Iran and the ongoing repression in Syria. The divide is deep even with regard to the Palestinian resistance, which for years had been a unifying legitimate struggle among Muslims. Now division is the rule, within and without, as Salafi activism (which does not care so much about the Palestinian cause) deepens among the Sunni as well as between Sunnis and the Shiites.

This strategic alliance with the Salafi literalists, on both religious and political grounds, is critical for the West as it is the most efficient way to keep the Middle East under control. Protecting the petromonarchies as well as their religious ideology while dividing any potential unifying political forces (such as alliances between secular and reformist Islamists or a popular front against Israeli policy) necessitates undermining the Muslim majority countries from within. The countries of the new Middle East, as well as those of North and West African, are facing serious dangers. The religious factor is becoming a critical one and if the Muslims, the scholars, the religious and political leaders, are not working for more mutual respect, unity and accepted diversity, it is quite clear there will be no successful Arab or African spring. The Muslims and their internal mismanagement and weaknesses will be exploited to protect Israel on the one hand and to compete with China and India on the other. Muslim majority countries should seek to exist as independent societies that no longer serve cynical concealed objectives. Muslims must decide, lest they end up divided by the very religion that calls upon them to unite.

Published in *Gulf News*, March 20, 2012

## 28  Egypt Goes to the Polls

If the Middle East is a complex region, Egypt is quite a complicated country. For more than a year now the entire world, and Egyptians in particular, have witnessed a major social upheaval. The masses have arisen, driven Moubarak from power and touched off a profound sense of arousal among peoples throughout the Arab world and far beyond. It was possible, they proved, to overthrow a despot, influence the course of events, and join forces in writing a fresh page in history.

No one can deny the urge for renewal, the awakening, and the newfound awareness. Whichever forces helped train the bloggers and the cyber-dissidents, whatever the foreign and domestic pressure, this new sense of collective awareness represents the best of the movements that have re-made the Middle East. But we must not be overcome by the optimism generated by the popular uprisings and rush to conclusions without an in-depth analysis of what is at stake economically and geopolitically on a national and regional scale. Since the uprisings began in 2010, I have warned that the forces that spurred on and supported them were neither spontaneous nor disinterested. Developments in each country, from Tunisia to Syria by way of Egypt, have born me out: we must remain prudently optimistic.

Egypt's presidential election has been particularly revealing. Recent parliamentary elections proved surprising, given the first-place finish by the Muslim Brotherhood and the even more startling emergence of a Salafi party, an-Nour, as a strong second. The country's new constitution has not yet been written; the committee responsible for drafting it has been all but dissolved. Candidates were often approved, and then rejected based on procedures that were far from clear and transparent. Political parties and individual candidates avoided polemics so as not to poison the atmosphere despite accusations that former regime holdouts and even the Armed Forces were tampering with the rules behind the scenes.

It was to be "Egypt's first free election." A dozen candidates faced off in the first round, with four among them seen as serious contenders: two, more or less, close to the autocratic regime, Amr Moussa and Ahmad Shafiq, and two Islamists, more or less, linked with the Muslim Brotherhood, Muhammad Morsi and Abd al-Mun'im Abul Futuh. Opinion polls and predictions presented one or the other as front-runner or second-place finisher. No one apparently was able to predict the winner. Strange alliances emerged: the Salafi party threw its weight behind Abul Futuh, even though he is considered "much more liberal" rather than Morsi. The role of the Salafis in the electoral process remains murky (since even before the Parliamentarian elections). Much was made of Amr Moussa, as though he represented the only secularist alternative while Ahmad Shafiq, who had actually already governed the country, was "forgotten." It is difficult to get a clear reading of the facts.

The scenario that appears to be unfolding could prove to be quite attractive for the former regime and the Armed Forces, whose economic and political clout remain determinant. The defeat of Abul Futuh, the candidate favored by the younger generation of Islamists and the bloggers who had originally supported Muhammad al-Baradei, and the disappearance of Amr Moussa, a secularist who might have proven difficult to control, has handed them an interesting situation, paradoxical though it might seem at first glance. A victory for the Muslim Brotherhood candidate, with Ahmad Shafiq close behind may well present them with the two best short or long-term options.

They could well brandish the specter of Islamism, and mobilize Egypt against the threat of Muslim Brotherhood control of both parliament and presidency. The Brotherhood could well lose the election to a representative of the old regime committed to protecting the interests of the oligarchy. Or, it could experience, in the long term, a loss of credibility in the exercise of power. There is little reason to believe that a Turkish-type outcome—modeled on the AKP's successful integration into the capitalist system—will come about in Egypt. The two countries cannot be compared, on economic terms, and with regard to regional issues such as the Israeli-Palestinian conflict and relations with the other Arab countries (from the petromonarchies to Syria and Yemen, not to mention the Sunni-Shia divide).

The Arab uprisings have not yet established political transparency. Political maneuvering, back stabbing and power seeking continue to be the rule; the hopes and aspirations of the people are barely considered, let alone respected. The road will be long, and today's apparent winners will not necessarily be those who we expect. The sense of awareness that has been awakened throughout the Arab world must not allow itself to be lulled to sleep. If indeed a revolutionary process is underway (though clearly incomplete), today it must muster its power of resistance and change. Nothing definitive has as yet been achieved; manipulation will continue. To those who believe Egypt's presidential vote will settle all outstanding questions, we say that these dangerous illusions must be discarded. It is precisely because Egypt is a great country deeply caught up in the main issues of the day that politicians and intellectuals, true democrats with demonstrated ethical credibility and determination are needed and must come to the fore.

The situation is critical. Without the awareness and courage needed to reject meddling, it may well be that the country's presidential election turn out to be less a new chapter in a democratic future than an old chapter complete with a stage-managed outcome. The worst possible result, after the fall of the dictatorship, would be an ostensibly democratic solution featuring real-life political figures on stage, playing out—while playthings—a production designed by a handful of economic and military operatives, foreign and domestic, who have learned from history that it is possible to deceive people with well-chosen words, by pandering to their illusions or exploiting their fears. The game is far from won in Egypt; that much is certain.

Published in *Gulf News* May 29, 2012

# Notes

## INTRODUCTION

1. www.tariqramadan.com (in English and French)

## CHAPTER 1

1. As it is repeated by Western analysts close to the "Reseau Voltaire" (www. voltairenet.org/en).
2. In his 1947 essay *What Is Literature?* or *Baudelaire*, where revolt implies opposing a system that holds power and thereby confirms the meaning of revolt, while revolution aims to bring down the system it opposes.
3. Statement by US President Barack Obama, February 10, 2011: "What is absolutely clear is that we are witnessing history unfold. It is a moment of transformation that is taking place because the people of Egypt are calling for change." See *AFP* video: www.youtube.com/watch?v=5NmhjL23d4I.
4. BBC article, November 6, 2003: http://news.bbc.co.uk/1/hi/world/middle_East/3248119.stm.Reagan said: "Sixty years of Western nations excusing and accommodating the lack of freedom in the Middle East did nothing to make us safe—because in the long run, stability cannot be purchased at the expense of liberty. As long as the Middle East remains a place where freedom does not flourish, it will remain a place of stagnation, resentment and violence ready for export."
5. The website CyberDissidents.org has been releasing reports about these trainings. A conference on Cyberdissidents took place in Dallas (April 19, 2010) organized by the George W. Bush Center and Freedom House (www.bushcenter.com/.../cyber-dissident-conference).
6. See his account on the Trustmedia website www.trust.org/trustmedia/multimedia/video-and-audio/detail.dot?mediaInode=31e1ea0a-bc95–429f-839f-e006faad3342 and the article about the relations with the Middle East: "La révolution pacifique serbe, modèle pour la jeunesse égyptienne" (The peaceful revolution in Serbia, a model for Egypt's youth), www.lesinrocks.com/actualite/actu-article/t/60772/date/2011–03–05/article/la-revolution-pacifique-serbe-modele-pour-la-jeunesse-egyptienne/.

7. "People & Power" broadcast February 9, 2011. In it, Adel confirms his visit to Belgrade. www.youtube.com/watch?v=QrNzodZgqN8&feature=playe r_Embedded#at=11.

8. Links exist between the Albert Einstein Institution and Otpor: Otpor members were trained beginning in spring 2000 by a former US Army colonel, Robert Helvey. See his interview in a Belgrade newspaper, published in January 2001 after the ouster of Milosević www.aforcemorepowerful.org/films/bdd/story/otpor/ robert-helvey.php.

9. Confirmed by Wikileaks notes reporting the January 2010 arrests in Egypt of people returning from training in the United States. Israa Abdel Fattah, a young woman belonging to the April 6 Movement and the al-Ghad party, attended the training course given by Freedom House (Project on Middle East Democracy program) with six other Egyptian bloggers and activists. In 2008, she had already made the headlines by drawing 70,000 on Facebook calling for a general strike on April 6 of that year, www.wikileaks.ch/cable/2010/01/10CAIRO99.html. Freedom House makes no secret of being funded by the United States Agency for International Development (USAID) and the State Department.

10. http://samibengharbia.com/2010/09/17/the-internet-freedom-fallacy-and-the-arab-digital-activism/.

11. In his article, Sami Ben Gharbia, aware of those facts, stresses the need to reject what he terms dangerous alliances and support: http://samibengharbia.com/2010/09/17/the-internet-freedom-fallacy-and-the-arab-digital-activism/.

12. Lina Ben Mhenni was among the individuals nominated for the 2011 Nobel Peace Prize. France Inter, Comme on nous parle program, 14 June 2011, www.franceinter.fr/em/comme-on-nous-parle/106013.

13. "Comme on nous parle," France-Inter, June 14, 2011, www.franceinter.fr/em/comme-on-nous-parle/106013.

14. The United States did not officially ask Bashar al-Assad to step down until six months after the uprisings began, on August 18, 2011, on the same day as France, Germany, and the United Kingdom. *Le Point*, 18 August 2011: www.lepoint.fr/monde/syrie-barack-obama-demande-a-bachar-el-assad-de-demissionner-18–08–2011–1363883_24.php.

15. Read Steve Cool, *Ghost Wars: The Secret History of the CIA, Afghanistan, and Bin Laden, from the Soviet Invasion to September 10, 2001*, New York: Penguin Press, 2004.

16. *Afrik* magazine, January 31, 2011, which quotes reports from several agencies: "Egypte: Israël soutient Hosni Moubarak" (Egypt: Israel supports Hosni Mubarak), www.afrik.com/breve27166.html.

17. Islamic slogans were not translated or referred to in Western media while the Islamic reference was always present in the Arab media coverage.

18. See my "Responsabilités historiques: La démocratie maintenant!" *Le Monde*, February 12, 2011, www.tariqramadan.com/Historical-Responsibilities.html.

19. See page 67.

20. I will return to this point at the end of the book.

21. Edward W. Said, *Orientalism*, New York: Random House, 1978.

22. Lecture at the Collège de France, "De la part des peuples sémitiques dans l'Histoire de la civilisation," du 23 février 1862, BNF, Paris 1995, p. 27.

23. Ibid., p. 17.

24. The term "Islamism" was used for Islam in the nineteenth century.

25. Ernest Renan and Henriette Psichari, *Œuvres complètes*, vol. 1, Calmann-Lévy, 1961, my translation, p. 957.

26. Samuel Huntington, *The Clash of Civilizations and the Remaking of World Order*, New York: Simon & Schuster, 1996.

27. Francis Fukuyama, *The End of History and the Last Man*, New York: Free Press, 1992.

28. For instance, well-known Sheikh Yusuf al-Qaradawi stated in a Friday sermon in Qatar (October 29, 2010) that he had long considered Kipling's claim to be wrong, but that over time and considering Western policies in the Middle East in particular he now tended to think it was true and supported by facts. See *Financial Times*, www.ft.com/cms/s/0/01d19166-fd65-11df-a049-00144feab49a. html#axzz1U6fccZ2p.

29. While forgetting, of course, decades of support for the most bloodthirsty of Arab dictatorships, in blatant contradiction with values preached both past and present.

30. Which is to be achieved, with no particular festivity, in the world order of the triumphant neo-liberal economy: a single civilization; a single common market.

31. Lecture at Beirut American University, April 1, 2011. Contrary to Emma Talon's report on the evening, the majority of the audience did not support Nasser Weddady, whose position was revealed to be marginal. Critical discourse *can* actually be heard in the Arab world, and more and more so.http://blogs.mediapart. fr/blog/emma-talon/210411/revolutions-arabes-quand-tariq-ramadan-franchit-la-ligne-rouge.

32. Jacqueline O'Rourke, *Representing Violence: Jihad, Theory, Fiction*, PhD dissertation, University of Newfoundland, Canada, September 2011. See the entire first chapter.

## CHAPTER 2

1. See Chapter 1.

2. See analysis by Srdja Popović, www.trust.org/trustmedia/multimedia/video-and-audio/detail.dot?mediaInode=31e1ea0a-bc95-429f-839f-e006faad3342.

3. He died of his wounds on January 4, 2011.

4. Vincent Geisser et Labri Chouikha, "Tunisie: la fin d'un tabou. Enjeux autour de la succession du président et dégradation du climat social," *L'Année du Maghreb*, VI,

Paris, CNRS-Éditions, 2010. See also "Tunisie: les coulisses de l'après Ben Ali," www. tunisiefocus.com/201101242947/politique/international/tunisie-les-coulisses-de-lapres-ben-ali.html).

5. Delphine Minoui, "Dans les coulisses du départ précipité de Ben Ali," *Le Figaro*, January 24, 2011. English translation: www.worldcrunch.com/behind-scenes-ben-ali-s-final-hours/2369

6. Morjane's involvement was confirmed by a high-ranking French official, *Le Figaro*, January 24, 2011.

7. The Egyptian Armed Forces, which kept in close contact with the American administration and military high command, would adopt exactly the same stance several weeks later.

8. She had to resign for that inappropriate statement (France has been supporting Ben Ali's regime for decades) and for having spent her holidays in Tunisia, paid by the Tunisian government.

9. *Le Figaro*, " www.worldcrunch.com/behind-scenes-ben-ali-s-final-hours/2369.

10. *Le Courrier international*, "Les dernières heures de Ben Ali," January 21, 2011: www. courrierinternational.com/article/2011/01/21/les-dernieres-heures-de-ben-ali. The article confirms the names of those involved in the Tunisian crisis as well as American pressure.

11. Ibid., and D. Minoui, www.worldcrunch.com/behind-scenes-ben-ali-s-final-hours/2369.

12. Reuters, January 14, 2011, 4.13 pm est, www.reuters.com/article/2011/01/14/tunisia-protests-obama-statement-idUSN1418664620110114.

13. http://foreign.senate.gov/press/chair/release/?id=33de444f-e50f-4497-a0bf-db42758b7409.

14. As stated by the members of the movement shown in the documentary produced by al-Jazeera English, "People and Power," aired on February 9, 2011, www.youtube. com/watch?v=QrNzodZgqN8&feature=player_Embedded#at=11

15. Joseph Mayton, "Police Day in Egypt a Troubling Holiday," January 25, 2010, a year before the demonstration: http://bikyamasr.com/wordpress/?p=7901.

16. Mayton, "Police Day," www.youtube.com/watch?v=QrNzodZgqN8&feature=player_Embedded#at=11.

17. See her video in Arabic with English subtitles: www.youtube.com/watch?v=SgjIgMdsEuk. See also her report on Inter Press Service (IPS): "Arab Women Lead the Charge," February 11, 2011 http://ipsnews.net/news.asp?idnews=54439; see also "Asmaaa Mahfouz, a woman behind Egypt's pro-democracy revolution," February 5 2011 (www.thecanadiancharger.com/page.php?id=5&a=774).

18. www.youtube.com/watch?v=SgjIgMdsEuk

19. *Asian Tribune*, February 11, 2011, www.asiantribune.com/news/2011/02/11/history-unfolding-egypt-hosni-mubarak-resigns-transfers-powers-supreme-military-coun.20 *Telegraph*, January 28, 2011, "Egypt Protests: America's Secret

Backing for Rebel Leaders behind Uprising," www.telegraph.co.uk/news/worldnews/africaandindianocean/egypt/8289686/Egypt-protests-Americas-secret-backing-for-rebel-leaders-behind-uprising.html.21*AlMasry Alyoum*, "6th April Waiting for El Baradei" shows a picture of activists holding up the closed fist symbol and a portrait of El Baradei, www.almasryalyoum.com/en/node/17220.

20. Telegraph, January 28, 2011, "Egypt Protests: America's Secret Backing for Rebel Leaders behind Uprising," www.telegraph.co.uk/news/worldnews/africaandindianocean/egypt/8289686/Egypt-protests-Americas-secret-backing-for-rebel-leaders-behind-uprising.html.

21. AlMasry Alyoum, "6th April Waiting for El Baradei" shows a picture of activists holding up the closed fist symbol and a portrait of El Baradei, www.almasryalyoum.com/en/node/17220.

22. *New York Times*, "U.S. Scrambles to Size Up ElBaradei," January 31, 2011, gives a lengthy analysis of the US administration's relations with El-Baradei, www.nytimes.com/2011/02/01/world/middleeast/01elbaradei.html

23. Ibid.

24. Ibid.

25. Ibid.

26. *Foreign Affairs*, "Is El Baradei Egypt's Hero? Mohamed El Baradei and the Chance for Reform," March 26, 2010, www.foreignaffairs.com/articles/66178/steven-a-cook/is-el-baradei-egypts-hero?page=2.

27. Tom Curry, "New Challenges for U.S.-Egyptian Military Ties," February 11, 2011, www.msnbc.msn.com/id/41521234/ns/world_news-mideast_n_africa/t/new-challenges-us-egyptian-military-ties/#.Tj5HqOaidWk.

28. Ibid.

29. Ibid.

30. "Iran's Twitter Revolution," *Washington Times,* June 16, 2009, www.washingtontimes.com/news/2009/jun/16/irans-twitter-revolution/.

31. Kate Allen, UK director of Amnesty International, "Rape in Iran's Prisons: The Cruellest Torture," *Telegraph*, November 1, 2010, www.telegraph.co.uk/news/worldnews/middleeast/iran/8102358/Rape-in-Irans-prisons-the-cruellest-torture.html.

32. "Je combattrai jusqu'à la dernière goutte de sang," Rue89, February 22, 2011,www.rue89.com/2011/02/22/kadhafi-je-suis-a-tripoli-pas-au-venezuela-191416.

33. "Amnesty Questions Claim that Gaddafi Ordered Rape as Weapon of War," June 24, 2011, *Independent*, www.independent.co.uk/news/world/africa/amnesty-questions-claim-that-gaddafi-ordered-rape-as-weapon-of-war-2302037.html.

34. Ghaddafi's privileged relations with Western countries are being gradually revealed by documents found in Tripoli. Britain collaborated closely with the Libyan regime to arrest an opponent who was returned to the dictator, see *Daily Mail*, "Torture," September 6, 2011, and BBC, "Libyan Torture Inquiry Dominates," www.bbc.co.uk/

news/uk-14799224. So did the CIA, see *Le Monde*: "La CIA et MI6 collaboraient avec les services libyens," September 6, 2011. Moreover France, with government support and help from private firms, installed the Internet and telephone monitoring system for the Libyan dictator; see *Libération*: "Kadhafi a espionné les Libyens grâce à la France," September 3, 2011, www.gnet.tn/revue-de-presse-internationale/kadhafi-a-espionne-les-libyens-grace-a-la-france/id-menu-957.html.

35. "Libya Opposition Launches Council," *Al-Jazeera*, February 27, 2011,http://english.aljazeera.net/news/africa/2011/02/2011227175955221853.html.

36. "Libye: Comment la France est entrée en guerre," *Le Journal du dimanche*, March 20,2011,www.lejdd.fr/International/Actualite/Libye-Les-coulisses-de-l-entree-en-guerre-de-la-France-286239.

37. Libyan authorities arrested spies they claimed worked for Moroccan intelligence and Mossad. Cf. "The Libyan Foreign Security Agency Accused Mossad and Morocco of Attempting to Break Algeria, Libya and Tunisia," www.amazighworld.org/eng/news/index_show.php?id=98. ).

38. Information confirmed by several sources, despite denials by the Obama administration. See *New York Times*: "C.I.A. Agents in Libya Aid Airstrikes and Meet Rebels," March 30, 2011, www.nytimes.com/2011/03/31/world/africa/31intel.html.

39. As operations dragged on and NATO blunders multiplied, public opinion slowly shifted to opposing the intervention: *l'Express*, "Une majorité de Français désapprouve l'intervention en Libye," August 8, 2011, www.lexpress.fr/actualites/2/actualite/une-majorite-de-francais-desapprouve-l-intervention-en-libye_1019123.html.

40. See Pierre Péan's fascinating—and sometimes debatable—analysis of the United States' and Israel's role in Africa: *Carnages, Les guerres secrètes en Afrique*, Fayard, October 2010. See also Pascal Boniface's discussion of the book in "Pierre Pean, à contre-courant sur l'Afrique," December 27, 2010, http://pascalbonifaceaffairesstrategiques.blogs.nouvelobs.com/archive/2010/12/27/pierre-pean-a-contre-courant-sur-l-afrique.html.

41. These three countries were among the most hesitant to approve of military intervention against the Libyan regime.

42. http://fr.rian.ru/infographie/20110222/188689447.html.

43. "Pétrole:l'accordsecretentreleCNTetlaFrance,"*Libération*,September1,2011,www.liberation.fr/monde/01012357324-petrole-l-accord-secret-entre-le-cnt-et-la-france.

44. "Dure chasse aux contrats en Libye," *Le Journal du Dimanche*, September 11, 2011.

45. "Gaddafi Tells Palestinians: Revolt against Israel," *Reuters*, February 13, 2011, http://af.reuters.com/article/tunisiaNews/idAFLDE71C0KP20110213?pageNumber=3&virtualBrandChannel=0.

46. See p. 35.

47. "Hugo Chavez and the Arab Spring," June 20, 2011, www.theworld.org/2011/06/hugo-chavez-arab-spring/.

48. Strict control is necessary to hold on to power and maintain order and privileges. Western powers made great use and profit of this during both the colonial and postcolonial eras.

49. See al-Jazeera's English-language website: "Thousands Stage Rally in Bahrain," March 3, 2011, http://english.aljazeera.net/news/middleeast/2011/03/201139175 95654981.html. and the *New York Times,*: "Bahrainis Fear the U.S. Isn't Behind Their Fight for Democracy," March 4, 2011, www.nytimes.com/2011/03/05/world/middleeast/05bahrain.html?_r=1. See also *European Times*: "More than 100,000 Demonstrate in Bahrain," February 23, 2011, www.eutimes.net/2011/02/more-than-100000-demonstrate-in-bahrain/.

50. See Amnesty International report, *Evidence of Bahraini Security Forces' Brutality Revealed,* March 17, 2011, www.amnesty.org/en/news-and-updates/report/evidence-bahraini-security-forces%E2%80%99-brutality-revealed-2011–03–16

51. See Aymane Chaouki's analysis, "L'Occident et le 'printemps arabe': un choix entre Realpolitik et Démocratie," IRIS, March 31, 2011, www.affaires-strategiques.info/spip.php?article4899.

52. Qatar was among the first to join France and had also welcomed regime changes in Tunisia and Egypt.

53. Saudi Arabia's fatwa council, headed by the country's Mufti, issued a fatwa branding street protests anti-Islamic.

54. Support for Palestinian resistance provided Shiites and Sunnis with a common cause. After the revolution in Iran, then the wars in Iraq, and finally the attacks on Lebanon, things have changed. Even Qatar-based Sheikh Yusuf al-Qaradawi referred to sectarian and religious strife to explain the conflict in Bahrain and thus implicitly justify support for the regime: www.dailymotion.com/video/xhs025_qaradawi-la-revolution-au-bahrein-est-sectaire-chiite_news. As if this could justify repressing and discriminating against Shiites!

55. "Sectarian Slants," *al-Ahram Weekly*, March 24–30, 2011, http://weekly.ahram.org.eg/2011/1040/re801.htm.

56. "Bahrain Protests to Qatar over al-Jazeera Film," *Guardian,* August 7, 2011, www.guardian.co.uk/world/2011/aug/07/bahrain-protests-qatar-aljazeera-film.

57. See Appendix 22, "Arab Spring: One Success, Many Failures?"

58. See Appendix 20, "Dead without Trial: Again."

59. American firms are already present in Libya, competing with major French conglomerates (Air France, Alcatel, Alstom, Peugeot, Bouygues or Vinci) that have successfully bid on reconstruction contracts; www.lemonde.fr/libye/article/2011/09/06/la-guerre-en-libye-coutera-320-millions-d-euros-selon-longuet_1568543_1496980.html.

60. See Appendices 19, 23, and 25: "Egypt in Danger," "Egypt: At the Crossroads," and "Egypt: A Complex Equation"; see also www.aljazeera.com/news/middleeast/201 1/12/201112188441092287.html.

61. Egypt's Salafists are anything but monolithic. Some have a national orientation while others are organically connected to Saudi groups and institutions. Influences are numerous, and the about-face of the Salafists (who only eight months earlier labeled participation in politics or working for democracy anti-Islamic) should in my opinion be interpreted in the light of a broader strategy (for instance, to limit Muslim Brotherhood influence in parliament). See also Appendix 25, "Egypt: A Complex Equation."

62. In an interview, one of the founding members of Attac-France and of the international altermondialist movement, Christophe Aguiton, uses the phrase while suggesting a balanced analysis of the role of the Internet, television, and the general state of society: "Les Révolutions à l'ère d'internet," March 9, 2011, http://revolutionarabe.over-blog.com/article-des-revolutions-a-l-ere-d-internet-69217128.html.

63. Manual available online, especially chapters 4 to 9: *Nonviolent Struggle: 50 Crucial Points. A Strategic Approach to Everyday Tactics,* by Srdja Popović, Andrej Milivojević, and Slobodan Djinović, www.canvasopedia.org/legacy/files/various/Nonviolent_Struggle-50CP.pdf

64. The Internet's impact was less substantial in Libya and Yemen; access is even less widespread there than in the above mentioned countries.

65. As France24 reports, the operator oddly claimed it was obliged to do so: "Des SMS pro-Moubarak envoyés 'contraints et forcés' par Vodafone," February 3, 2011, www.france24.com/fr/20110203-vodafone-sms-egypt-pro-moubarak-defense-obligation-mobilnil-etisalet-manifestation-tahrir.

66. Elizabeth Hunter, "The Arab Revolution and Social Media," February 24, 2011, http://flipthemedia.com/index.php/2011/02/the-arab-revolution-and-social-media/.

67. Quoted by Elizabeth Hunter, ibid.; see also Philip Howard, *The Digital Origins of Dictatorship and Democracy: Information Technology and Political Islam,* New York: Oxford University Press, September 21, 2010.

68. "Al-Jazeera's Coverage of Egypt Protests May Hasten Revolution in World News," *Guardian,* February 7, 2011, www.guardian.co.uk/media/2011/feb/07/al-jazeera-television-egypt-protests.

69. Ibid.

70. "Egypt Shuts Down Al-Jazeera Bureau," al-Jazeera, January 30, 2011, http://english.aljazeera.net/news/middleeast/2011/01/201113085252994161.html; also *Le Monde*: "La chaîne Al-Jazira interdite en Égypte," January 30, 2011, www.lemonde.fr/proche-orient/article/2011/01/30/la-chaine-al-jazira-interdite-en-egypte_1472733_3218.html.

71. http://english.aljazeera.net/news/middleeast/2011/02/201126202228183972.html.

72. "A Beirut-Based Newspaper Raises Questions about Al Jazeera's Coverage," April 8, 2011, http://blog.camera.org/archives/2011/04/an_arab_newspaper_raises_quest.html.

73. "Les démissionnaires d'AlJazira créent leur propre chaine: Al-Mayadine," July 29, 2011, www.alterinfo.net/notes/Les-demissionnaires-d-AlJazira-creent-leur-propre-chaine-AlMayadine_b3167055.html.

74. "Les Nouvelles d'Orient, Syrie-Bahreïn, Causes Communes," May 10, 2011, http://blog.mondediplo.net/2011–05–10-Syrie-Bahrein-cause-commune.

75. "Selon le 'Daily Mirror', M. Bush a envisagé de bombarder Al-Jazira," *Le Monde,* November 22, 2005, www.lemonde.fr/ameriques/article/2005/11/22/selon-le-daily-mirror-m-bush-a-envisage-de-bombarder-al-jazira_712792_3222.html.

76. "Hillary Clinton Calls al Jazeera 'Real News', Criticizes US Media," *Huffington Post,* March 3, 2011, www.huffingtonpost.com/2011/03/03/hillary-clinton-calls-al-_n_830890.html, as well as *Business Insider,* "Hillary Clinton Says Al Jazeera Is Putting American Media to Shame," March 2, 2011, www.businessinsider.com/hillary-clinton-al-jazeera-2011–3#ixzz1UoS394AI.

77. The channel's managing director Waddah Khanfar was invited to resign on September 20, 2011. Interpretations are contradictory: the government suspects him of being too close to the Americans (according to a Wikileaks report); or, on the contrary, he may have gone too far in covering events in Syria and Bahrain. He was replaced by a member of the ruling family who was trained and worked in France with Total, as well as in the United States and Britain.

78. Internet surveillance for political and/or economic ends is constant. American firms that aggregate and classify information are the almost exclusive owners of search engines. Social networks permanently monitor, watch, and categorize user profiles. Nonviolent political movements using alternative means of communication are obviously monitored and watched: the only question is to what extent, and what latitude they still possess. For more information seewww.lunil.com/fr/actualite.php?id_article=1027&PHPSESSID=f1d9cab179618fe6daf9b595231824e9.

79. "Bin Laden Is Dead, Obama Says," *New York Times,* May 2, 2011, www.nytimes.com/2011/05/02/world/asia/osama-bin-laden-is-killed.html?_r=1&pagewanted=all.

80. The wildest and most contradictory interpretations have been suggested as to the choice and meaning of that moment. I will stay far from these sterile—and sometimes most counterproductive—debates. Yet it seems important to read this event in light of the United States' internal politics as well as of events on the Arab and international scenes.

81. "Popularity Boost for Obama," *Independent,* May 2, 2011, www.independent.co.uk/news/world/americas/popularity-boost-for-obama-2277896.html; see also "La popularité d'Obama bondit après la mort de Ben Laden," *Le Monde,* May 4, 2011, www.lemonde.fr/mort-de-ben-laden/article/2011/05/04/la-popularite-d-obama-bondit-apres-la-mort-de-ben-laden_1516901_1515627.html.

82. *Huffington Post*: www.huffingtonpost.com/2011/03/03/hillary-clinton-calls-al-_n_830890.html.

83. A well-known example is that of university professor Dr. Sami al-Arian, who has been under house arrest for the past three years in Washington after spending more than five years in jail. With each successive trial the case is losing ground but the "emergency situation" allows outrageous treatment of an activist thinker who never supported terrorism but made the mistake of being too supportive of the Palestinian cause and too critical of Israeli policies. This case is representative of many other instances of unfair treatments (arrests, deportations, etc.).

84. See Appendix 12, "President Barack Obama: Words and Symbols."

85. See Appendix 11, "From Bin Laden to the Arab Springs."

86. "Osama bin Laden Dead: Arab Reaction," *Guardian*, May 2, 2011, www.guardian.co.uk/world/2011/may/02/osama-bin-laden-arab-reaction, and "What the Arab Papers Say," *Economist*, May 7, 2011, www.economist.com/blogs/newsbook/2011/05/osama_bin_ladens_death.

87. "Le choix américain du Qatar," *Le Monde*, 31 March 2003, www.mafhoum.com/press5/139P52.htm.

88. On the US 5th Fleet's website, see the description of its missions and area of responsibility and the address of its Bahrain office: "Commander, U.S. Naval Forces Central Command/Commander, 5th Fleet's area of responsibility encompasses about 2.5 million square miles of water area and includes the Arabian Gulf, Red Sea, Gulf of Oman and parts of the Indian Ocean. This expanse, comprised of 20 countries, includes three critical choke points at the Strait of Hormuz, the Suez Canal and the Strait of Bab al Mandeb at the southern tip of Yemen," www.cusnc.navy.mil/mission/mission.html.

89. "Chomsky: Arab Spring's Threat to Western Colonialism," May 11, 2011, http://forafreeegypt.blogspot.com/2011/05/chomsky-arab-springs-threat-to-western.html.

90. "La Ligue arabe, la Russie et la Chine critiquent l'intervention," *Le Monde*, March 20, 2011, www.lemonde.fr/afrique/article/2011/03/20/la-ligue-arabe-la-russie-et-la-chine-critiquent-l-intervention_1495991_3212.html; and "Arab League Condemns Broad Western Bombing Campaign in Libya," *Washington Post*, March 20, 2011, www.washingtonpost.com/world/arab-league-condemns-broad-bombing-campaign-in-libya/2011/03/20/AB1pSg1_story.html.

91. "Arab League Calls for No-Fly Zone over Gaza," *Reuters*, April 10, 2011, www.reuters.com/article/2011/04/10/us-palestinians-israel-arabs-idUSTRE73923020110410.

92. Turkish Prime Minister Erdoğan's visits to Egypt on September 13, 2011, then to Tunisia, were interesting and revealing. The Turkish government's popular support (due in particular to its firm stance on the Israel-Palestine issue) should not obscure the fact that Erdoğan came with over a hundred entrepreneurs seeking markets and contracts. Turkey's economic health and its regional and strategic weight elicit both awe and concern.

93. H. Rafik.

94. BBC News, 15 April 2000, http://news.bbc.co.uk/2/hi/middle_East/714796.stm.

95. "Israel Censures China over Invitation to Hamas," *Financial Times*, May 19, 2006, www.ft.com/cms/s/o/d8f2b57e-e750–11da-9046–0000779e2340. html#axzz1V54ANzEM.

96. "China Criticizes U.S. over Human Rights, Cites Abu Ghraib," *Seattle Times*, March 4, 2005, http://seattletimes.nwsource.com/html/nationworld/2002196432_china04.html.

97. See the Center for International and Strategic Studies (CSIS) website, program presentation and lead sentence: "At the same time, the Chinese experience of economic growth without significant political liberalization remains an interesting, if not outright attractive, example for some Middle Eastern regimes"; http://csis. org/program/china-middle-east.

98. Ibid.

99. See figures and graph drawn up by the International Monetary Fund in *The Vital Triangle: China, the United States, and the Middle East* (CSIS, 2008), p. 84 (the full book is available in PDF format: http://csis.org/files/media/csis/pubs/080624-alterman-vitaltriangle.pdf). See also Abdulaziz Sager, "Saudi-Chinese Relations: Energy First, but Not Last," *Arab News*, January 23, 2006, http://archive.arab-news.com/?page=7&section=0&article=76692&d=23&m=1&y=2006&pix=0 pinion.jpg&category=Opinion.

100. International Monetary Fund, *The Vital Triangle*, pp. 94–114.

101. "As Middle East Erupts in Protest, India Finds Comfort on the Fence," *Washington Post*, February 18, 2011, www.washingtonpost.com/wp-dyn/content/article/2011/02/18/AR2011021802699.html.

102. About 157 million Indians are Muslims, that is, 13.4 percent of the population. Among those, 50 million are Shiites, that is more than in Iraq: a crucial element in India's involvement in the Middle East.

103. In particular during President Barack Obama's visit and his address to Parliament on human rights and India's relations with China and Burma (see "As Middle East Erupts in Protest").

104. "Arundhati Roy, tornade indienne," interview by Vanessa Dougnac, *Le Soir* (Belgium), May 7, 2011, http://archives.lesoir.be/arundhati-roy-tornade-indienne_t-20110506–01DTUG.html).

105. "Obama's Mideast Speech," *New York Times*, May 19, 2011, www.nytimes. com/2011/05/20/world/middleeast/20prexy-text.html?_r=4.

106. "Obama n'a pas séduit la twittosphère arabe," *Le Monde*, May 20, 2011, http://printempsarabe.blog.lemonde.fr/2011/05/20/obama-na-pas-convaincu-la-twittosphere-arabe/.

107. Debate over the Constitution began, then was momentarily suspended in Tunisia. The role, membership, and voting procedures of the Constituent Assembly gave rise to heated discussion. The notion of male-female parity was also a source of tension. See Isabelle Mandraud: "La Tunisie se débat entre difficultés économiques et tensions politiques," *Le Monde*, April 6, 2011. See also, on Egypt, Mohammed

Mahmud, "Proposed Constitutional Amendments in Egypt Generate Heated Debate," Al-Shorfa.com, March 16, 2011.

108. Isabelle Mandraud, "En Tunisie, le report des élections ne bride pas l'élan démocratique," *Le Monde*, 10 June 2011, and the France24 article: "Coup d'envoi de la campagne électorale du 23 octobre," www.france24.com/fr/20111001-tunisie-election-assemblee-constituante-politique-campagne-electorale-ben-ali.

109. "New Political Parties in Egypt," *World*, April 18, 2011, www.theworld.org/2011/04/egypt-political-parties/ and "Egypt the Day after Mubarak Quits," *Guardian*, February 18, 2011, www.guardian.co.uk/world/blog/2011/feb/12/egypt-day-after-mubarak-quits.

110. Larry Diamond and Marc F. Plattner, eds., *Democratization in Africa (A Journal of Democracy Book)*, Baltimore: Johns Hopkins University Press, 1999, and its critical analysis by Cheikh Fall, "Regard sur l'évolution de la démocratie en Afrique, " www.esspri.net/Regard_sur_l_Evolution_de_la_democratie_En_Afriqu.html.

111. These issues and the terms of debate will be examined more fully in Chapter 3.

112. Vali Nasr, *The Shia Revival: How Conflicts within Islam Will Shape the Future*, New York: Norton, 2006.

113. Ibid., p. 106.

114. "Around the World, Distress over Iran," *New York Times*, November 28, 2010, www.nytimes.com/2010/11/29/world/middleeast/29iran.html.

115. "Mahmoud Ahmadinejad Criticizes Arabs over Gaza Crisis," *European Union Times*, January 5, 2009, www.eutimes.net/2009/01/mahmoud-ahmadinejad-criticizes-arabs-over-gaza-crisis.

116. "Iran, Syrian Leaders Laud Hezbollah 'Victory,'" Associated Press, August 15, 2006, www.msnbc.msn.com/id/14356871/ns/world_news-mideast_n_africa/t/iran-syrian-leaders-laud-hezbollah-victory/#.TktM2WOjw2U.

117. Transcript of Vali Nasr interview, *Shi'a Revival*, Carnegie Council Public Affairs Program, October 18, 2006, www.carnegiecouncil.org/resources/transcripts/5400.html.

118. "By curious accident of history and geography, the world's major energy resources are located primarily in Shiite regions. They're a minority in the Middle East, but they happen to be where the oil is, right around the northern part of the Gulf. That's eastern Saudi Arabia, southern Iraq and southwestern Iran. And there's been a concern among planners for a long time that there might be a move towards some sort of tacit alliance in these Shiite regions moving towards independence and controlling the bulk of the world's oil. That's obviously intolerable." (http://forafreeegypt.blogspot.com/2011/05/chomsky-arab-springs-threat-to-western.html)

119. "Iran Criticizes Saudi Involvement in Bahrain," *Washington Post*, April 6, 2011, www.washingtontimes.com/news/2011/apr/6/iranian-lawmakers-condemn-saudi-action-in-bahrain.

120. "Saudi Switch against Syria's Assad Is Blow to Iran," *Reuters*, August 9, 2011, www. reuters.com/article/2011/08/09/us-saudi-syria-idUSTRE7781QS20110809.

121. See the notes of Menas Associated Limited, November 3, 2008, www.localcontent-online.com/pubsamples/Qatar%20Politics%20and%20Security%20-%20 03.10.08.pdf.

122. See "Rafsanjani and al-Qaradawi Call upon the Nation to Unite and Reject Fighting," Iumsonline.net, February 15, 2007, www.usislam.org/SunniShia/ Al-Qaradawi%20and%20Rafsanjani.htm.

## CHAPTER 3

1. See Edward Said's response after the 9/11 attacks: "There Are Many Islams," CounterPunch.org, 16 September 2001 www.counterpunch.org/saidattacks.html, as well as Robert Bistolfi and François Zabbal, *Islams d'Europe: integration ou insertion communautaire?* Editions de l'Aube, 1995.

2. For my proposed categories, see *Western Muslims and the Future of Islam*, New York: Oxford University Press, 2004, pp. 24–30.

3. For my critique of binary oversimplification, see "Good Muslim, Bad Muslim," *New Statesman*, February 12, 2010, www.newstatesman.com/religion/2010/02/ muslim-religious-moderation. The article can be found in Appendix 1.

4. This is a well-known rule in the field of the "fundamentals of Islamic Law and Jurisprudence" (*usûl al-fiqh*) regarding social affairs (*muâmalât*)

5. Elie Kedouri, *Afghani and 'Abduh*, London: Cass, 1966; and my *Aux sources du renouveau musulman*, Paris: Bayard, 1998; repr. Lyons: Tawhid, 2002.

6. Ramadan, *Aux sources du renouveau musulman*, part 2, chapter 1.

7. Robert Mitchell, *The Society of the Muslim Brothers*, Oxford: Oxford University Press, 1969, and Ramadan, *Aux sources du renouveau musulman*, part 2.

8. Ramadan, *Aux sources du renouveau musulman*, p. 200.

9. Contrary to the claims of some intellectuals who promote a biased rereading of history, while Hassan al-Banna supported the mufti of Jerusalem in opposing the extremist Zionist groups Irgun and Stern, his position on fascism was quite unambiguous: he described it as the dangerous drift of European nationalisms. (See Ramadan, *Aux sources du renouveau musulman*, pp. 357–364.) In contrast, the leaders of the Stern Gang concluded an agreement with Hitler to facilitate the exodus of German Jews to Palestine. See Eugene Rogan, *The Arabs, a History*, New York: Penguin, 2010, pp. 248–250.

10. For al-Banna's speech distinguishing between the Muslim Brothers and more radical Egyptian groups, see Rogan, *The Arabs*, p. 215.

11. Ibid., pp. 204–210.

12. Ibid., pp. 430–438, and François Burgat, *L'islamisme en face*, Paris: La Découverte, 1995.

13. Hassan al-Hudaybi, *Du'at, lâ Qudâ'* (in Arabic), Cairo: Dâr al-Tawzi' wa an-nashr al-Islamiyyat, 1977.

14. For my analysis of the evolution of thought from al-Banna to Qutb, see *Aux sources du renouveau musulman*, part three, chapter 2 ("Se penser minoritaire"), pp. 416–446.

15. See the positions of Yusuf al-Qaradawi since the 1980s and of Rached Ghannouchi, the leader of the Tunisian party Ennahda. See also Azzam Tamimi, *Rachid Ghannouchi: A Democrat within Islamism*, New York: Oxford University Press, 2001.

16. Olivier Roy, "Révolution post-islamiste," *Le Monde*, February 12, 2011. www.lemonde.fr/idees/article/2011/02/12/revolution-post-islamiste_1478858_3232.html.

17. See my, *The Quest for Meaning: Developing a Philosophy of Pluralism*, London: Allen Lane, 2010, pp. 40–51.

18. Initially restricted to men, these ideals were much later extended to women. For example, voting rights were granted women only in the twentieth century in Western countries.

19. Applicable to all secularization processes in Europe or the United States. Although in the United States secularization aimed at protecting religions from state interference (as opposed to France), the parallel introduction of democratization and pluralism was everywhere experienced as the direct, almost automatic result of the secularization process.

20. Thierry Zarcone, *La Turquie. De l'Empire ottoman à la République d'Atatürk*, Paris: Gallimard, 2005, pp. 68–75 and 138–140; Paul Dumont, *Mustafa Kemal invente la Turquie moderne*, Brussels: Complexe, 1983, repr. 2006.

21. Zarcone, *La Turquie*, p. 131.

22. President Habib Bourguiba's speech to the Turkish parliament, *Le Monde*, March 27, 1965. See also Alexandre Jevakhoff, "Le kémalisme, cinquante ans après," *Centre d'études sur la Méditerranée orientale et le monde turco-iranien*, no. 8, July–December 1989, p. 4, www.ceri-sciencespo.com/publica/cemoti/textes8/jevakhoff.pdf.

23. Augustin Jomier, "Laïcité et féminisme d'État: le trompe-l'œil tunisien," *LaViedesidees*, April 12, 2011, www.laviedesidees.fr/Laicite-et-feminisme-d-État-le.html#nb9.

24. Habib Bourguiba, "Les nations ne durent qu'autant que durent leurs valeurs morales," Tunis: State Secretariat for Information, August 13, 1973.

25. Jomier, "Laïcité et féminisme d'État."

26. François Burgat, *L'Islamisme au Maghreb: la voix du Sud*, Éditions Karthala, 1988, and Jomier, "Laïcité et féminisme d'État."

27. Quoted in Jomier, "Laïcité et féminisme d'État." See France Info website: www.france-info.com/chroniques-les-invites-de-france-info-2011-01-18-si-nous-ne-devions-parler-qu-aux-regimes-democratiques-nous-ne-509768-81-188.html

28. Whatever Abdelwahab Meddeb may have said in a debate about Tunisia in which, as a Tunisian, he legitimized dictatorship in the name of secularism, his position has

shifted since the Tunisian people's uprising. See our debate on "Ce soir ou jamais" January 31, 2008, www.dailymotion.com/video/x484ns_ce-soir-ou-jamais-abdel-wahab-meddeb_news; see also Alain Gresh, "La maladie d'Abdelwahab Meddeb et la révolution tunisienne," July 27, 2011, http://blog.mondediplo.net/2011–07–27-La-maladie-d-Abdelwahab-Meddeb-et-la-revolution.

29. Jean Baubérot, *La laïcité, quel héritage?* Paris: Labor & Fides, 1990; Jean Boussinesq, Michel Brisacier, and Emile Poulat, *La laïcité française*, Paris: Seuil, coll. "Points Essai," 1994.

30. Roy, "Révolution post-islamiste."

31. "Tunisian Islamist leader Rachid Ghannouchi returns home," BBC News, January 30, 2011, www.bbc.co.uk/news/world-africa-12318824.

32. "Egypt's Muslim Brotherhood Creates Political Party," *Los Angeles Times*, April 30, 2011, http://articles.latimes.com/2011/apr/30/world/la-fg-egypt-brotherhood-20110501.

33. "Egypt Brotherhood Member Says to Seek Presidency," *Saudi Gazette*, May 13, 2011, www.saudigazette.com.sa/index.cfm?method=home.regcon&contentID=2011051131005, and "Egypt Elections Cause Brotherhood Rift," CairoOnLine.com, June 20, 2011, http://getcairoonline.com/2011/06/20/egypt-elections-cause-brotherhood-rift.

34. As stated by Turkish Prime Minister Erdoğan during his visit to Egypt on September 13, 2011. "Erdoğan défend un État laïc en Égypte" www.gnet.tn/revue-de-presse-internationale/video-erdogan-defend-letat-laic-en-egypte/id-menu-957.html. He also suggested Arab societies explore a third way by setting up a secular model of their own. See also Appendix 17.

35. Edward Said defined himself as "a Christian wrapped in a Muslim culture"; see "Philosophers of the Arabs: Edward Said," www.arabphilosophers.com/English/philosophers/modern/modern-names/eEdward_Said.htm.

36. The Pope recently repeated his statement, criticizing some for their "amnesia" and their "denial" of the "Christian roots" of their culture. See "Pope Sees European Amnesia about Christian Roots," CatholicCulture.org, April 11, 2011, www.catholicculture.org/news/headlines/index.cfm?storyid=9949.

37. *Secularism, Religion and Multicultural Citizenship*, coordinated by Tariq Modood, introduction by Charles Taylor, Cambridge: Cambridge University Press, 2008.

38. See my *Radical Reform*, New York: Oxford University Press, 2009, where I summarize the history of the science of *usûl al-fiqh* (the fundamentals of Islamic law and jurisprudence).

39. Alain de Libera, *Penser au Moyen Âge*, Paris: Seuil, 1991.

40. Ibn Rushd, *Decisive Treatise and Epistle Dedicatory*, translated by C. Butterworth, Provo: Brigham Young University Press, 2001.

41. John Locke, *A Letter Concerning Toleration and Other Writings*, London: Liberty Fund, 2010.

42. Sigrid Hunke, *Allahs Sonne über dem Abendland. Unser arabisches Erbe*, Frankfurt: Fischer, repr. 2001.

43. This is what the people are expressing and hoping in the Muslim majority countries.

44. I have criticized the reductive character of Islamic finance and its often disturbing and counterproductive objectives; see my *Western Muslims and the Future of Islam*, and *Radical Reform*, chapter 14.

45. *The Ordinances of Government (al-Ahkâm al-Sultaniyya)*, translated from Arabic by Wafaa H. Wahaba, Beirut: Garnet Publishing, 1996, and *Le Traité de droit public d'Ibn Taimiya (al-Siyâsa al-Shar'iyya)*, French translation by Henri Laoust, Beirut (n.p.), 1948.

46. Ayatollah Khomeini constantly arbitrated among Mehdi Bazargan, Abolhassan Bani-Sadr, and the more traditionalists in the early 1980s.

47. "Primacy of Islam and Shari'a Law Expected to Remain in Egypt's Constitution," CNSNews.com, February 21, 2011 www.cnsnews.com/news/article/primacy-islam-and-shari-law-expected-rem, and an article about the positions of the Egyptian Salafi Front (literalists, and not "Salafists," a term that today generally refers to violent extremists): "The Salafi Front in Egypt: Shari'a Is the Basis of National Consensus," July 29, 2011, www.tahrirdocuments.org/2011/08/the-salafi-front-in-egypt-sharia-is-the-basis-of-national-consensus.

48. The concept of shari'a can be understood differently according to field of application and/or to the angle from which its use is justified (Ramadan, *Western Muslims and the Future of Islam*). See also Dr. Jasser Awda, "As'ila Hawl al-Shariah Fi Marhalat Ma Ba'd al-Thawra al-Misriyya" ("Questions about the shari'a in Egypt's post-revolutionary era"), Cairo: Al-Shurouq Al-Dawliyyah, 2011 (in Arabic).

49. About Saudi Arabia's constitution and its reference to the shari'a, see http://jurist.law.pitt.edu/world/saudiarabia.htm.

50. See my debate with Abdelwahab Meddeb, "De la charia à l'islamophobie, de l'homosexualité au statut de la femme," *Le Monde*, April 22, 2011, www.lemonde.fr/idees/article/2011/04/22/de-la-charia-a-l-islamophobie-de-l-homosexualite-au-statut-de-la-femme_1511640_3232.html.

51. See Appendix 26, "Pondering over 2011."

52. The mufti of Saudi Arabia, Abdul-Aziz al-Sheikh, and his Islamic Legal Council ruled that protesting against rulers in the streets was against Islam. This official fatwa (legal ruling) was "political" and implied formal support for the ruling regime. He was not alone: in Egypt, mufti Sheikh Ali Jum'a called on protesters to stop demonstrating and to go to the mosque on Friday, since this was the "just Islamic position." He criticized Sheikh al-Qaradawi who supported the protests but "who lives in Qatar and does not know the Egyptian reality." Yusuf al-Qaradawi himself criticized Bahrain's demonstrators, as noted earlier, claiming that their movement was sectarian, exclusively Shiite, and thus illegitimate. In Syria as well, Sheikh Said Ramadan al-Bûtî criticized the protesters' "un-Islamic" action and urged them to stop demonstrating and to recognize "the legitimate authority of President Bashar al-Assad" (to whose father he had already shown unfailing

support). These made-to-order, highly political fatwas come from theologians who present their political opinions as religious rulings and who sometimes use their status in support of disreputable regimes. This is one of the dimensions of the crises undermining Muslim majority societies.

53. Lecture organized by Oxford students.

54. Marc Lynch, "Tahrir Turning Points," *Foreign Policy*, August 1, 2011, http://lynch.foreignpolicy.com/posts/2011/08/01/tahrir_turning_points, and "Tahrir Updates: 28 Secular Parties and Coalitions Pulling Out from Square," US Copts Association, July 29, 2011, www.copts.com/english/?p=2538.

55. This was the substance of Erdoğan's speeches during his visits to Egypt, Tunisia, then Libya, in mid-September 2011. Insisting on democracy and rejecting timid rhetoric on secularism, he called on the people to take their fate into their own hands, and on political leaders and intellectuals to face up to real challenges (see Appendix 17).

56. Over thirty Turkish embassies have recently been opened on the African continent alone.

57. The Muslim Brotherhood sharply criticized Turkey's claim as excessive interference in Arab affairs, "which have nothing to do with Turkish history." See "Egypt's Muslim Brotherhood Criticizes Erdoğan's Call for a Secular State," September 14, 2011, http://english.alarabiya.net/articles/2011/09/14/166814.html.

58. www.francemondexpress.fr/turquie-croissance-record-de-8-1-pour-2010,1020. html. The International Monetary Fund forecasts a 2.9% GDP growth for Turkey, versus 1% for advanced European economies. See also "La Turquie sera la meilleure croissance économique européenne," Turquie-fr.com, 21 April 2010, www.turquie-fr.com/la-turquie-sera-la-meilleure-croissance-economique-europeenne/21/04/2010.

59. The Syrian opposition sharply criticized the media for their scanty coverage of events, particularly al-Jazeera, which failed to report that a National Syrian Council (NSC)—like that which had been so quickly recognized in Libya—had been set up in Istanbul on September 14–15, 2011. Even self-proclaimed free media clearly made strategic choices in giving events varying treatment: the founding of the Syrian Council was similarly ignored by Western media. Only after a unified National Council (headed by Burhan Ghalioun) was finalized in Istanbul, on October 2–3, 2011, did the media finally begin to report on the Syrian opposition. However, the political positions expressed by other countries remained purely verbal. On October 5, China and Russia again opposed using sanctions to punish Bashar al-Assad's repressive policies.

60. Meant, said an adviser to the prime minister, as an alternative to the training provided by American and European institutions (see Chapter 1). A meeting on democratic reform was organized by the Turkish prime minister's office in Istanbul: see "Arab Spring to Be Debated in Istanbul," www.hurriyetdailynews.com/n. php?n=arab-spring-to-be-debated-in-istanbul-2011–10–04.

61. Prime Minister Erdoğan is accused by American neo-conservative critics of being an Islamist intent on implementing shari'a, hence their biased interpretation of his commitment to reduce interest rates close to zero.

## CHAPTER 4

1. In a debate I had with him in Estoril, Portugal, during the Estoril Conference, May 7–9, 2009. www.portugalglobal.pt/PT/geral/Documents/ EstorilConferences2011_ProgrammeENG.pdf.

2. Jean Ziegler, *La victoire des vaincus: oppression et résistance culturelle*, Paris: Seuil, 1988.

3. Olivier Roy, *L'Échec de l'Islam politique*, Paris: Seuil, coll."Esprit," 1992. Interviewed by Rue89 during the Arab uprisings, Roy asserted: "As a political solution, Islamism is finished." www.rue89.com/entretien/2011/02/20/olivier-roy-comme-solution-politique-lislamisme-est-fini-191153.

4. By virtue of such a definition the oil-rich monarchies, which are not against the West, would not be "Islamist."

5. The substance of Moussavi's criticism in his debate with Ahmadinejad before Iran's 2009 elections: "Moussavi vs. Ahmadinejad: Examining Iran's First Major Presidential Debate," June 9, 2009, www.irantracker.org/analysis/mousavi-vs-ahmadinejad-examining-irans-first-major-presidential-debate.

6. "Obama: Not Much Difference between Ahmadinejad and Moussavi," *Haaretz*, June 17, 2009, www.haaretz.com/news/obama-not-much-difference-between-ahmadinejad-mousavi-1.278259.

7. "Erbakan: D8 summit Is in Spring," *Turkish Daily Press*, December 13,1996, www.hurriyetdailynews.com/h.php?news=erbakan-d8-summit-is-in-spring-1996–12–13.

8. Ibid.

9. Tariq Ramadan, *Western Muslims and the Future of Islam*, New York: University Press, 2004, pp. 102–110.

10. Tariq Ramadan, *Aux sources du renouveau musulman*, Paris: Bayard, 1998, section one.

11. Ibid., pp. 317–321.

12. See my comparative analysis, ibid., pp. 261–267.

13. Ali Rahnema, *An Islamic Utopian: A Political Biography of Ali Shariati*, London: I. B. Tauris, 1998.

14. These were the terms of a lecture I delivered in Abu Dhabi on September 20, 2011. My critique of the various trends in contemporary political Islam (their internal crises and divisions and their frequent inability to provide answers to contemporary challenges) touched off sharp reactions in Egypt, particularly among the Muslim Brotherhood, when the newspaper *al-Masry al-Yawm* reported on my

analysis (September 22, 2011). The substance of this criticism has been developed in similar terms in Chapter 3 of this book, "Interlocking Crises."

15. Muhammad Abduh, and after him Hassan al-Banna, believed that the British parliamentary model could be borrowed and was not contrary to Islamic principles. The principles of elections and of elective tenure could be integrated into an eventual "Islamic state." Accepting these principles implies acceptance of the idea of pluralism in managing political forces. See Ramadan, *Aux sources du renouveau musulman*, pp. 314–317.

16. According to Abd ar-Razzaq Makri (the movement's current scond-in-command), during a discussion in Paris in April 2011. See also Yassin Temlali's more recent critical article, in which accepting the "civil state" is seen more as a compromise than as a self-critical advance of the movement: "L'islamisme algérien: le MSP entre modération et compromission," September 24, 2008, www. babelmed.net/Pais/Alg%C3%A9rie/l%C3%A2islamisme_alg%C3%A3rien. php?c=3594&m=36&l=fr.

17. Erdoğan's remarks about secularism during his September 13, 2011, visit to Egypt were badly received by the Muslim Brotherhood and by Islamists in general. Yet Mr. Erdoğan merely associated secularism with the process leading to democratization and pluralism.

18. Muhammad Imara, *Thawrat 25 Yanayir wa kasr hajiz al khawf*, Cairo: dar al-salam, 2011.

19. Ibid., p. 86.

20. Ibid., pp. 89–93.

21. *Financial Times*, January 18, 2011, www.ft.com/intl/cms/s/0/24d710a6–22ee-11-e0-adob-00144feab49a.html#axzz1ZKlaW7aC.

22. "Our conception of the civil state does not stem from a secular conception of the state. It nevertheless results from the necessity to guarantee the rights of minorities, the separation of powers, the pacific alternation of power, and attachment to dialogue," (*Akhbar al-Yaoum*, Morocco, March 25, 2011). See also the statement in the spirit of the February 20th Movement: "We are calling for the inception of a modern civil state with no divine right, where nobody can claim to be sacred and nobody has divine delegation; a state where the people will hold sovereignty and power, according to their beliefs and choices" ("Al Adl Wal Ihssane plaide pour un 'État civil,'" Lakome.com, March 25, 2011, http://fr.lakome.com/politique/42-actualites-politique/241-al-adl-wal-ihssane-plaide-un-qetat-civilq.html).

23. "Nous sommes plus proches du modèle turc," Lakome.com, March 23, 2011, http://fr.lakome.com/politique/42-actualites-politique/232-nadia-yassine-nous-sommes-plus-proches-du-modele-turc-video.html.

24. El-Hassan bin Talal, "A New World Order without Ideologies," February 4, 2003, http://ecumene.org/hassano203.htm.

25. Halim Rane, *Islam and Contemporary Civilisation: Evolving Ideas, Transforming Relations*, Melbourne: Melbourne University Publishing (MUP), July 2010,

chapter 4 ("Issues on Legal Thought," pp. 75–100) and chapter 6 ("The Struggle for Democracy," pp. 123–147). The author writes of the renewal of contemporary Islamic thought made possible through the "higher objectives" (*maqâsid*).

26. New York: Oxford University Press, 2009. See chapters 5, 7, and 15.

27. "Al Adl Wal Ihssane plaide pour un 'Etat civil.'"

28. "L'islam n'est pas irrationnel," *Aujourd'hui le Maroc*, December 28, 2001, www. aujourdhui.ma/imprimer/?rub=actualite&ref=6265.

29. "Meeting with Heba Ezzat," *Open Democracy*, May 11, 2005, www.opendemocracy. net/faith-europe_islam/article_2497.jsp.

30. On the crisis of democracy, see Marcel Gauchet: *L'Avènement de la démocratie*, Paris: Gallimard, 2007–2010. He has repeatedly developed the notion of a "growth crisis of democracy": see, for example, his April 2008 interview, http://gauchet.blog-spot.com/2008/06/la-democratie-traverse-une-crise-de.html, as well as "Crise dans la démocratie?" November 2010, http://marcelgauchet.fr/blog/?p=488.

31. Dominique Wolton, *Il faut sauver la communication,* Paris: Flammarion, 2005; *Télévision et Civilisations,* with Hugues Le Paige, Brussels: Labor, 2004; *L'Autre Mondialisation,* Paris: Flammarion, 2003; as well as an earlier study, *La Dernière Utopie. Naissance de l'Europe démocratique,* Paris: Flammarion, 1993.

32. The title of Daniel Bell's *The End of Ideology: On the Exhaustion of Political Ideas in the Fifties*, Cambridge, MA: Harvard University Press, 1960; repr. 2000.

33. Naomi Klein, *The Shock Doctrine: The Rise of Disaster Capitalism*, London: Penguin, 2007.

34. "Let Them Come," *Economist*, 27 August–2 September 2011, www.economist. com/node/21526893, about the necessity and economic benefits of immigration.

35. See my "The Global Ideology of Fear or the Globalization of the Israel Syndrome," December 2005, www.tariqramadan.com/the-global-ideology-of-fear-or-the. html.

36. While also developing far-fetched conspirationist theories about the "plot to control the world." The Internet culture amplifies such phenomena to an extraordinary extent.

37. Ramadan, *Western Muslims and the Future of Islam*, pp. 165–171.

38. Chapter 1, this volume, "When the Other Is no Longer the Other."

39. Particularly when speaking of "Islamic democracy," an ambiguous notion that refers to a model located somewhere between the Islamic state and secular democracy. I do not endorse this formula: I prefer clarity on the principles and methods of managing political power to formulas and slogans that blur analysis.

40. Not even a "secular theocracy" according to Massignon's rather tortuous formula, as discussed by Régis Blachère, www.persee.fr/web/revues/home/prescript/ article/ridc_0035-3337_1959_num_11_4_11293.

41. Ramadan, *Aux sources du renouveau musulman*, pp. 433–436.

42. *In the Footsteps of the Prophet: Lessons from the Life of Muhammad*, New York: Oxford University Press, 2006.

43. Qur'an, Surah 17, verse 70.

44. John Rawls, *A Theory of Justice*, Cambridge, MA: Belknap Press, 1971; repr. 1999.

45. Qur'an, Surah 2, verse 256.

46. See my *Islam, the West and the Challenges of Modernity*, Leicester, UK: Islamic Foundation, 2003, pp. 155–175, and *Radical Reform*, New York: Oxford University Press, 2009, pp. 259–285.

47. See discussion and definition in *Western Muslims and the Future of Islam*, pp. 31–62.

48. See my *Radical Reform*, chapter 13: "Women: Traditions and Liberation," pp. 207–232.

49. Reforms in women's status have often been used to legitimize positions (on both sides) in the struggles between secularists and Islamists, or between governments and their oppositions. Unfortunately, they have not always resulted in concrete results. In Tunisia, Morocco, and in other countries mentioned (starting with the petro-monarchies), women are still being discriminated in education, the job market, and of course families. A literalist, decontextualized reading of scriptural sources, as well as cultural projections (from Arab and Asian patriarchal societies) explain a situation that requires in-depth reform: the law alone cannot change age-old individual behavior.

50. See my *Islam, the West and the Challenges of Modernity*, p. 139; *Western Muslims and the Future of Islam*, pp. 174–200; and *Radical Reform*, pp. 239–258.

51. Fridays had an important function in mobilizing populations during the uprisings in Tunisia, Egypt, Libya, Syria, and Yemen. Both day and occasion are fraught meaning in citizens' religious and civic conscience. See Appendix 10, "Freedom Fridays."

52. *Islam, the West and the Challenges of Modernity*, pp. 86–105.

53. *Radical Reform*, pp. 259–292.

54. *Islam, the West and the Challenges of Modernity*, pp. 135–187; *Western Muslims and the Future of Islam*, pp. 174–199; and *Radical Reform*, chapter 14, pp. 233–258.

55. My *Western Muslims and the Future of Islam* was banned in Malaysia (often presented as an "Islamic" economic mode) because it criticized Malaysian-style Islamized capitalism or "Islamization" of the economy, finance, and bank transactions.

56. On the difference between "adaptation reform" and "transformation reform," see Ramadan, *Radical Reform*, pp. 26–38.

57. One of the Prophet Muhammad's first initiatives when he arrived in Medina was to reconstitute tribal and political alliances as well as the rules regulating transactions in the city's central market. The link between the two powers is as old as human societies, and there can be no ethics in politics without concern for ethics in economy. See my *In the Footsteps of the Prophet*, pp. 87–109.

58. See my presentation of those founding principles in *Islam, the West and the Challenges of Modernity*, pp. 135–155.

59. In Libya, the uprising was shaped, encouraged, and used by France, with the "international community" following suit despite the resistance and refusal of a few Arab and African countries.

60. As suggested by the calls for a "dialogue of civilizations," a religious and cultural dialogue is indeed taking place, but it barely considers political and economic power relations.

61. In Washington, on December 1, 2010, during the celebration of "The world's 100 most influential intellectuals," former US presidential candidate and Senator John Kerry took part in the debate.

62. To be one of the research projects of the Research Center on Islamic Legislation and Ethics which I head, sponsored by the Contemporary Islamic Studies chair at Oxford University and the Faculty of Islamic Studies in Qatar. Research will focus on seven fields: medicine, education, gender issues, ecology, economy, the arts, and food. Allied ethics in economy (which I do not call "Islamic economy") is one of the main areas of study.

63. Their observations and their analyses of facts are often to the point; the solutions they offer require critical examination.

64. See Ramadan, *Radical Reform*, pp. 127–155.

65. Ibid., pp. 183–206.

66. Ramadan, *Islam, the West and the Challenges of Modernity*, part three, particularly pp. 264–294.

67. Ibid., pp. 264–272.

68. The substance of his analysis of the success of Islamists among the populations of the Global South. Challenging the monopoly of universality goes hand in glove with religious affirmation as cultural and identity affirmation. See François Burgat, *Face to Face with Political Islam*, London: I. B. Tauris, 2003.

69. Ramadan, *Islam, the West and the Challenges of Modernity*, pp. 201–264.

70. Except for the great tradition of combatant Sufi orders that shaped the history of Islamic civilization, with the mystics of East Africa, North Africa, the Caucasus, Turkey or Asia. Such emblematic figures as Algeria's Adbelkader or Chechen Sheikh Shamil are but two among thousands of Sufis who resisted colonial rulers and despots.

71. As in the title of Amin Maalouf's *Les Identités meurtrières,* Grasset, 1998. Maalouf understands the cost of populations when they close themselves off, seen against the background of Lebanon, a source of meditation for the Arab world.

72. See my *Islam, the West and the Challenges of Modernity*, pp. 233–236, and *Radical Reform*, pp. 293–313.

73. The month of Ramadan, which should be a month of privation, is the busiest in terms of food production and sales in all Muslim majority societies.

74. See Chapter 1, this volume.

75. A statistical index of the United Nations Development Program, based on life expectancy, education, and standard of living, meant to measure a society's development through qualitative data.

76. Abû Hâmid al-Ghazâlî, *The Revival of Religious Sciences (Ihyâ' 'ulûm al-dîn),* Cambridge, UK: Islamic Texts Society (al-Ghazâlî series).

77. International Movement for a Just World, www.just-international.org/index.php/ profile-of-dr-chandra-muzaffar.html.

78. On the Muslim question in China: http://topics.nytimes.com/top/reference/ timestopics/subjects/u/uighurs_chinese_Ethnic_group/index.html; on the Chechnya conflict: www.cbc.ca/news/background/chechnya/.

79. Human Rights Watch report, April 2002, vol. 14, no. 3, "'We Have no Orders to Save You': State Participation and Complicity in Communal Violence in Gujarat," www.hrw.org/reports/2002/india/gujarat.pdf; Elaine Audet: "Un massacre ciblant les femmes," Sisyphe.org, October 2002, http://sisyphe.org/spip. php?article126.

80. The same prism can be seen in a number of Edward Said's articles and major contributions after *Orientalism.* See, for instance, *Covering Islam,* rev. ed., New York: Vintage, 1997, the collection of interviews *Power, Politics and Culture: Interviews with Edward Said,* New York: Gauri Viswanathan, 2001, p. 416, as well as *Peace and Its Discontents: Essays on Palestine in the Middle East Process,* New York: Vintage, 1996, where he surprisingly disqualifies "political Islam" as a—right or wrong—way to resist Western hegemony.

81. *Building Moderate Muslim Networks,* by Angel Rabasa, Cheryl Benard, Lowell H. Schwartz, Peter Sickle, ed. Rand Corporation, Washington, 2007.

82. www.islamicpluralism.org/521/cip-recommends-rands-building-moderate-muslim-networks.

83. "Good Muslim, Bad Muslim," *New Statesman,* February 12, 2010, www.newstatesman.com/religion/2010/02/muslim-religious-moderation.

84. "Netanyahu Says Egypt Peace Stands Despite Embassy Riot," BBC, September 10, 2010, www.bbc.co.uk/news/world-middle-east-14867867.

85. John J. Mearsheimer and Stephen M. Walt, *The Israel Lobby and US Foreign Policy,* New York: Farrar, Straus and Giroux, 2007.

86. Roger Cohen: "Israel Isolates Itself," *New York Times,* September 6, 2011, www. nytimes.com/2011/09/06/opinion/06iht-edcohen06.html.

87. "Le message politique des 'indignés' israéliens," *Le Monde,* September 5, 2011, www.lemonde.fr/idees/article/2011/09/05/le-message-politique-des-indignes-israeliens_1567790_3232.html.

88. Meeting with the Dalai-Lama, 2nd Annual Conference on Global Peace and Religions, Montreal, September 7, 2011, www.ledevoir.com/societe/ethique-et-religion/330937/conference-sur-les-religions-le-dalai-lama-defend-le-fait-religieux.

CONCLUSION

1. "The Turkish elections," www.tariqramadan.com/The-Turkish-Elections.html.

# Index

27.95                              10/11/12.